Reconsidering the American Way of War

Reconsidering the American Way of War

US Military Practice from the Revolution to Afghanistan

Antulio J. Echevarria II

GEORGETOWN UNIVERSITY PRESS
Washington, DC

Library of Congress Cataloging-in-Publication Data

Echevarria, Antulio Joseph, 1959–
    Reconsidering the American way of war : US military practice from the Revolution to Afghanistan / Antulio J. Echevarria II.
        pages cm
    Includes bibliographical references and index.
    ISBN 978-1-62616-067-5 (pbk. : alk. paper)
    1. Strategic culture—United States—History. 2. United States—Military policy—Case studies. 3. United States—History, Military. 4. Strategy. I. Title.
        U21.2.E32 2014
        355'.033573—dc23

                                                        2013034006

This book is printed on acid-free paper meeting the requirements of the American National Standard for Permanence in Paper for Printed Library Materials.

15 14   9 8 7 6 5 4 3 2 First printing

Printed in the United States of America

To Jorge, who fought well.

Contents

Acknowledgments

I began framing the chapters of this book while on a visiting research fellowship through Oxford University's Changing Character of War program. I enjoyed the better part of a year at Nuffield College, which afforded me access to Oxford's vast research facilities and a collegial environment in which to work. My warmest thanks go to Sir Hew Strachan, Rob Johnson, Andrea Baumann, and Sibylle Scheipers, whose perspectives greatly enriched my own. I would also like to thank my friends and colleagues from the Society of Military History, many of whom gave of their valuable time to consider or debate some of the points in this study. All were helpful in that special way the society has of encouraging the research of its members, but Bianka Adams, Conrad Crane, Brian Linn, Randy Papadopoulos, Jill Russell, and Janet Valentine deserve particular mention. I am also grateful to Don Jacobs of Georgetown University Press for his professionalism in preparing this manuscript for publication.

Last and never least, my deepest appreciation goes to my family, whose patience was limitless over the long months I spent writing this book. To my wife Laurie and our children I owe a debt I can never repay.

Preface

This book of history . . . is based on an assumption that what we
believe and what we do today is governed at least as much by the
habits of mind we formed in the relatively remote past as by what we
did and thought yesterday."
Russell Weigley, The American Way of War, 1973

THIS BOOK CHALLENGES several longstanding notions about the American
way of war. It examines American military practice from the War of Independence to the campaigns in Iraq and Afghanistan to determine what patterns,
if any, exist in the way Americans have used military force against their adversaries. It argues that many beliefs concerning the American way of war—
such as its alleged apolitical and astrategic character and its reputation for
using overwhelming force to achieve decisive results—do not, in fact, hold
up to scrutiny.[1] American uses of force were typically driven more by political considerations than military ones, and the amount of force employed
was rarely overwhelming or decisive. Whereas Russell Weigley's celebrated
work, *The American Way of War*, traced ideas about military strategy, this
study concentrates on strategic and operational practice. Its premise is that
what people did historically is just as revealing as, if not more than, what they
thought or said. Accordingly this book closes the gap between Weigley's novel
effort to represent America's way of war as a history of ideas and the more
grounded narratives of America's diverse wars and military actions.

Focusing on strategic and operational practice helps strip away some
of the rhetoric of the age, such as Gen. William T. Sherman's oft-repeated
phrase "hard hand of war."[2] Such rhetoric obscures both the complexity and
the simplicity of what took place. Peeling it away is especially necessary because the language of the so-called transformation and counterinsurgency
"revolutions" has misrepresented the American way of war for more than a
decade. Each tried to lay claim to the American style of fighting, though in

different ways and for different reasons. Since those revolutions are behind us, we can now take a more objective look at what the American way of war was and in some ways still is. Hence the title of this book.

Weigley's *American Way of War* remains a classic. Even so, and even with his considerable skills as a historian, his history of ideas necessarily omitted much. We find little discussion of America's supposed small wars, except for the campaigns against Native Americans, and those were not small when their geographic scope and duration are considered.[3] Almost no mention is made of the Barbary Wars, the antipiracy actions in the Gulf of Mexico and the Caribbean, the Banana Wars, the border wars with Mexico, and the various interventions in the Philippines, China, and Russia. Weigley's focus was decidedly on major wars and more precisely on the strategic ideas underpinning them. However, since the late eighteenth century, the United States has employed force overseas roughly two hundred times to protect or promote its interests.[4] That number increases when one adds the three dozen or so covert operations undertaken during and after the Cold War, as well as some 150 domestic military operations short of war. Admittedly, many of these actions did not escalate to bloodshed, yet they represent a Clausewitzian "continuation of policy by other means."[5] Collectively they create a truer picture of how and why Americans used military force. For that reason, this book covers not only America's major conflicts, but also many of its smaller wars and military actions (it was simply not possible to examine all of them) to offer a more comprehensive treatment of the American way of war.

This more comprehensive picture reveals that, of the many factors that drove American uses of force, perhaps the most important was an administration's desire to reduce its political risk. Rarely was the use of overwhelming force seen as a way to reduce risk. Instead, political leaders typically focused on committing only sufficient force. This rationale is counterintuitive from a military perspective, which considers it beneficial to enter a conflict with a preponderance of force. Ultimately what constituted an acceptable level of political risk to an administration was a subjective call. Presidents and their advisers took any number of internal and external factors into account when determining the degree of risk they were willing to accept. Such factors included an administration's sense of itself, how strong its mandate appeared, its assumptions regarding the efficacy of military force, and how confident it felt about its ability to fight a war while advancing its other policies. Thus the chief characteristics of the American way of war—and how they changed over time—were determined largely by the major tensions and dialectical turns in American politics. The American way of war was, and still is, thoroughly political.

To underscore the point further, Americans have used war as a political instrument not only to advance their foreign policies, but also to promote their domestic agendas. Successes and failures on the battlefield clearly affected how international rivals (and partners) dealt with one another. However, US policymakers also readily leveraged such outcomes to strengthen their parties' standings at home and to weaken those of their opponents. As interesting as it would be to explore such dynamics, this book is an analysis of American military, not political practice. The latter would require a study organized along completely different lines. Instead, this work examines the strategic and operational practice that made up the American way of war—defined for purposes of this study as how the United States used military force to protect or promote its interests.[6]

Contrary to the received view, the American way of war was also not astrategic. American strategic and operational practice became more fused over time. The latter incorporated the former in war plans and campaign plans or, more precisely, within the various sections detailing the schemes of maneuver for such plans. This development did not mean that military strategy was consumed by operational art, as some claim.[7] Rather, it meant that military strategy—the art of the general as it has been called—had become more diffuse. Instead of one general or field commander directing armies or navies in wartime, the scope of modern war required that many generals and admirals assume responsibility for specific sectors or functions within geographically defined theaters or operational areas. In short, it meant American military strategy became more "nested" in practice. It was possible, for instance, for the United States to pursue an overall military strategy of attrition against the Japanese, as articulated by President Roosevelt in 1943: "We set as a primary task in the war of the Pacific a day-by-day and week-by-week and month-by-month destruction of more Japanese war materials than Japanese industry could replace."[8] Yet within that overarching strategy, it was also possible for Gen. Douglas MacArthur and Adm. Chester Nimitz to pursue strategies of position in designing their respective campaigns, even as they carried out force-oriented strategies aimed at destroying Japanese combat power. Strictly speaking, strategies of position and control do not preclude the use of force-oriented strategies or vice versa. Yet the distinction provides a useful framework for discussing the variety of military strategies that made up American military practice. The downside of such variety is that, without strong coordination at the top, nested military strategies can become disjointed, with each of the armed services pursuing separate strategic agendas. That, in fact, happened to a degree in several American conflicts.

Another observation supported by an analysis of American military practice is that the anatomy of war—the operational phasing—currently followed by American campaign planners is misleading.[9] It places too much emphasis on the phase referred to as decisive operations. If such operations were truly decisive, there would be little need for studies concerning war termination. And yet such studies abound, caused largely by the need to understand why military victory does not always compel an opponent to act in accordance with our wishes.[10] The American way of war, though manifold in its features and characteristics, is at root a way of battle precisely because it places decisive operations at the core of its conception of war and often expects to win wars by virtue of winning battles. This is not to say that winning or losing battles is trivial or irrelevant. Battles or engagements are often the principal currency in the exchanges that take place among belligerent parties. Nevertheless, the link between victory on the battlefield and overall success is not automatic, as contemporary US doctrine tends to assume.

This book is divided into two parts. Part I, "Preludes," consists of three chapters, each of which sets the stage for discussions in part II. Chapter 1, "American Ways of War: Turns in Interpretation," lays out the many versions of the American way of war that have appeared since the publication of Weigley's book and the uses to which they have been put. Chapter 2, "American Strategic Culture: An Elusive Fiction," analyzes the notion of strategic culture and its uses. Despite four decades of research and scholarship, the proponents of strategic culture and its American derivative have yet to show how their concept can bridge the tensions between change and continuity and between uniqueness and commonality. Chapter 3, "American Military Art: A Misleading Analogy," rejects the term *art* as a descriptor for an activity that relies more on scientific processes than on imagination and creative impulses. Instead, this chapter makes use of the term *practice* as a way of combining the disparate, yet interdependent activities of art and science. It also describes the various types of military strategy that will be discussed in part II, "American Military Practice." This part examines American strategic and operational practice from the American War of Independence to the campaigns in Iraq and Afghanistan.[11] Chapter 4 covers the period from the Revolutionary War to the Mexican War. Chapter 5 considers the interval from the American Civil War to the Boxer Rebellion. Chapter 6 addresses the half century from the Caribbean Wars to the Korean War. Chapter 7 examines the decades from the coup in Guatemala to the War on Terrorism. The book's conclusion offers collective observations from each of these four chapters.

To date, no way of war has had as much written about it or has been as influential or as controversial as the American one. That is likely to remain the case because the contemporary American use of force is too important to too many people for the opposite to occur. For that reason, the phrase "American way of war" will probably remain strong currency within defense circles for some time.[12] However, its buyers would do well to beware. As Weigley reminded us several decades ago, what we believe and do today is influenced in part by our historical habits of mind. This book aims to challenge those habits, whether recent or remote, by examining what the American way of war was like in practice.

Notes

1. An example is found in Clark, *Waging Modern War*, 450, which states: "There is an American way of war, developed in the two world wars, last practiced in the Gulf War: muster an overwhelmingly large force: prepare and train it; then use it to achieve militarily decisive results." This characterization is sometimes referred to as the "true" American way of war.

2. See Weigley, *American Way of War*, 149. This phrase is often used to underscore the brutality of war or of Sherman's approach, but it is easy to give it too much weight.

3. Though controversial, Boot, *Savage Wars of Peace*, attempts to fill this gap.

4. Grimmett, *Instances of the Use*.

5. Clausewitz's most famous observation, this has been translated in various ways. It reflects the sense that war is an instrument (or weapon) of policy, as well as a continuation of political intercourse, albeit with violent means. Clausewitz, *Vom Kriege*, bk. 1, chap. 1, 210. Cited from Clausewitz, *On War*, 87.

6. The term *United States* (or the adjective *US*) is used in this study even for the Revolutionary era, as the political and military institutions established during this period provided the foundations for those developed later.

7. See Kelly and Brennan, *Alien*. For a rebuttal, see Van Riper, "Foundation of Strategic Thinking." Strachan, "Strategy or Alibi?," argues the operational level of war assumed strategic significance since the end of the Cold War.

8. Roosevelt, "State of the Union," 1943.

9. The US military has used a number of phasing constructs over the years but all have followed the basic sequencing of the one depicted in *Joint Publication 3-0*, v–6, which consists of five phases: shape, deter, seize initiative, dominate (i.e., conduct dominating or decisive operations), stabilize, and enable civil authority.

10. Cf. Caraccilo, *Beyond Guns and Steel*; Rose, *How Wars End*; Moten, *War Termination*; and Pillar, *Negotiating Peace*.

11. Since the West Point campaign atlases (now public domain) are tough to beat in terms of accuracy and detail, readers are encouraged to make use of them while perusing chapters 4–7: www.westpoint.edu/history/sitepages/our%20atlases.aspx.

12. Kaplan, *Insurgents*, is a recent example.

PART I

Preludes

1

American Ways of War

Turns in Interpretation

There is emerging a distinctive American style of war, a style that is
essentially joint, drawing on the unique capabilities of each service
via centralized planning and decentralized execution.

Gen. William DePuy, 1991

IN THE WAKE OF DESERT STORM, retired US Army general William DePuy
made some observations about a distinctive American way of war that were
both belated and premature. A distinctive American style of war had already
been described by the preeminent military historian Russell Weigley two
decades earlier. Yet it was too soon to characterize that style as "essentially
joint," as DePuy had done. Jointness was still a distant goal, as the after-action
critiques from Desert Storm made clear.[1] DePuy was, nonetheless, correct
in stating that the American way of war was "distinctive." Unfortunately, the
characteristics that made it distinctive were largely in the eye of the beholder.
Many interpretations of the American style of war have, in fact, emerged
since the publication of Weigley's *American Way of War* in 1973. Yet most
of them did not appear until some thirty years after his book was in print.
Fewer than a dozen works on the American way of war were published in the
twenty-five years between 1973 and 1999. However, more than three times
that number were printed since the beginning of the new millennium, a trend
that began well before 9/11.[2]

There are two major reasons for this imbalance. The first of these is that
from the start, Weigley's study has been hailed as the definitive account of
American strategic thinking from George Washington to Rear Adm. J. C.
Wylie.[3] His argument that the American way of war settled on a military
strategy of annihilation after the Civil War, though inaccurate, was intellectu-
ally appealing. Even as early as the mid-1970s, this interpretation held sway
in academe and the defense community, offering a cogent explanation for

what had gone wrong with the US involvement in Vietnam. To many, the complexity of that involvement required a less-heavy-handed approach than a strategy of annihilation offered. Still, even counterguerrilla methods were not, in Weigley's view, likely to result in victory because such techniques had their own "special problems of indecisiveness."[4] In short, Weigley's *American Way of War* was readily accepted in part because it was as political as it was historical. It was not only a seminal work for readers of American history— it was also a call for policymakers and military strategists to broaden their thinking at a time when both nuclear and conventional weapons were, as he claimed, bringing the "history of useable combat" to an end.[5]

Second, interest in the American way of war rose sharply after the Gulf War (1990–91), the interventions in Bosnia (1995–96) and Kosovo (1999), and the increase in speculations about a revolution in military affairs (RMA) based on the union of precision-strike and information technologies. This military revolution became associated with an entirely new American way of waging war. The phrase "way of war" quickly became popular as an analytical or rhetorical trope.[6] As the crisis in Iraq intensified after the summer of 2003, much of the literature on the new American way of war took a decidedly polemical turn, reflecting increased frustration with US and coalition policies and the seemingly slow progress of the counterinsurgency campaigns. This frustration was due in part to the belief that the US military was not adapting quickly enough to Iraq's insurgency, but it was also due to impatience with the pace of such campaigns in general.[7] In other words, while the underlying message in Weigley's classic was clearly political, by the beginning of the twenty-first century the expression "American way of war" had itself become politicized, an instrument used by pundits and scholars alike in the recurring debates regarding the direction of US strategy.

Over the last four decades, interpretations of the American way of war have taken three distinct but interrelated turns. The first turn, which began in the mid-1970s and continues still, is marked by the general acceptance (and criticism) of Weigley's thesis. The second turn, which occurred between the mid-1990s and early 2004, involved comparing the "old" American style of war to a "new" one closely identified with the unfolding revolution in military affairs and the subsequent transformation of the US military. The third turn began in the late spring of 2004, as the new American way of fighting— geared perhaps too much toward conventional conflicts—appeared to have bogged down in Iraq. It was characterized by efforts to revisit the main traits of the American style of war to identify why it seemed to be failing and how to fix it. This period also saw a tendency to link the American way of war to the notion of strategic culture in an effort to argue that the causes of failure were deeply rooted in American values or assumptions about the use of force.[8]

Acceptance and Criticism

Weigley's *American Way of War* was essentially a "history of American strategic thought" and—for those periods where strategic writings were too thin for analysis—a "history of ideas expressed in action."[9] His definition of a way of war was centered on the use of military force in support of policy aims, and he was particularly concerned with the "habits of mind" that appeared to be shaping modern American strategic thinking. He traced the historical development of the American way of war through two basic types of military strategy: annihilation, which he defined as the overthrow of the enemy's military power, and attrition, which he saw as the pursuit of military objectives short of overthrow and often as what British historian and strategist Basil H. Liddell Hart famously called the "indirect approach."[10] Weigley's principal argument was that, after the Civil War, as the United States experienced a "rapid rise from poverty of resources to plenty," the American way of war tended to opt for strategies of annihilation.[11] As a result, the further evolution of strategies of attrition was cut short, and American military strategy became one-sided or imbalanced. This habit of mind subsequently slowed the search for strategic alternatives from the 1950s through the Vietnam War era. It also appeared, as Weigley claimed, to have delayed recognition of the fact that "technological and social developments" since the age of Napoleon were making wars less decisive: "The use of combats has had to seem less and less a rationally acceptable means for the pursuit of national objects."[12] This was a significant statement because Weigley's analysis of US military strategies did not address how useful they might be in turning tactical victories into policy successes.

Other scholarly studies of the American way of war written in the 1970s and 1980s reflected similar concerns, though not all of these cited Weigley's work or even mentioned it.[13] One noteworthy study of "The Wilsonian Way of War" by Frederick Calhoun argued that President Woodrow Wilson "imposed his own definitions and his own restrictions on the employment of armed power," which in turn "prohibited force from getting out of control, regardless of the advice of his military experts."[14] For Calhoun a way of war had to do with "how armed power is used to implement policies," which clearly resembled Weigley's definition.[15] The study filled an important gap because Weigley had very little to say about Wilson's use of force in pursuit of the purposes of policy. Most such works during this period were concerned with demonstrating how the use of military power can and should be limited and that escalation need not be inevitable. They illustrate how easily interest in the history of the American way of war went hand in hand with concerns over the contemporary use of US military power. That relationship helps explain why Weigley's argument met with little scholarly criticism initially.

The first (and to date only) serious criticism of Weigley's work did not come until Brian Linn's critique of it in 2002, nearly thirty years after its publication.[16] It is worth noting that the Cold War was well over by then, as was the Vietnam conflict, even though the ghosts of both may linger still.[17] Linn was able to bring a fresh perspective to the American way of war and in so doing raised four objections to Weigley's argument. The first objection concerned Weigley's confusion over the definitions of annihilation and attrition (about which more will be said below). The second issue was that Weigley's book gave too little attention to the alternative strategies and war aims discussed in American military thinking. Linn's third point was that the period between the end of the Civil War and the middle of the Second World War was actually more strategically ambivalent than Weigley admitted. The fourth objection was that the US military's "propensity for improvisation and practicality" in its peacetime thinking, as well as its wartime performance, suggests that it was not as committed to strategies of annihilation as Weigley maintained.[18]

The first objection was essentially the foundation for the other three. Not only did Weigley get the definitions and thus the concepts wrong—a serious problem for any historian of ideas—he also later admitted to "trying to shoehorn" almost all US strategic thinking into those two categories.[19] Such oversimplification makes for an even greater problem because it undermines a study's authority and persuasiveness. Weigley identified two general categories of military strategy—annihilation and attrition—which he borrowed from the German historian Hans Delbrück, but he ought to have found at least three, the third being exhaustion.[20] As will be explained in chapter 3, Weigley defined annihilation as seeking the complete destruction of the enemy's military power and attrition as the pursuit of any military objective short of that. A strategy of exhaustion, by comparison, aims to make an adversary believe the probable costs of winning a conflict outweigh the likely gains. George Washington and Nathanael Greene followed strategies of attrition against the British armies in North America during the Revolutionary War, while the overall American military strategy was one of exhaustion.

To be sure, pinning down military definitions can be difficult and not only for civilians. However, Weigley's argument regarding the American way of war required such distinctions in order to show that one type of strategy was dominant. Linn suggested instead that if there is an American way of war, it might lie more in the practical combination of political-strategic aims, operational considerations, and military concepts as they are understood historically.[21]

Linn's critique effectively demolished Weigley's argument, and Weigley, for his part, essentially conceded as much.[22] He had managed to pull two hundred years of American military history into a coherent narrative and in the process had analyzed more than a dozen variations of US military strategy: Washington's strategy of attrition, Greene's partisan war, Robert E. Lee's Napoleonic strategy, Ulysses S. Grant's strategy of annihilation, Stephen B. Luce's and Alfred Thayer Mahan's sea-power strategy, Billy Mitchell's strategy of air power, Douglas MacArthur's and George C. Marshall's strategies in the Korean War, strategies of deterrence and action on the part of America's intellectuals, and strategies of action as attempted in Vietnam. Nonetheless, he had neglected some key traditions in American strategic thinking, one of which was the emphasis on deterrence. That tradition, as Linn pointed out, had influenced the development of US coastal artillery, provided a rationale for the long-range bomber, and reinforced US attitudes toward isolationism into the early twentieth century. Again, the core military strategies are largely about different ways or methods. They can be matched to a range of war aims, depending on the means available. Some methods are clearly better suited to specific aims than others. Put differently, Weigley's portrayal of the American style of war was altogether too tendentious.

An American Way of War—Sui Generis?

On the one hand, Weigley's historical analysis engendered further research into the origins of the American style of fighting. Whereas his story begins with the American War of Independence, other scholars have examined how seventeenth-century European settlers made war and in the process have given us a better understanding of the "early American ways of war."[23] For instance, Armstrong Starkey's *European and Native American Warfare, 1675–1815* (1998) offers a comparison between the technologies, tactics, and customs followed by European settlers and those that might be loosely described as the "Indian way of war."[24] As one might expect, all parties tended to adopt elements of the others' ways of war, even as they adapted to the evolving conditions of early modern warfare in the North American forests.[25] Starkey contended that Native American wars were not merely ritualistic volleys of insults and taunts culminating in a few physical casualties, nor were they simply exercises in ambushing and raiding—often referred to as the "skulking way of war"—though these tactics were much preferred over frontal assaults and similarly direct methods.[26] Instead, Indian wars were often bloody and extirpative, and the Indians' methods gave them an upper hand over their European counterparts in unconventional or "frontier war" for more than a century. According to Starkey, the Indian way of war had, until 1675, evolved in a fashion not unlike a revolution in military affairs.[27] Timothy Shannon has subsequently pushed that thesis further to include the period 1754–1814, while Wayne Lee has argued that these claims have to be tempered.[28] In Lee's view, changes in warfare in the American context, though pronounced, were not on the scale of the seventeenth-century European revolution in military affairs sparked by the Swedish king Gustavus Adolphus.

John Grenier's *The First Way of War: American War Making on the Frontier, 1607–1814* (2005) looked more carefully at the character of this style of warfare and argued that "early Americans created a military tradition that accepted, legitimized, and encouraged attacks upon and the destruction of noncombatants, villages, and agricultural resources."[29] In contrast to Weigley, Grenier defined a "way of war" to mean a concrete set of practices, rather than a history of ideas, and the specific tradition in this case was the practice of combining unlimited aims with irregular means. America's "first" way of war was first in the sense that it came before the period in which Weigley's story began and that it was also the first choice, or preferred, way of fighting. Grenier's argument was as political as Weigley's, though perhaps more explicit: Grenier urged American military leaders to "look at all the ways, even if they seem brutal and out of character, that we wage war."[30] The message was that early Americans were not reticent about attacking and killing noncombatants and laying waste to villages and crops—a point that stands in complete contrast to the accepted characteristics of the contemporary Western way of war in general and to the American way of war in particular, both of which seek to minimize noncombatant casualties and collateral damage.

Other historians recently suggested that several of the more distinctive practices that defined the early American ways of war had antecedents in the sixteenth-century wars of Ireland, the English Civil War, and the Thirty Years' War of the seventeenth century. Along this line, Lee's *Barbarians and Brothers: Anglo-American Warfare, 1500–1865* (2011) maintained that "three distinct ways of war" existed during the American Revolution: "one against the British, one against the Indians, and a third, middle way for the partisan war between rebels and Loyalists."[31] Lee did not use the phrase "way of war" in the book's title, but he addresses the topic nonetheless. *Barbarians and Brothers* is an example of a historical study with a contemporary political message: Americans waging war in the twenty-first century confront a problem similar to that which the early colonists faced—namely, distinguishing between friends, or "brothers," on the one hand, and the enemies, or "barbarians," walking among them on the other.[32] The book is also a cultural history, exploring what armies believed and how those beliefs shaped actions in the field. As a result, a more complex picture of the origins of the American way of war has emerged, one that depicts several ways of war at work in America's early history—each defined by who was fighting whom, when, where, and why.

Michael Bonura's *Under the Shadow of Napoleon: French Influence on the American Way of Warfare from the War of 1812 to the Outbreak of WWII* (2012) took up the story from the War of 1812 to the beginning of the Second World War and concluded that French military ideas dominated the American *"way of warfare"* during that time.[33] Bonura attempted to distinguish between a "way of war" and a "way of warfare." The former he described as "a nation's strategic and military traditions"; the latter he defined as "the underlying ideas concerning the relationship between citizen, state, and war and acceptable types of soldiers, armies, practices, and traditions."[34] In contrast, Mark Grotelueschen's *The AEF Way of War: The American Army and Combat in World War I* (2007) did not discuss French dominance of American operational doctrine directly but rather examined what its author referred to as the "war of ideas" in play *"within* the AEF [American Expeditionary Force] between those who adhered to the traditional, human-centered ideas of the prewar army and those who increasingly appreciated the modern, industrial ideas more prevalent in the European armies."[35] He used the phrase "way of war" to describe the ongoing alignment and realignment of weapons and ideas for their employment. For Grotelueschen, European and especially French influence over AEF doctrine was hotly contested. For Bonura, it was warmly embraced.

Brian Linn captured other tensions in his *Echo of Battle: The Army's Way of War* (2007), which traced the major intellectual traditions, or schools of thought, that have made up the US Army's way of war for the better part of two centuries.[36] Linn described these traditions as "guardians," or those officers who saw war as an engineering problem to be solved through the correct application of accepted principles; "heroes," for whom war was simply battle on a larger scale—chaotic, violent, and emotional; and "managers," who saw war as an organizational problem requiring the rational coordination of human and material resources.[37] It is not clear that these traditions would be limited only to the army, even though the navy and the air force are generally considered to be more technically oriented. This characteristic might suggest only that their heroic traditions are different, not less powerful. One could also imagine similar schools of thought to have been at work within the US Marine Corps. Considering the high caliber of some of the works published recently by marines and former marines, this task is just as interesting. The larger point, however, is that the US Army, like any other military institution, is hardly monolithic. Its views of past battles, of present threats, and of the best ways forward are all contested.

The early American way of war was in other words neither a single way of war nor wholly American, and the same holds true of its nineteenth-century counterpart. As Weigley once remarked, "The particular emphases that Americans drew from European methods of war-making were to help shape American strategy into the twentieth century, when Americans ceased to be simply pupils of Europe."[38] Indeed, we find a number of similarities regarding how the American and European styles of war unfolded historically. Each responded to the Industrial Revolution in similar ways, developing tactics that emphasized the use of mass to achieve superiority at the decisive point and combining firepower and maneuver to accomplish an opponent's annihilation. Each also held that battles and wars were invariably linked: Winning wars necessitated winning battles. Each also appeared to harbor similar aversions to political interference, admitting that policy had every right to establish the ends of war but also insisting that those ends could be achieved most effectively—and most efficiently—if the influence of politicians were filtered or, better, eliminated during the actual conduct of war. Each one also appears to have seen war principally as a means of "doing what politics cannot."[39] Politics brought war into being but existed as a violent alternative to it, rather than as its logical extension. Such attitudes became more common as Western militaries developed into professional institutions and as the study of warfare became more systematic and widespread. Consequently, many of the characteristics Weigley attributed to the American way of war in the latter half of the nineteenth century would also apply to European methods of warfare.[40] The dissimilarities were as likely due to each power's unique economic, geographic, and political conditions as to the influence of its national culture.

Put differently, some evidence exists to support the argument for an overall Western way of war. Victor Davis Hanson's *The Western Way of War: The Infantry Battle in Classical Greece* (1989), perhaps the most widely cited and most controversial work on this topic, argued that the Western style of war is patterned on that of the Greek hoplites. Although Hanson's thesis, which relies on drawing stark contrasts between Western and other cultures, was popular for some time, that popularity is fading. In *Carnage and Cultures: Landmark Battles in the Rise of Western Power* (2001), Hanson argued that the victory of Hernán Cortés's conquistadors over Cuauhtémoc's Aztecs in 1520–21 was due largely to the West's traditions of rationalism, individualism, and civic duty, which led to significant advantages in "military organization, discipline, morale, initiative, flexibility, and command."[41] All of these purportedly contributed to Western dominance in warfare in the modern era. However, one could easily argue that each of these traditions can actually work against the development of essential martial virtues, especially discipline, obedience, and organizational cohesion. Other scholars have countered that Central and South America were already alive with shifting alliances and patterns of conquest well before the arrival of the Spaniards. These patterns simply continued, with the Spaniards contributing as auxiliaries to the Indians' plans of conquest, rather than the other way around.[42]

Other historians have taken on Hanson's thesis more directly, offering intriguing counterexamples in the form of successful Chinese and Indian armies, which were obviously remotely removed from Western values.[43] The debate will surely continue, especially as the effects of smallpox and other diseases continue to be reassessed and further research uncovers more about how Amerindians and other indigenes actually conceived of and practiced war.[44] The larger point, therefore, is that individual ways of war may be only as unique as combinations of political, economic, geographic, cultural, and other factors allow them to be.

Contrasting the "Old" and "New" American Ways of War

Throughout the 1990s, speculations ran high that a revolution was under way in the conduct of war and consequently in the American way of war. As General DePuy stressed in a letter to Gen. Colin Powell in September 1991, this RMA "certainly figured in the Soviet decision to end the Cold War."[45] As with any technological revolution, the much anticipated RMA would not necessarily benefit all services or combat functions equally. By extension, maximizing the power of the RMA might well require some services to accept diminished roles, missions, and force structures. Despite DePuy's reference to jointness, most claims regarding the new way of war concerned the increasing effectiveness of US air power—which some Pentagon briefings heralded as America's asymmetrical advantage.[46] Resource debates intensified in the face of large-scale downsizing measures designed to realize a "peace dividend." As they got under way, the phrase "new American way of war" appeared more frequently in defense literature to highlight enhanced capabilities, which in turn added to the phrase's increasing politicization. Counterarguments also appeared, noting that the effectiveness of US air power did indeed give the American way of war an image of potency that US diplomacy would do well to foster. However, air power was too limited in nature to solve most strategic problems.[47]

By the mid-1990s, efforts were being made to carry the story of the American way of war beyond Vietnam, where Weigley's book ends. Some of these efforts opined that a "new" American way of war was emerging based on the principle of "decisive force"—or the use of enough military power "to defeat an opponent swiftly and decisively"—which amounted to a subtle but important modification of Weigley's characterization of the US style of fighting as the use of overwhelming force to "grind down opponents with firepower and mass."[48] In contrast to the ideational study of military strategy that Weigley provided, others defined a way of war to mean "the military's orientation and preferred operational style."[49] These attempts also inadvertently raised the question as to which institutions—military or civilian—ought to determine the character of the American way of war. Moreover, an increasing number of analysts began to express concern that this way of war would not fit well in the post–Cold War security environment, a view Weigley also supported.[50] As a result, there was a growing sense that a composite, yet fundamental change was under way in both the means for waging war and the environments in which it would occur.[51]

By the beginning of the new millennium, the phrase "new American way of war" was used more frequently to describe a smaller, yet presumably more responsive force capable of meeting the challenges of the twenty-first century. In 2000, Michael Ignatieff connected the RMA and the American style of war directly, claiming that Desert Storm had demonstrated just "how far the RMA had transformed the American way of war."[52] The following year, Eliot A. Cohen described the key differences concerning the traditional American way of war and the new one.[53] The former, he said, was characterized by a desire to take the fight to the enemy, by the resolute pursuit of a decisive battle, by an overt dislike of diplomatic interference, and by a low tolerance for anything but clear political objectives. In contrast, the new style of warfare was marked by an aversion to casualties—as evidenced by a growing preference for precision bombing and long-range stand-off weapons—and a willingness to set aside the restrictions inherent in the doctrine put forth by Defense Secretary Caspar Weinberger and General Powell and participate in humanitarian interventions, which the reduced risk of casualties, in turn, made more acceptable. Cohen's comments revealed the extent to which the idea of the American way of war had become politicized: The traditional American way of war was associated with the residue of the industrial age and perhaps a stubborn military culture resistant to change, whereas the new one was believed to reflect the cutting-edge principles of the information age and to be more open to being deployed as an instrument of quick strikes and limited interventions that eschewed long-term commitments.

In the summer of 2002, other warnings appeared. Some historians cautioned that the new way of war would prove irresistible to American political leaders precisely because it appeared to offer low-risk solutions to a range of strategic problems.[54] What might be less obvious, however, is that the success of this approach, as the campaigns in Kosovo and Afghanistan initially had shown, depended greatly upon the availability of local ground forces willing and able to fight as a complement to US air power. The problem was that in most areas where the US military could expect to intervene, local ground forces were likely to be willing but not capable. Some defense scholars suggested that the new style of war was already passé: Its strategic premises were "no longer valid."[55] One of these obsolete premises was the alleged American aversion to casualties. Defense analysts such as Stephen Biddle rightly pointed out that, in the wake of thousands of lives lost in the attacks of September 11, 2001, Americans were now more willing to return to a more aggressive style of warfare and to bear whatever costs were necessary—including significant US casualties—to defeat al-Qaeda and its affiliates. Indeed, a number of opinion pieces seemed to affirm this shift in attitude.[56] The coalition's campaigns in Afghanistan appeared to have demonstrated that a capable ground force was essential for achieving military success. Historians and defense scholars alike were beginning to see the American way of war as the product of military techniques as well as popular attitudes.

The rapid defeat of the Taliban in 2001 and 2002 by this seemingly aggressive style of war encouraged Max Boot to make a case for imperial policing in his *Savage Wars of Peace: Small Wars and the Rise of American Power* (2002). "Yes, there is a danger of imperial overstretch and hubris," he admitted, "but there is an equal, if not greater, danger of undercommitment [sic] and lack of confidence."[57] By giving air to America's other way of war—its tradition of fighting so-called small wars—Boot set aside the premises of the Weinberger-Powell doctrine and attempted to remove the stigma that has been associated with small wars at least since the Vietnam era. He defined small wars in the spirit of Charles E. Callwell: "campaigns undertaken to suppress rebellions and guerrilla warfare."[58] For Boot, a way of war was not a history of ideas, as it was for Weigley, but a historical pattern or tradition reflecting how and why force has been used. He further maintained that, with respect to the pattern of America's small wars, there were four such purposes: inflicting punishment, as in the armed expedition to capture Pancho Villa (1916); ensuring protection, as in the Barbary Wars (1801–5 and 1815); achieving pacification, as in Haiti (1915–34) and the Dominican Republic (1916–24); and benefiting from profit-making, as in the other so-called Banana Wars of the early twentieth century, which furthered America's "dollar diplomacy."

Boot's *Savage Wars of Peace* actually attempted to do more than broaden the "traditional" American way of war. It tried to redefine that tradition as one that had always confronted head-on the particular risks and difficulties inherent in fighting small wars. "In most cases," he declared, "our armed forces, however ill-prepared for the job at hand, quickly adapted, figured out what they had to do, and did it with great success. . . . The bottom line is that the American armed forces should not be unduly afraid of small wars."[59] This statement completely overlooked the political costs typically incurred when a major power proves incapable of defeating a small, irregular force. Moreover, as reviewers quickly pointed out, American interventions often required the US military to occupy some places—such as the Philippines, Haiti, Nicaragua, and the Dominican Republic—many times and for many years at a time, in order to impose any kind of enduring stability. Indeed, even after long occupations, stability sometimes collapsed soon after US forces departed.[60] Many years later, it was still not clear whether the benefits of such interventions were worth the costs.

Nonetheless, by January 2003, the Office of the Secretary of Defense (OSD) had officially embraced an air-centric model of warfare, intending to exploit America's primacy in air power and to achieve quick results with minimal casualties and collateral damage.[61] The swift success of military operations in Iraq in the spring of 2003 seemed to validate this choice and to enhance the mystique surrounding the new American way of war even further. As historian Victor Davis Hanson declared, "there was no typical 'American Way of War' anymore, in the textbook sense of traditional armored drives supported by overwhelming firepower." Instead, a complete transformation was under way.[62] Throughout the spring and early summer of 2003, rhetoric proclaiming the success of the new model continued to escalate with public speeches and articles by Vice President Dick Cheney, Chairman of the Joint Chiefs of Staff Gen. Richard Myers, and the Defense Department's Chief of Transformation, Retired Admiral Arthur Cebrowski.[63] The principles underpinning the new model were briefed to Congress by Secretary Donald Rumsfeld and Gen. Tommy Franks in the summer of 2003.[64] Boot gave further articulation to these principles: "precision firepower, special forces, psychological operations, and jointness," which corresponded with the US Department of Defense's efforts to enhance the "speed, maneuver, flexibility, and surprise" of US forces and thereby reduce dependence on the industrial-age principles of mass and concentration.[65] The sum of these advantages meant, or was supposed to mean, that the United States could now wage the "savage wars of peace" more effectively and more efficiently. Still, to many it was not clear how the new principles and capabilities actually expanded America's strategic options when compared to the "old" way of war. Indeed, the new ones seemed to be effective only under limited circumstances.[66] Nonetheless, by this point in time the differences between the old and the new American ways of war were firmly, if inaccurately, established in the literature.

Failings in the American Way of War

Although some early accounts of operations in Afghanistan, such as in Norman Friedman's *Terrorism, Afghanistan, and America's New Way of War* (2003), were positive, by the autumn of 2003 it was becoming clear that claims concerning the potency of the new way of war had been oversold. As one former senior officer noted, postconflict security operations had apparently fallen to the wayside in the much-touted new American style of fighting.[67] By early 2004, the new way of warfare had also come under fire for, among other things, resembling a way of battle more than a way of war— treating military victory mainly as an end in itself, rather than as a means to an end.[68] The intervention in Iraq was being increasingly portrayed in defense literature and the media as a failure, and not just for the Bush administration or for the American way of war, but also, according to some critics at least, for the entire Western way of war. In short, the question had shifted from what the new American way of war was to what had gone wrong with it.

There were two immediate and diametrically opposed answers to this question. The first was that the US military had not transformed quickly or thoroughly enough: If some of the services had not reaped the benefits of the RMA, it was largely because they had failed to appreciate its potential. The second answer was that the RMA had gone too far: It was preoccupied with high-technology weaponry and developed concepts appropriate for only a narrow slice of the spectrum of conflict.

In 2005, Boot published an article, "The Struggle to Transform the Military," favoring the first answer and charging that some of the services had essentially blunted the transformative potential of the RMA. He then changed course in *War Made New: Technology, Warfare, and the Course of History* (2006), arguing that the Pentagon failed to invest in human capital because "senior leaders, such as Donald Rumsfeld, believed that the future of warfare lay in high-tech informational systems, not lowly infantrymen."[69] Some authors blamed the army more directly, claiming it was responsible for shaping American strategic culture in the direction of conventional warfare rather than along the path of dealing with nonstate actors.[70] Robert Tomes's *US Defense Strategy from Vietnam to Operation Iraqi Freedom: Military Innovation and the New American Way of War, 1973– 2003* (2007) appeared to support the first position, arguing that the RMA was not to blame for the slow transition to a counterinsurgency mind-set in Iraq and Afghanistan.[71] Tomes associated the idea of a way of war with the combination of military capabilities and doctrine and asserted that there was a close relationship between it and strategic culture.[72] He was not alone in this view. He also maintained that the American military had been drifting away from counterinsurgency capabilities and doctrine since Vietnam due to three reasons: the declining utility of nuclear defense strategy; the run of successful quick-strike interventions in the late 1980s and 1990s, which brought conventional warfare back into vogue; and the conservative nature of the innovation processes used by the Department of Defense. Tomes aptly reminded readers that precision-strike and information-based warfighting capabilities did not suddenly become available in the early 1990s but rather had been under development since the 1970s. The story of the transformation of the US military had taken place over three decades, not three years. While that is correct, the RMA was, in essence, about developing fundamentally "new ways of thinking" that would permit employing evolutionary capabilities in revolutionary ways.[73] It was the thinking, and specifically the thinking of the late 1990s and early 2000s, that had become the issue.

Thomas Mahnken's *Technology and the American Way of War since 1945* (2008) also seemed to support the first answer, maintaining that the "culture of the armed services has tended to shape which technologies they have pursued as well as how they have employed new weapons on the battlefield."[74] Expectations that information technology would produce revolutionary change in the American way of war, whether for good or ill, were, accordingly, too high and had to be revised. Mahnken also remarked that innovations—such as GPS and Blue Force Tracking—made possible by information technology were, on the whole, positive and that the information revolution was in fact bringing about fundamental changes in the "character of war."[75] Most scholars and practitioners would have agreed that the new technology brought immense benefits—the only items they might debate would be which elements of war had not changed. For Mahnken, a "nation's way of war flows from its geography and society and reflects its comparative advantage. . . . It represents an approach that a given state has found successful in the past."[76] He too asserted that there was a close relationship between a nation's way of war and its strategic culture. In his view, American strategic culture reflected a predilection for waging wars for unlimited aims while spurning limited wars, for demonizing its adversaries, and for relying on advanced technology.[77]

Frederick Kagan's *Finding the Target: The Transformation of American Military Policy* (2006) held to the second position, that the RMA was primarily about the expansion of air power capabilities and that it explicitly downplayed the need to hedge against chance and uncertainty, two inalienable properties associated with war's nature. As Grant Hammond's "The US Air Force and the American Way of War" (2005) also pointed out, the army had little influence, if any, over the development of navy or air force doctrines and, as a review of the defense literature of the 1990s shows, it was largely air-power concepts that had shaped the new American way of war. In short, both sides of the debate saw transformation as the problem. Whereas one side contended that some services had resisted transformation or had gone about it in ways that diluted its revolutionary potential, the other countered that a single service had essentially hijacked the process, due in part to the way it had aggressively marketed its capabilities.

By the autumn of 2006, however, a third view had emerged that went beyond the debate over the nature and consequences of transformation. According to this view, the answer to what had gone wrong with the US style of fighting was to be found deeply ingrained in Americans' long-standing habits of thinking about and waging war. One such critic, historian Jeffrey Record, maintained that the problem was "rooted in American political and military culture. Americans are frustrated with limited wars, particularly counterinsurgency wars, which are highly political in nature." The Pentagon's "aversion" to such wars, he went on to say, was "deeply rooted in the American way of war."[78] Along similar lines, Adrian Lewis's *The American Culture of War: The History of U.S. Military Force from World War II to Operation Iraqi Freedom* (2007) revealed that culture—whether national-, strategic-, or service-oriented—had become a popular explanation for why the American way of fighting failed at times. He asked "why Americans fight the way they do" and found the answer in the concept of national culture.[79] He identified ten key tenets of American culture, all of which, just as Mahnken argued, made the United States better at fighting traditional wars rather than modern, "limited" ones. These tenets were respect for human life, equal opportunity and burden sharing, pride in technology, optimism, a tendency to devalue military service in peacetime, isolationism, unilateralism, and ready acceptance of America's status as a great power.[80] All of these tenets would indeed seem to make the United States more prone to fighting crusades than to intervening in "quagmires." In 2010, Dominic Tierney's *How We Fight: Crusades, Quagmires, and the American Way of War* made a similar point. Tierney argued that there were two contradictory tendencies in the American way of war. One was typified by a "Crusader" mentality that embraced wars fought in defense of democracy for the overthrow of tyrants. The other was characterized by an aversion to potential quagmires, which tended to involve nation-building tasks and their sometimes heavy costs in lives and dollars. However, there is nothing peculiarly American about wanting to avoid quagmires. It is simply common sense.

All told, culture is a seductively convenient answer. Nonetheless, it is more a way around the problem than a cause or a solution. One either has to change the culture or avoid getting involved in sticky conflicts like Vietnam and Iraq. It is worth noting that Mahnken, Record, and many others have drawn heavily from a detailed description of the American way of war by Colin Gray, who once argued that the American style of fighting could adapt to the challenges of irregular warfare "but only with difficulty."[81] According to Gray, the American approach to war was distinguished by thirteen characteristics closely linked to US strategic culture. Gray held that the American way of war is (1) apolitical, paying little heed to how military operations will affect the peace; (2) astrategic, rarely thinking in strategic terms; (3) ahistorical, learning little from history; (4) problem-solving and optimistic; (5) culturally challenged; (6) technology-dependent; (7) focused on firepower; (8) large-scale; (9) aggressive and offensive; (10) profoundly regular; (11) impatient; (12) logistically excellent; and (13) highly sensitive to casualties.[82] Historical analyses would likely show periods in which all of these characteristics were present to some degree, as well as many cases in which they were not. European styles of warfare too, one would have to admit, would reflect many of these traits.

As discussed earlier, it is difficult to draw firm lines between ways of war. A case in point is Martin Shaw's New Western Way of War: Risk-Transfer War and Its Crisis in Iraq (2005), which attempted to equate the new American style of warfare—described as the effort to make war "precise, clinical, spatially and temporally discreet" and without serious ramifications for Western society and politics—to the larger Western way of war.[83] Shaw argued that the Western approach to waging war had developed a system or "economy" of "risk transfer" over the quarter century since the Vietnam conflict that reduced risks to soldiers and their political leaders by transferring them onto enemy combatants and onto noncombatants, "those whom the West agrees are 'innocent.'"[84] Whereas some scholars might see noncombatants as included in the Western goal of reducing casualties, Shaw argued differently, claiming that the risk-transfer economy breaks down in interventions such as Iraq, which he described as a hopeless quagmire, one of the "brutal struggles we cannot win."[85] What he actually captured with his theory of a risk-transfer economy, however, was not the Western way of war per se, but the growing sophistication of the West's collective strategic communications efforts, which are designed to elicit public consent to the use of violence in wars of choice.

Other works seemed to challenge Gray's sixth and seventh points, the American reliance on technology and firepower. Reuben Brigety's *Ethics, Technology and the American Way of War: Cruise Missiles and US Security Policy* (2007) maintained that the use of cruise missiles and other stand-off technologies was "logical and innovative," especially given the new international environment and American domestic concerns regarding casualties.[86] According to Brigety, "increased international attention on the protection of civilians in armed conflict has elevated the incidence of so-called 'collateral damage' from the status of a vexing moral dilemma to a serious strategic problem."[87] In other words, the American way of war has in some ways had to accept international as well as domestic restrictions. While some voices have suggested that the American way of war ought to reject such restraints, it is often clearly counterproductive to do so.[88]

A number of military experts and analysts would agree completely with Gray's description of the first two characteristics of the American way of war—namely, that it was apolitical and astrategic. Isaiah Wilson's *Thinking beyond War: Civil-Military Relations and Why America Fails to Win the Peace* (2007) explored the "ideas and mechanizations of the American way of war" in an effort to understand why it seemed "prone to winning all its battles but losing its wider wars."[89] His conclusion was that, as a nation, Americans had only a limited understanding and a partial definition of war. It was a definition that stopped at military victory. In his view, the American style of warfare failed to internalize Clausewitz's contention that war was the continuation of politics by other means. As a result, Americans tended not to think through the consequences that military actions might have for the peace that followed.

Similarly, Benjamin Buley's *New American Way of War: Military Culture and the Political Utility of Force* (2008) examined the cultural assumptions about armed conflict underpinning the new American style of war. The American "failure to convert its astonishingly rapid decapitation of the Iraqi regime into a stable political outcome," he maintained, was rooted in a military culture that "refused to accept the full implications of Clausewitz's insight that war is a true continuation of politics."[90] Buley held that the new American way of war differed in important respects from its predecessor but that there were essential cultural continuities linking them, one of which was the tendency to confuse military successes for political victories.

Michael Lind's *The American Way of Strategy: US Foreign Policy and the American Way of Life* (2006) offered a different interpretation, one that suggested the American way of war might not be as apolitical or astrategic as it seemed. In Lind's view, the American way of strategy reflected a historic balance, albeit with some failures, between the legitimacy politics of international liberalism and the power politics of realism.[91] Accordingly, the inconsistencies in American foreign policy and strategy are explained by the competing tensions created by upholding the values of self-determination and nonintervention on the one hand and addressing the threats posed by imperial powers or anarchy on the other. Lind also introduced the phrase "American way of world war," which he described as achieving the "economic exhaustion of the enemy by a coalition of great powers whose combined military and economic resources dwarfed those of the enemy."[92] Although the American tradition of limited war might be more relevant to the present and future, Lind saw a role for the American way of world war under a "concert of power" approach to grand strategy.

Although much has been written on the connections between warfare and economics, Hugh Rockoff's *America's Economic Way of War: War and the US Economy from the Spanish–American War to the Persian Gulf War* (2012) offered a much more detailed analysis of the relationships between the American way of waging war and US fiscal policies and economic realities. It showed, for instance, that America's twentieth-century wars, whether big or small, have tended to become more "cruel" in character as financial costs rise and human casualties mount.[93] This observation suggests that Sherman's "hard hand of war" approach to strategy may be more a function of rising costs in blood and treasure than an a priori characteristic of the American way of war.[94] However, it also begs the question as to whether those characteristics attributed to the American way of war are also found in other approaches to using force.

Indeed, the lack of comparative analyses regarding other ways of war has in many respects given rise to more than a few unsubstantiated claims about the uniqueness of the American way of war, its ills, and its cures. For instance, whereas Liddell Hart's *The British Way in Warfare* attributed rather more flexibility to the British approach to waging war than most historians believe it possessed, Weigley's *American Way of War* did the opposite for American strategic thinking. Both authors were clearly trying to shape contemporary policy through their historical analyses—Weigley by portraying the American style of fighting as he wished it were not, Liddell Hart by describing the British way of war as he wished it had been.[95] Nonetheless, both authors would inspire subsequent generations of historians to examine for themselves what the distinguishing characteristics of each way of war might be.[96]

Despite its lack of comparative basis and definitional flaws, Weigley's *American Way of War* has served ably as the point of departure in the search for the American style of war for more than forty years. That remains true even though his thesis was demolished more than a decade ago by Brian Linn. The search for the American way of war has continued, going further into those periods and themes Weigley omitted or barely touched. We now know more about the origins of the American way of fighting, its chief characteristics, how they changed over time, and their similarities with other ways of war. As one might expect, however, the more we know, the more we seek to know. Our definitions of ways of war have expanded from military patterns, to customs and practices, to what armies believed, and how those beliefs shaped their actions in war. The methods scholars have used have also changed, from the history of ideas that Weigley employed, to the identification of concrete strategic and tactical patterns, to the rather more amorphous cultural analyses. Those methods also included linking ways of war to strategic cultures, which became more popular as the American way of war became more politicized. This politicization both helped and hurt the general understanding of how America has fought its wars. On the one hand, it stimulated greater interest in the American style of war and encouraged research into underexplored areas. On the other, it prompted normative arguments claiming that the American style of fighting is not what it should be: It ought to be more political, more strategic, less sensitive to casualties, and more open to technological change, for instance, while at the same time being less technocentric.

Inevitably, historical analyses of the American way of war—including Weigley's—will reflect some of the political concerns of the period in which they were written. However, such efforts differ sharply from many of the works produced during the politicization of the American way of war at the end of the twentieth century. The new way of war that emerged at that time became almost inseparable from the US military's transformation agenda, and as a result the successes and failures of coalition campaigns in the field were often attributed to the soundness of that agenda and to the validity of the principles underpinning the RMA. The new American way of war was, in essence, the RMA in action.

Clausewitz's definition of war has figured large in the overall effort to understand the American way of war. Ironically, Weigley disagreed with Clausewitz's famous observation that war was a continuation of policy by other means and instead maintained that war tended to create policies of its own.[97] Presumably this disagreement was based at least in part on his study of America's wars over two centuries. Yet the chief failing of the American way of war is considered by many to be its inability to understand this particular doctrine of Clausewitz. Clearly our interpretations of the American way of war have been as fluid as the American style of fighting itself, changing not only as new weapons and new ideas about war were introduced, but also as the political stakes changed. If a way of war is the search for historical patterns, then strategic culture is presumably the glue that holds those patterns together. However, as will be shown in the next chapter, that adhesive has given the American way of war an artificial coherence.

Notes

1. Votaw and Weingartner, *In the Wake*, 12–14.

2. To be sure, these numbers do not tell the whole story. Some studies did not use the phrase "American way of war" in their titles but addressed it nonetheless. Others dealt with US internal politics, rather than the American way of war. See Engelhardt, *American Way of War*, and Jarecki, *American Way of War*.

3. Several reviews suggested the work was definitive. See Snell, "Review of *The American Way of War*," and Coffman, "Review of *The American Way of War*."

4. Weigley, *American Way of War*, 467.

5. Ibid., 477.

6. For example, see Johnson, *Afghan Way of War*; Melville, "Last Campaign"; Hayward, *For God and Glory*; and Cann, *Counterinsurgency in Africa*.

7. For an example of a coalition officer's frustration with the US approach, see Aylwin-Foster, "Changing the Army."

8. The linkages between strategic culture and ways of war are discussed in Sondhaus, *Strategic Culture*, 1.

9. Weigley, *American Way of War*, xx.

10. Bond, *Liddell Hart*.

11. Weigley, *American Way of War*, 36.

12. Ibid., xxiii.

13. One PhD dissertation, for instance, analyzed the events of the Korean War in light of an American cultural style of war but made no reference to Weigley: Toner, "Candide as Constable," ii. Toner appears to have borrowed less from Weigley than Pusey, *Way We Go to War*.

14. Calhoun, "Wilsonian Way of War," 2. Weigley's *American Way of War* is included in the bibliography but is not cited in the text. Later published as *Power and Principle* and *Uses of Force and Wilsonian Foreign Policy*.

15. Calhoun, "Wilsonian Way of War," 11.

16. Linn, "*American Way of War* Revisited."

17. Fitzgerald, *Learning to Forget?*

18. Linn, "*American Way of War* Revisited," 502–3.

19. Weigley, "Response to Brian McAllister Linn," 531.

20. Ibid. According to accepted military sources, the principal difference between the three basic strategies lies in their methods, not in their aims. Annihilation seeks to destroy the enemy force quickly, ideally in one or two battles. In

contrast, attrition seeks to destroy it gradually, while the third type, exhaustion, does not aim at military force directly but rather seeks to wear down an opponent's "will to resist." For updated definitions, see Department of History, *History of the Military Art*, 8, in which annihilation is the "complete and immediate destruction of the enemy's combat power," and attrition is the "gradual erosion of the [enemy's] combat power."

21. Linn, "*American Way of War* Revisited," 530.

22. Weigley, "Response to Brian McAllister Linn," 531.

23. Lee, "Early American Ways of War." This is an update of Higginbotham, "Early American Way of War."

24. Starkey, *European and Native American Warfare*, esp. 17–35.

25. Laramie, *European Invasion*, and Cohen, *Conquered into Liberty*.

26. Starkey, *European and Native American Warfare*, 19, and Malone, *Skulking Way of War*, 6.

27. Starkey, *European and Native American Warfare*, 14, 37–42.

28. Shannon, "Native American Way of War," and Lee, "Military Revolution."

29. Grenier, *First Way of War*, 10.

30. Ibid., ix, 223–25.

31. Lee, *Barbarians and Brothers*, 2–3.

32. Ibid., 3.

33. Bonura, *Under the Shadow*, 3; italics in original.

34. Ibid., 4.

35. Grotelueschen, *AEF Way of War*, 6; italics in the original.

36. Linn, *Echo of Battle*.

37. Ibid., 5–8.

38. Weigley, "American Strategy from Its Beginnings," 408.

39. Hanson, "American Way of War," 22.

40. Cf. Matheny, *Carrying the War*; Citino, *Blitzkrieg to Desert Storm* and *German Way of War*; and Harrison, *Russian Way of War*.

41. Hanson, *Western Way of War*, 20–22. There were also various multimedia presentations describing several key aspects of the Western way of war. See Centano, *Western Way of War*.

42. Matthew and Oudijk, *Indian Conquistadors*; Hassig, *Mexico and the Spanish Conquest*; and Clendinnen, "'Fierce and Unnatural Cruelty.'"

43. Lynn, *Battle*, esp. 1–28.

44. Estimates still vary widely concerning the impact of European diseases on Amerindian populations. See Mann, *1491* and *1493*.

45. Letter from DePuy to Powell dated September 26, 1991, in Swain, *Selected Papers*, 466.

46. Fogelman, "Airpower and the American Way of War." Cf. Hammond, "U.S. Air Force and the American Way of War."

47. Cohen, "Mystique of U.S. Air Power."

48. Hoffman, *Decisive Force*, xii.

49. Ibid., 1.

50. Weigley, "New Way of War?"

51. For some, this change had more to do with rebuilding the US military's morale, its operational doctrine, and its organizational structure after Vietnam. See Kitfield, *Prodigal Soldiers.*

52. Ignatieff, "The New American Way of War," surveyed new contributions to the existing literature.

53. Cohen, "Kosovo and the New American Way of War."

54. Record, "Collapsed Countries."

55. Biddle, "New Way of War?"

56. Robert L. Bartley, "Thinking Things Over," asked not whether Americans could "abide body bags," which surely they had, but rather why "hesitancy at the decisive moment" seems more frequent in the American way of war than "incisiveness."

57. Boot, *Savage Wars,* 352.

58. Ibid., xv, 287. See Callwell, *Small Wars,* 21.

59. Boot, "Everything You Think You Know."

60. Schwartz, "Post-Powell Doctrine."

61. Cebrowski and Barnett, "American Way of War."

62. Hanson, "American Way of War."

63. Cheney, "New American Way of War"; Meyers, "New American Way of War" (article) and "New American Way of War" (speech); Scott, "New Way of War"; Cebrowski, "New American Way of War"; and "Champion of 'A New American Way of War.'"

64. Rumsfeld and Franks, "Summary of Lessons."

65. Boot, "New American Way of War."

66. Owens, "Unlikely Partners."

67. Atkeson, "Adapting." The Defense Department's Office of Force Transformation responded by quickly commissioning a study to address this deficiency, but it was not clear from where the resources would come to implement its recommendations. Binnendijk and Johnson, *Transforming.*

68. Echevarria, *Toward an American Way of War,* and "Principles."

69. Boot, *War Made New,* 467.

70. Lock-Pullen, "U.S. Way of War."

71. Tomes, *US Defense Strategy,* 1.

72. Ibid., 4.

73. Rumsfeld, "Transforming the Military," 21.

74. Mahnken, *Technology,* 220. The exceptions to the rule were nuclear weapons and long-range ballistic missiles.

75. Ibid., 223–25.

76. Ibid., 3.

77. Ibid., 4–6.

78. Record, "American Way of War," 1.

79. Lewis, *American Culture of War*, xvii.

80. Several of the tenets were reminiscent of Hanson's Western traditions; see Lewis, *American Culture of War*, 34–35.

81. Gray, *Irregular Enemies*, vii, and "American Way of War," which listed twelve characteristics.

82. Gray, *Irregular Enemies*, 30–49.

83. Shaw, *New Western Way of War*, 3.

84. Shaw claimed that there were fifteen "rules" by which this system of risk-transfer war operated. Wars must (1) be plausible responses to risks to Western interests, norms, and values; (2) be limited in the risks they create; (3) anticipate the problems of global surveillance; (4) be strictly time-limited, quick-fix wars; (6) be limited spatially; (7) minimize casualties to Western troops, above all; (8) rely heavily on air power; (9) kill the enemy efficiently, quickly, and discreetly; (10) minimize civilian casualties, but "massacres must be regarded as inevitable"; (11) rely on precision weaponry to sustain their legitimacy; (12) conceal suffering and death; (13) spread long-term, postwar risks as widely as possible internationally; (14) annex "humanitarianism" to compensate for violence against civilians; and (15) manage the media. *New Western Way of War*, 71–94.

85. Ibid., 1.

86. Brigety uses case studies of four operations: Southern Watch, January 1993; Bushwacker, June 1993; Deliberate Force, August–September 1995; and Desert Strike, September 1996.

87. Brigety, *Ethics, Technology*, 2.

88. Peters, "Speed the Kill."

89. Wilson, *Thinking beyond War*, xiv.

90. Buley, *New American Way of War*, 5.

91. Lind, *American Way of Strategy*, 23.

92. Ibid., 210.

93. Rockoff, *America's Economic Way of War*, 4.

94. Weigley, *American Way of War*, 149.

95. For British critiques, see Howard, "British Way in Warfare," and Strachan, "British Way in Warfare Revisited." For recent takes on the British style of war, see Neilson and Kennedy, *British Way in Warfare*; McInness, *Hot War, Cold War*; Freedman, "Alliance and the British Way"; and French, *British Way in Warfare*.

96. Linn, "American Way of War," and Owens, "American Way of War."

97. Weigley felt that armed conflict introduced a new set of political dynamics that placed the winning of war above other goals. "War once begun," he wrote, "has always tended to generate a politics of its own: to create its own momentum, to render obsolete the political purposes for which it was undertaken, and to erect its own political purposes." "Political and Strategic Dimensions," 341.

2

American Strategic Culture
An Elusive Fiction

> [All interpretations of culture are] fictions in the sense that they are "something made," "something fashioned"—in the original meaning of *fictiō*—not that they are false [or] unfactual.
>
> *Clifford Geertz,* The Interpretation of Cultures, *1973*

IF THE AMERICAN WAY OF WAR is a history of contending interpretations, the story of American strategic culture is one of elusive fictions. This is true not only because the concept of strategic culture has been too variously and too broadly defined, but also because it rests on contradictory and as yet unresolved tensions between continuity and change and between uniqueness and commonality. Put differently, if strategic culture is likened to the glue that holds patterns of war together, then interpretations of American strategic culture lack the power to adhere. They are at best what Clifford Geertz said all interpretations of culture must be: "fictions in the sense that they are 'something made,' 'something fashioned.'"[1] They are not necessarily false as such. However, they have yet to be reconciled with the historical record, and as this chapter argues, it is not likely they can be.

Problematic Origins

The concept of strategic culture was originally advanced by Jack Snyder in a monograph titled *The Soviet Strategic Culture: Implications for Nuclear Options*, which was published in 1977.[2] Snyder used the concept to challenge the core assumption underpinning the US policy concerning "limited nuclear options"—namely, if deterrence failed, both sides would still act with restraint by selecting targets and weapons that would minimize damage. As a counter to that assumption, Snyder argued that the Soviets "may be more favorably inclined toward unilateral damage limitation strategies than toward cooperative ones." American and Soviet strategic thinking, he said, "had developed in different organizational, historical, and political contexts, and in response to different situational and technological constraints." Mirror-imaging, in other words, was risky.[3]

It is worth noting that Snyder's monograph was published by the RAND Corporation, and as was typical of its products at the time (and still is), his piece addressed a specific policy issue—in this case, potential vulnerabilities in US nuclear flexibility doctrine. It is also worth noting that an underlying theme in Snyder's study was the credibility of "game theory," a widespread but controversial analytical approach that tended to represent opponents as "generic strategists" who were "culture-free and preconception free." Snyder's concept of strategic culture was one way of highlighting the vulnerability of that theory. In his view, Soviet responses might well surprise American strategists because the two sides could be thinking along different lines or from within different belief structures. Moreover, these differences might possess a quality of "semipermanence" that placed them on the level of "'culture' rather than mere 'policy.'"[4]

Snyder's theory was, in retrospect, more useful not as a separate field of study, which it inadvertently became, but as a means to expose the limitations of mirror-imaging in strategic analyses. The tone of his monograph is tentative: It discusses strategic culture as a theoretical counterweight rather than as an established fact. The theory itself was based on two broad but ultimately indefensible assumptions. The first of these was that historical circumstances and experiences are, by definition, unique, and they thus lead to distinct concepts or ways of thinking. However, this assumption overlooks the fact that many historical experiences are shared, such as wars fought by alliances against common enemies or intellectual movements such as the Enlightenment or economic and technological transformations such as the Industrial Revolution. To be sure, shared experiences would in some respects have to pass through separate cultural filters, but those filters also expand in the light of shared experiences. In contrast, Snyder's assumption of cultural uniqueness inclined too far in the direction of impermeability or insularity. While all cultures are surely unique in some respects, the historical record shows that their modes of thinking are not necessarily insular. Russian and Western cultures, for instance, interacted over many centuries and influenced each other in various ways, despite many obvious differences.[5] As a result, both cultures developed methods of understanding each other, however imperfect. A search for cultural differences will in fact yield cultural differences, in other words. Still, the resulting picture will be a distorted one.

Snyder's second assumption was that substantial continuity persists despite significant change. Indeed, the essence of strategic culture is the idea that a "large residual degree of continuity" remains in place and influential despite changes in "objective conditions." Snyder's term for this was "semipermanence" (a neologism). However, readers would do well to remember that semipermanence does not describe a real condition. A thing can either be temporary or permanent, not both. To use this term is to set aside or eliminate the impact of change rather than taking it into account. Once change is so removed, the influence of purported constants, such as geography or climate, is left unchallenged. Ignoring the tension between change and continuity thus leads to a different kind of distorted picture. It is one thing to search for unique and enduring attitudes or values; it is another thing to create the conditions for them.

Snyder's theory of strategic culture not only rested on dubious assumptions—it also suffered from the definitional vagueness and tautological snares that have plagued the general concept of culture. He defined culture as "the sum total of ideas, conditioned emotional responses, and patterns of habitual behavior that members of a national community have acquired through instruction or imitation and share with each other."[6] According to the wording here, without knowledge of the "sum total" it is not possible to talk about culture. Moreover, the sum total, if such a thing exists or can be known, would be impossible to represent. In addition, Snyder's definition contains terms such as "conditioned emotional responses" and "habitual behavior," which convey a sense that culture both defines behavior and determines it.

Snyder's tendency toward inclusion rather than exclusion is not unusual among definitions of culture. One example of such a definition appears in an official publication of the US military, which refers to culture as the "distinctive and deeply rooted beliefs, values, ideology, historic traditions, social forms, and behavioral patterns of a group, organization, or society."[7] It should not be surprising, then, that we find the same tendency carried over to definitions of strategic culture, which one scholar recently defined as "a nation's traditions, values, attitudes, patterns of behavior, habits, customs, achievements and particular ways of adapting to the environment and solving problems with respect to the threat or use of force."[8] Similarly, any number of variables are said to constitute strategic culture: geography, climate, natural resources, organization, traditions, historical practices, political structures, ideology, myths, symbols, generational change, and technology.[9] Such broad definitions and limitless variables make it impossible to determine what strategic culture is.

While scholars have long admitted defining culture (or strategic culture) is difficult, they have not entirely acknowledged the implications of saying it. Clearly such definitions are tautological, but circular reasoning is more than an intellectual embarrassment or a minor inconvenience for the discipline. If an object of study cannot be defined and isolated, then genuine scientific analysis cannot begin, and defensible conclusions cannot be drawn. Precise definitions are also a safeguard against determinism, which makes an idea both a cause and an effect. To be sure, some definitions of strategic culture are more selective. However, one cannot compare Soviet strategic culture to American strategic culture unless they are defined in the same way— otherwise the concept is useless to policymakers and strategists. Nor can one compare an approach defining strategic culture as the "context" within which strategic debate and formulation take place to one that defines it as the way in which "members of a military or political elite approach the problem of winning."[10] Drawing general conclusions from such approaches is not possible, and the field of study cannot advance, despite its popularity. Ironically, neither of these approaches needs the label of strategic culture. It adds nothing to their efforts. Definitions of strategic culture have thus not only confounded the study of it—they have diverted worthy endeavors from other topics.

Problematic Applications

The theory's flaws notwithstanding, it was enthusiastically embraced and too hastily applied. The literature concerning the concept's use describes it in terms of three waves or generational shifts.[11] These follow a loose thesis-antithesis-synthesis progression. However, a fourth shift has also occurred that is not mentioned in the literature, and it will be described here. Not surprisingly, none of the shifts resolved the underlying tensions in the theory.

The first wave (or thesis) began in the early 1980s as scholars picked up Snyder's original concept and applied it in a search for other "distinctly national" approaches to strategy and their core determinants.[12] To be sure, it is reasonable to expect that Russians, Americans, Chinese, and others would think differently about strategy. However, as discussed earlier, the search for uniqueness—for "distinct modes of strategic thinking"—went too far.[13] Also, removing change from the search for core determinants meant that strategic culture was seen as predictive.[14]

The second shift, or antithesis, began in the early 1990s with Snyder's criticism of the manner in which his initial theory was being applied.[15] Rather than serving as an alternative to rational-actor models as he had intended, it was being used to predict strategic behavior and to justify specific defense policies precisely because, as previously noted, Snyder's theory and the pictures it created facilitated such use. Snyder was joined in his criticisms by a number of other scholars, who also added that strategic cultures were rarely as unique as assumed and that many were, in fact, subjectively constructed.[16] The concept was not abandoned, however, nor did its growing popularity appear to have suffered in any way.

The third shift began in the late 1990s in response to the criticisms offered by Snyder and others. In essence, it was an attempted synthesis that recast strategic culture as an explanatory "context," rather than the determinant, of strategic behavior.[17] The synthesis did not succeed entirely because contextual factors that explain must also to some degree determine, otherwise they lack explanatory power. Despite Snyder's denials, his original concept did have deterministic elements in it, as we have seen. To be valid, any theory of strategic culture would have to be able to do both—explain and predict—at least broadly. And yet none has.[18] Constructivism has also been part of the synthesis, as recent studies of British, Chinese, Japanese, and Israeli strategic cultures show.[19] In some respects, the influence of constructivism has merely returned anthropological studies to the classic frames of reference established by Geertz and others, who opined that culture is the product of dynamic social processes with participants often acting as interpreters and vice versa.[20]

The fourth shift is characterized by the concept's politicization and its subsequent use in the public sphere. An example is how prominent political figures, such as former secretary general of the Council of the European Union (EU) Javier Solana, have publicly used "strategic culture" to make policy announcements and to create or manage expectations.[21] Solana announced that the EU had embraced a "strategic culture that fosters early, rapid, and when necessary, robust intervention."[22] In this case, the term signified a seemingly broad agreement to put in place mechanisms that would facilitate certain kinds of strategic interventions, while also reaffirming some of the EU's collective values. Another example is found in Robert Kagan's provocative assertion that "Americans are from Mars and Europeans are from Venus."[23] Kagan essentially claimed that the United States and Europe had developed diverging strategic cultures. Americans, in his view, were more comfortable using hard power—military force—to extend the reach of policy. Europeans, in contrast, saw the reliance on military force as crude and naive and instead preferred diplomatic measures marked by "subtlety and indirection."[24] His subsequent elaboration of the argument in *Of Paradise and Power: America and Europe in the New World Order* (2003) revealed that, as with the

American way of war, the phrase "American strategic culture" had become an extension of politics by rhetorical means.

Kagan's *Of Paradise and Power* presumed to speak for American strategic culture, and his rendition of it promoted his worldview as broadly representative. Absent from his discussion were the dialectical tensions that have defined American politics and strategy from the start. What emerged was little more than a one-dimensional representation, a caricature, of the American worldview that was perhaps true of the administration of George W. Bush but not of the administrations immediately before or after it. The fact that the concept of strategic culture facilitates such facile representations is another one of its major flaws. Snyder's attempt to distinguish between "mere policy" and strategic culture only begs the question as to whether the latter is not better thought of as a form of grand or meta-policy, since it lacks particulars as well as the durability to span different administrations.

Kagan's assertion regarding the celestial origins of Americans and Europeans also shows that the boundaries between waves or generational shifts are not rigid. The search for distinctly national approaches to strategy often went hand in hand with the politicization of the concept. Perceived differences between American and European political perspectives shaped the concept of strategic culture. Those applications, in turn, influenced what the major differences were perceived to be and subsequently what American strategic culture was and was not. As the campaigns in Iraq and Afghanistan wore on, the question of what American strategic culture was or was not became increasingly associated with identifying what was wrong with it.

American Fictions

Although Snyder's concept of strategic culture provided a theoretical counterweight to the reflexive sterility of rational-actor models, its dubious assumptions kept it from being more than that. It provided the intellectual rationale for acknowledging asymmetry in strategic thinking. However, because it overlooked the influence of shared experiences, the impact of change, and the dialectical tensions of politics, it was never able to describe specific strategic cultures. After four generations of effort, it could manage little more than assertions based on vague generalities, stereotypes, and caricatures. These errors carried over into interpretations of American strategic culture. The search for a distinctly American approach to strategy, and its core determinants, was based more on myth and conventional wisdom than fact. The United States was assumed, for instance, to have developed a unique strategic culture because it has had unaggressive neighbors to its north and south, as well as major water "barriers" to its east and west, essentially giving it a history of "free security."[25]

However, even seemingly elemental factors such as geography do not hold up well as determinants, particularly in the case of the United States. America's so-called constants have actually changed more frequently and more completely than such claims appreciate. Not only was armed conflict present every step along the way, but the United States was never as isolated as this fiction suggests. By the time the Treaty of Paris was signed in 1783, the land area of the United States was approximately 888,900 square miles. Within twenty years, it had doubled, due largely to the Louisiana Purchase in 1803. The purchase of Alaska in 1867 doubled the territory of the United States yet again—to 3,615,000 square miles. From the late nineteenth century on, the United States acquired territories in much the same way as the Europeans did, though in Latin America and the Pacific rather than Africa and Asia. As a result, the geography of the United States (the territory it controlled) has changed dramatically over the preceding centuries, even if the geography of North America itself has not.

Even before the United States was established, North America was more a "land of war" than one of peace, partly because the European struggle for power had carried across the Atlantic.[26] By the time of the Louisiana Purchase, the United States had already waged an undeclared naval war with France, was engaged in the First Barbary War, and had put down several rebellions and insurrections, which, though tiny in comparison to the French Revolution, had seriously tested the fledgling American government. It had also fought protracted wars against the Chickamaugas (1776–94) and the Northwest Indian tribes (1785–95), who had inflicted humiliating defeats on US troops in 1790 and 1791.[27] Over the following six decades, the United States fought conflicts against France (1798–1800), England (1812–15), the Barbary pirates (1801–2, 1815), and Mexico (1846–48), as well as the Seminoles, Apaches, Cheyennes, Comanches, Dakotas, Osages, Navajos, Sioux, Paiutes, Pawnees, and other Native American tribes.[28] To that total we must add US military expeditions into the Gulf of Mexico, the coasts of Florida, the Caribbean, and as far away as Asia, Africa, South America, Greece, and Turkey, which were intended to punish pirates and bandits and to protect American commercial interests. Even such small military actions were important to a relatively young government attempting to earn the respect of its own citizens, as well as the regard of Europe's more established regimes.

Although conventional wisdom might claim that the Atlantic and Pacific oceans served as barriers, they actually functioned more as conduits. Until the expansion of the railroad in the mid-nineteenth century, seaborne travel was essentially four or five times faster than travel by land, and it entailed less physical strain for people and animals. Even before the age of steam, seagoing vessels could typically cover 100 to 120 miles per day, while horse-driven pack trains could manage only 20 to 30 miles per day, and ox-driven wagons only half that much. The distance from London to Boston is about the same as from Boston to Los Angeles (about three thousand miles as a crow flies), but a seagoing vessel could complete three or four round-trips between Boston and London in the same time that an ox-driven wagon train would need to travel once from Independence, Missouri, to San Francisco.[29]

Demographic and economic changes were also significant over the last two centuries. The population of the United States grew from an estimated 2.5 million people in 1776 to more than 275 million by the end of the twentieth century, more than 61 million of whom were immigrants who had arrived after 1840.[30] Such changes make it difficult for claims regarding the emergence of a particular American national character to find firm purchase. Economically the United States transformed from an agrarian-based society to an industrial-based economy to a service- and production-based economy. As a result, the surface area of the United States was altered through urbanization and the growth of networks of rail and water transportation infrastructures. In short, the original thirteen states (circa 1783) cannot be compared to the United States of the early twenty-first century in almost any category. Accordingly, evidence supporting claims regarding long-term continuities and "semipermanent" values in American strategic thinking remains elusive.[31]

As the concept of strategic culture became more politicized, the search for American strategic culture evolved into a question not of what it might be, but rather what had gone wrong with it. Three popular fictions emerged as answers. The first of these claimed that the flaw in American strategic culture was that it viewed wars naively as crusades or "fights to the finish" rather than as untidy scrums requiring negotiation and compromise.[32] The second popular answer suggested that American strategic culture was too technocentric—too prone to search for technological solutions for complex political and military problems.[33] The third and most popular fiction argued that the problem was that Americans were overly sensitive to casualties and that this adversely affected their strategic choices and operational methods.[34] However, as will be shown, none of these fictions holds up to historical scrutiny or to cross-cultural comparisons, raising the question once again as to whether meta-policy is a more accurate term for the phenomenon Snyder tried to identify. Each is instead a by-product of the tendency to see contemporary problems as rooted in the past.

Crusades and Limited Wars

Historical evidence is also elusive with respect to the view that Americans have an aversion to fighting limited wars and prefer instead to fight "wars to the finish." Between 1798 and 2009, the United States used military force more than 280 times in conflicts and potential conflicts abroad.[35] (It has also used military force more than 170 times in domestic situations during the same time frame.) Strictly speaking, only two of these—the Civil War and the Second World War—qualify as wars to the finish, if the term is taken to mean that the aim was the "extinction of a nation-state" or unconditional surrender.[36] In each of these cases, maintaining support for the war required considerable effort once the initial swell of "war fever" had passed. In the first case, "war weariness and the grim realities of army life" had set in by 1863 to the extent that the Union had to institute a draft of sorts to maintain recruitment quotas.[37] However, the conscription system that was implemented by the North in 1863, which was also similar to that instituted in the South, allowed for commutation (payment for exemption from the current draft) and substitution (hiring a substitute), such that "of the 207,000 men who were drafted [in 1863], 87,000 paid the commutation fee and 74,000 furnished substitutes, leaving only 46,000 who went personally into the army."[38] This system was not uniquely American, as the commutation-substitution provisions had deep European roots, even deeper than the levee en masse. It did work in a sense, producing several hundred thousand recruits over the remainder of the war, but it did so with federal and local authorities paying substantial bounties in order to meet recruitment quotas. Many recruits were willing to serve and to reenlist for bounties. Yet the point is that support for the war to preserve the Union had to be subsidized by the government. It also had to be aggressively nurtured through propaganda and other means of opinion shaping. Pamphleteering was a private enterprise until 1863, when organizations were established specifically for the purpose of diffusing political knowledge. The cities of New York and Philadelphia produced over five million copies of two hundred different pamphlets.[39]

In the case of the Second World War, new research suggests that support for the war was different in nature than once believed. Public support was contingent on the "unusual durability of elite consensus on the correctness of the war."[40] It was not the type of war (limited or unlimited) that mattered per se but whether American citizens perceived Germany, Italy, and Japan as threats. Before the war, America's "greatest generation" was divided along ethnic lines: Citizens with ties to Allied countries were more likely to want to help, while those with roots in Axis countries were more likely to prefer minimal or no involvement.[41] The attack on Pearl Harbor did not entirely eliminate these differences, nor did it galvanize the American public to move from iso-lationism to interventionism so much as it muted partisan resistance to Presi-dent Franklin D. Roosevelt's interventionist policies, which of course were bearing fruit before the war. Once the United States was attacked, partisan opposition lost its rationale for not intervening. Moreover, administration officials undertook extensive efforts to nurture public support, particularly after the Allied victories in 1942 at Midway, El Alamein, and Stalingrad, lest American citizens grow complacent believing victory was close.[42] Deliberate efforts were also undertaken to conceal the prospective costs of the so-called good war from the American public. These included debt financing, print-ing money, instituting wage and price controls, rationing, controlling pro-duction control, and deferring taxation.[43] Rather than Americans being "un-comfortable with wars for limited political aims," it seems more accurate to say that the United States, like most nations, is uncomfortable with what it perceives to be disproportionate disruptions to its economic and daily life. Most of America's small wars or military interventions caused little or no discomfort and were not opposed on principle or otherwise.

Technocentrism

This claim is curious because, if viewed historically, technocentrism could hardly be described as a long-term characteristic of either the American way of war or American strategic culture. By the end of the nineteenth century, the United States was clearly a leading economic power, but it did not hold the lead with regard to military technology. Instead, Germany and the United Kingdom had set the pace in the development of naval technologies, largely as a result of their mutual antagonism and participation in the global arms race under way since the late 1880s.[44] France clearly led the way in field ar-tillery during this time, introducing a fully recoilless gun in 1898, and after 1905 the French broke one record after another in aviation, despite the fact that Americans had recorded the first ever heavier-than-air flight in 1903.[45] In short, at the beginning of the twentieth century American technological contributions to warfare were, on the whole, uninspiring. The general West-ern attitude toward technological innovation was ambivalent, torn between optimism on the one hand and apprehension on the other.[46]

French technological advances before the Second World War were also notable. Even though the Maginot Line has been much derided by critics, it was a superior technological achievement for its day. Also, French tanks are widely recognized as having been qualitatively superior to their German counterparts. Technological achievement and its integration into the pro-cesses of war, in other words, were not notable American characteristics in the interwar years. During the war, American military hardware was arguably not much better overall than that of its allies and adversaries. The Soviet T-34 tank was, in fact, superior to its American counterparts and may well have been the best overall tank produced during the war. American technology had the edge in warships and, by the end of the war, in aircraft with the P-51 fighter and B-17 and B-29 bombers. However, the Germans made numerous qualitative innovations in jet-propelled aircraft and rocket and missile technologies. Technology had clearly been an integral part of the ways of war of all the major powers during the industrial age. None stood out as culturally disposed to technology more than any other. All of them also employed styles of war that used vast amounts of firepower to facilitate the maneuver of friendly forces over land or sea, while at the same time using air interdiction and long-range bombing in attempts to destroy production facilities and morale.

During the Cold War, both the North Atlantic Treaty Organization (NATO) and the Warsaw Pact competed aggressively to expand the quantity and quality of conventional weapons, as well as weapons of mass destruction. However, in the 1970s, Americans also began actively developing long-range precision munitions and information technologies, which by the early 1990s would give rise to speculations regarding an emerging revolution in military affairs. It is true that technocentrism became a characteristic of many of the Pentagon's military theories at the time, such as network-centric warfare (NCW) and effects-based operations (EBO). However, they also quickly became part of the rest of NATO's military thinking as well. NCW was eagerly embraced by European militaries, and EBO became EBAO in NATO doctrine (the added *A* being for "approach"). Moreover, US military thinking also included a counterculture represented by theories, such as fourth-generation warfare, which, however flawed, still stood in direct opposition to those promoted by RMA advocates.[47]

Casualty Aversion
As with the other fictions discussed here, the belief that casualty aversion is a characteristic of American strategic culture is fairly recent. However, it has no historical foundation. Moreover, recent research suggests that American support for military action is tied more to the public's perceptions of the way the war is unfolding and the prospects for success rather than directly to the number of casualties.[48] Casualty aversion differs from a general concern over minimizing friendly casualties in that the former can force policymakers and military planners to consider only those options that keep casualties close to zero. Otherwise, it is feared, support for the war will collapse and force the mission to be terminated before it has a full chance to succeed. Casualty

aversion was not a factor in any of America's wars up to the Vietnam War. American casualties (dead and wounded) in the Civil War and the First and Second World Wars, for instance, numbered 647,000 (Union only), 321,000, and 1,100,000, respectively.[49] The costs were high, but the aims were considered worth the price. In contrast, in wars of choice, such as the Korean and Vietnam conflicts, it was more difficult to establish where the cost threshold was or ought to have been. American casualties in the Korean and Vietnam Wars were 140,000 and 212,000, respectively; the latter is only somewhat lower than World War II when viewed as a percentage of troops in service.[50] In truth, the threshold can be viewed differently across the political spectrum: Conservatives and liberals may disagree on how much the policy aims in a particular conflict are worth.[51] Again, new research suggests that public support does not reflexively collapse with the occurrence of casualties, but rather with falling expectations of success.[52] Of course, the rhetoric of the political opposition will connect the incidence of casualties to the likelihood of failure, thereby turning the mission into a liability. It is up to government officials to disassociate casualties from expectations of success by pointing to other indicators. In short, casualties become a political instrument in time of war, regardless of the type of conflict, and this is part of the legacy of the First World War. It is surely not unique to the American context. How powerful that instrument becomes is dependent upon the stakes and how well governments are able to manage the public's reception of adverse news against the prospects for success.

As mentioned earlier, casualty aversion is commonly associated with the contemporary Western way of war. Whether one accepts the argument that risk transfer is a characteristic of "postheroic" warfare and its related "culture of restraint," the risk-benefit calculus has changed since the end of the Cold War largely because neither the political stakes nor the benefits of intervention are high.[53] Casualty aversion is thus more a policy choice in response to changed conditions than a semipermanent aspect of culture.

Conclusion

It was Clifford Geertz who first described interpretations of culture as fictions: not necessarily untrue or "unfactual" but clearly something fashioned or made. The key differences between the fiction of an invented story and that of a subjective account of an event, as he explained, are the conditions of their creation and the purposes for which they were created.[54] Fictions succeed if they achieve their purposes. These range from entertainment (storytelling) to conveying information (recounting).

By Geertz's criterion, the fictions surrounding American strategic culture have failed. They have informed discussions of different national, political, or military perspectives in misleading ways, having misrepresented or invented traits that are supposed to be either enduring or uniquely American. This is true despite the fact that some of the interpreters of American strategic culture are part of the culture they purport to interpret. These efforts have succumbed to cultural determinism brought on by the concept's basic definitional vagaries and underlying tensions, which after several decades remain unresolved. In still other cases, the concept's popularity has induced individuals to assign the label of strategic culture to their works unnecessarily. Strategic culture, in short, went from being something fashioned, in Geertz's words, to something fashionable. While the concept may remain intriguing to academics, its flaws make it too risky for policymakers and strategists.

Notes

1. Geertz, *Interpretation of Cultures*, 15. The field has expanded greatly since Geertz's classic was published in 1973, but his description of interpretations of culture as fictions is still valid.

2. Snyder, *Soviet Strategic Culture*, v. Whether Snyder was actually the first to coin the term "strategic culture" is not clear, but his monograph is generally cited as the source.

3. Ibid., 39.

4. Ibid., v.

5. Some of these ways were reexamined in an Oxford University conference, "Was There a Russian Enlightenment?," held on November 10, 2012.

6. Snyder, *Soviet Strategic Culture*, 8.

7. Mullen, *Officer Professional Military Education Policy*. Compare this definition to Geertz's description of culture as a "historically transmitted pattern of meanings" in *Interpretations of Culture*, 4.

8. Booth, "Concept of Strategic Culture," in Sondhaus, *Strategic Culture*, 5.

9. Howlett, "Strategic Culture."

10. Cf. Gray, *Nuclear Strategy*, to Lee, *Warfare and Culture*, 5. Underpinning this definition is the assumption that leaders' decisions are influenced by "past experience, beliefs, and expectations about the nature of war and what actions would not only define victory but also produce it." While the approach clearly brings up useful topics for study, it does not distinguish how an individual's personal experiences, beliefs, and expectations differ from those shared by the group.

11. The three shifts are summarized in Adamsky, *American Strategic Culture*, 8–12. See also Sondhaus, *Strategic Culture*, 1–13, which summarizes the debates, and Lantis, "Strategic Culture."

12. Cf. Gray, "National Style," and Booth, *Strategy and Ethnocentrism*.

13. Adamsky, *American Strategic Culture*, 8.

14. For a rejection of the notion of strategic determinants, see Strachan, "Operational Art," 100.

15. Snyder, "Concept of Strategic Culture," 4, 7.

16. Cf. Klein, "Theory of Strategic Culture," and Johnston, "Thinking about Strategic Culture." Johnston, in *Cultural Realism*, makes the case that the Chinese approach is closer to that of the West. For an opposing view, see Wang, *Harmony and War*. Porter, *Military Orientalism*, warns that the perception of difference may matter more than the reality.

17. Gray, "Strategic Culture." See Poore, "What Is the Context?"

18. Katzenstein, *Culture of National Security*; Gray, *Out of the Wilderness*; and Farrell, *Norms of War* and "Strategic Culture."

19. Baylis and Stoddart, "British Nuclear Experience"; Wang, *Harmony and War*; Forrest, *Compellence*; Kober, "What Happened," which defined Israeli strategic culture as belief in the efficacy of experience and experience-based intuition, improvisation, material strength, and technology; Lantis, "Strategic Culture"; and Hopf, "Promise of Constructivism."

20. Geertz, *Interpretation of Cultures*, 15n2, explains that most interpretations of culture are only second- and third-order ones, though anthropological works based on other anthropological works can be fourth-order or higher.

21. Cornish and Edwards, "Beyond the EU/NATO Dichotomy" and "Strategic Culture."

22. Solana, "Secure Europe." Cf. Cornish and Edwards, "Strategic Culture," 801.

23. See Kagan, "Power and Weakness," as well as Kagan, *Of Paradise and Power*. For reactions to Kagan's argument ten years on, see Kagan, "A Comment on Context"; Cooper, "Hubris and False Hopes"; Drezner, "Power of Economics"; Kupchan, "Still-Strong Alliance"; and Sarotte, "Deciding to Be Mars."

24. Drezner, "Power of Economics," 18.

25. Arms, "Strategic Culture," and Mahnken, *United States Strategic Culture*, 5–6.

26. Laramie, *European Invasion*, and Cohen, *Conquered into Liberty*.

27. Skaggs and Nelson, *Sixty Years' War*.

28. Morrison, *Oxford History*.

29. Ox-driven wagon trains in the mid-nineteenth century could take four to six months to travel from Independence to San Francisco, a distance of nearly two thousand miles along the Oregon and California trails. Cf. the classic Jefferson and Stewart, *Map of the Emigrant Road*.

30. These numbers do not reflect Native American populations, which fluctuated from about 600,000 in 1800 to 250,000 in 1890 to 1.9 million in 1990, nor does the 1776 estimate include African-descendant slave populations. Boyer, *Oxford Companion*, 179–81, 359–61.

31. Black, *Rethinking Military History*, 142, reminds readers that any interpretation of culture is likely to have an artificial coherence but that at some point artificiality becomes invention.

32. Mahnken, *Technology*, 4–6, and *United States Strategic Culture*, 6; Lewis, "American Culture of War" and *American Culture of War*, 33; and Tierney, *How We Fight*, 3–9.

33. Mahnken, *Technology*, 5–6, and Farrell, "Strategic Culture."

34. See Adamsky, *American Strategic Culture*; Thomas Mahnken, *United States Strategic Culture*; Farrell, "Strategic Culture"; Record, "Collapsed Countries"; Burk, "Public Support"; and Lord, "American Strategic Culture."

35. Grimmett, *Instances of the Use*.

36. The official war aims of both the Union and the Confederacy were limited at the outset but escalated into a war to the finish. McPherson, "From Limited War." Japan's surrender was, of course, not completely unconditional, as the Japanese emperor was allowed to retain his symbolic position. Murray and Millett, *War to Be Won*, 524–25.

37. McPherson, *Battle Cry of Freedom*, 600–611.

38. Ibid., 601.

39. Paludan, "'Better Angels,'" 362.

40. Berinski, *In Time of War*, 209.

41. Ibid., 8.

42. Roeder, *Censored War*, 1.

43. Rockoff, *America's Economic Way of War*, 317–19.

44. Sondhaus, *Naval Warfare*.

45. Echevarria, "Arms Race."

46. Echevarria, *Imagining Future War*.

47. In brief, the theory of fourth-generation war (4GW) holds that warfare has evolved through four generations: the use of massed manpower, firepower, maneuver, and an advanced form of insurgency. However, it tends to portray the insurgent of tomorrow in larger-than-life terms. Its other flaws are noted in Echevarria, *Fourth-Generation War*.

48. Gelpi, Feaver, and Reifler, *Paying the Human Costs*, 1–2.

49. Leland, *American War*.

50. Ibid., table 2.

51. Berinski, *In Time of War*, argues that public opinion in wartime reflects many of the same predilections it displays in peacetime.

52. Gelpi, Feaver, and Reifler, *Paying the Human Costs*, 2–3.

53. Luttwak, "Toward Post-Heroic Warfare" and "Post-Heroic Military Policy."

54. Geertz, *Interpretation of Cultures*, 16.

3

American Military Art
A Misleading Analogy

Strictly speaking, war is neither an art nor a science, and using such concepts as points of departure . . . results in a host of misleading analogies.

Carl von Clausewitz, On War, *1832*

MILITARY ART, the sum of strategic and operational practice, is clearly central to any way of war. However, the term "art" itself is misleading. As Clausewitz noted, war is neither an art nor a science. To think of it as either is to obscure its violent and dialectical aspects. Unlike painting or sculpture, war is a clash of opposing wills that *"react"* when force is directed against them.[1] Today the word *strategy* (from *strategía*) may still mean what it did in ancient Greece: the art of the general (*strategós*).[2] Yet the success of generalship has always owed at least as much to the methods of science as it does to the skills of the individual. Even the most celebrated displays of American operational art—Winfield Scott's campaign against Mexico City in 1847, the invasion of Normandy in June 1944, and the landings at Inchon in September 1950—could not have succeeded without the groundwork, the operational science, provided by diligent staff officers. The functions of military staffs—mission analysis, intelligence gathering, course-of-action development, coordination and contingency planning, execution and adjustment, and after-action reviews—are the fundamentals of operational science. They also parallel the basic steps of the scientific method: analysis of the problem, development of hypotheses, experimentation, observation, and assessment.[3] It would be wrong to think of military science merely as the knowledge of military hardware and its capabilities; for science, whatever its brand, is but the scientific method followed to its logical conclusion.[4] Nor is military science the search for formulas or recipes for victory.[5] These have more in common with the fashions of art than they do with the methods of science.

Military practitioners, even including Clausewitz, have long preferred the phrase "art of war" to "science of war." Through the first decade of the twenty-first century, American operational doctrine highlighted the element of art, claiming that operational art was foremost "the application of creative imagination by commanders and staffs."[6] The rationale has been that, even if victory requires some knowledge of military science, the application of that knowledge requires skill, and skill belongs more to the realm of art than to science. Only art, it seemed, could account for a commander's genius and its role in penetrating the fog of war in planning and executing military operations.[7] And only art could appreciate the influence of other intangibles such as morale and courage, as well as arational factors such as chance. Yet what this rationale overlooks is that when commanders apply their skills in war, they do so with the disciplined judgment of practitioners, rather than the unfettered imagination of artists. Gen. Stanley McChrystal's "find, fix, finish, exploit, and analyze" is a contemporary example of such skill applied in iterative cycles.[8] Like lawyers and doctors, military practitioners solve problems replete with risk, and their collective status as professionals depends on the public's trust in their ability to solve those problems. It is a status artists do not enjoy. Nor do artists have a corpus of professional knowledge, or doctrine, to guide their practice. Clausewitz's *On War* was based on a variant of the scientific method, and it is largely because of that method that we have a base of knowledge regarding war's intangibles.[9] The aforementioned fundamentals of operational science are the reason innovation and adaptation can occur at all in war. The former should be thought of as any measure taken to gain a competitive edge, while the latter is any measure taken to adjust to an environment.[10] Contrary to conventional wisdom, therefore, art is not essential for military success—only for military glory.

Nevertheless, Americans will likely continue to celebrate their operational artists, and well they should. The wartime exploits of Winfield Scott, George S. Patton Jr., and Douglas MacArthur offer some timeless insights for military professionals. Scott, for instance, carried out a successful campaign against Mexico City in 1847, one that allowed military and political pressure to be exerted gradually. He may also have been among the first true American strategists, as exemplified by the integrated nature of his much-derided but ultimately effective Anaconda Plan for defeating the South in the Civil War. Among other things, Patton is credited with turning around the performance of II Corps in 1943 and for carrying out successful offensives in North Africa, Sicily, and northern France. During the latter he was commander of the Third Army, which was especially notable for its historic contribution to the breakout from Normandy in August 1944, resulting in the encirclement and destruction of the German Seventh Army and Fifth Panzer Army (ten thousand dead and fifty thousand prisoners) as cohesive fighting formations.[11] Clearly a controversial figure, Patton consciously and aggressively cultivated his personal image, which in turn obscured just how much his operational successes were due to the diligence of his staff officers.[12] Similarly notable was General MacArthur's surprise amphibious attack at Inchon on September 15, 1950, which recaptured Seoul, severed most of the lines of communication and supply running to the North Korean army, and temporarily reversed the course of the war.

As noted, that maneuver required wide-ranging staff work, or operational science, in the form of asking and answering questions about the landing conditions at Inchon, the tides, the strength of the defenses, planning of the preparatory assault and main assault, logistical support, air cover, and follow-on reconnaissance needs. By continuing to push for complete military victory in the winter and spring of 1950–51, even when it was clear his troops could no longer achieve it and his political leaders no longer desired it, MacArthur revealed the ineluctable flaw of the artist—the tendency to regard his personal views as infallible and his inspiration as coming from a higher source.[13] To avoid such errors, military practitioners would do well to match their celebration of history's military artists with a sober appreciation for the full range of operational science that went into each maneuver or campaign.

Toward that end, this book's remaining chapters use the term *practice* rather than *art*. Military practice is thus the sum of two things: military strategy and its supporting operations. Military strategy, as previously stated, is the "art of the general." It is how generals and admirals employed their forces to defeat their opponents pursuant to accomplishing the war's purpose. It is important to note that military strategy differs in scope from national or grand strategy. Grand strategy deals not only with military power, but also with economic power and diplomacy, as well as other tools of statecraft. Put differently, if military strategy is regarded as the art of the general, then grand strategy is the "art of the monarch or head of state." Each art, nonetheless, rests on broad, if not always firm, scientific foundations.

American Military Strategy

Weigley drew from Clausewitz's definition of strategy—"the use of combats to attain the objects of the war"—to discuss American military strategy.[14] Clausewitz's definition distinguished between the purview of *tactics* as the winning of battles and the realm of *strategy* as the use of battles or engagements for the purpose of the war.[15] It was clearly battle-centric in nature: to use battles or engagements, one has to bring them about or threaten to do so. Thus, Weigley's use of this framework led him to a battle-centric appreciation of American military strategy. That in itself was problematic, as American military strategy writ large has been much more open-ended in practice. In addition, Weigley further limited his analysis by embracing Hans Delbrück's division of military strategy into two basic types: annihilation (*Niederwerfungsstrategie*) and attrition or erosion (*Ermattungsstrategie*), which Weigley also likened to Liddell Hart's indirect approach.[16] That linkage was an error. Liddell Hart made "the strategy of the indirect approach" a popular phrase with the publication of his book of the same title in 1941.[17] His principal argument was that doing the unexpected—the "indirect" rather than direct—was more profitable in war precisely because an adversary would not expect it. The indirect approach relied heavily on the principles of surprise and psychological dislocation, which applied as much, if not more, to strategies of annihilation as to strategies of attrition.

Delbrück defined a strategy of annihilation as seeking the complete defeat of an opponent by means of major engagements or battles, and he declared that it had a single focus or "pole": battle. He cast a strategy of attrition more broadly as wearing down an opponent by means of a combination of maneuver and battle to achieve limited aims and assigned it two "poles": battle and maneuver. Delbrück's categories were contrived, however. Both strategies often involve a great deal of activity among their so-called poles. A strategy aimed at achieving a decisive battle, for instance, often requires a well-planned maneuver or series of maneuvers to force an opponent into accepting battle under unfavorable conditions. Moreover, as Otto von Bismarck and Helmuth von Moltke the Elder demonstrated in the 1860s and 1870s, this type of strategy could also be used to achieve any number of limited aims. Conversely, strategies of attrition can involve very large and very costly engagements, which might be fought among trenches and fortifications with little room for maneuver. Furthermore, Delbrück's category of *Ermattungsstrategie* actually conflated a strategy of attrition with a strategy of exhaustion. The former is best thought of as eroding an opponent's physical capacity to resist by relentlessly destroying his military forces at a rate greater than they can be replaced. A strategy of exhaustion, by comparison, is best thought of as wearing down an adversary's will to resist, rather than his physical capacity.

Despite these flaws, Weigley accepted the artificial duality in Delbrück's strategic categories without reservation and recast them in the form of a simple dichotomy: annihilation, aiming at conquest through the complete destruction of an opponent's capacity to resist, and attrition, achieving limited objectives by wearing down an opponent. Both historians had defensible reasons for wanting to expose the limitations and the vulnerabilities of strategies of annihilation, which they saw as reflective of doctrinaire military thinking. Nonetheless, in Weigley's case, the use of these categories precluded the development of a truly representative account of the many types of military strategies—the various ways—Americans have used military force as an instrument of policy. This was true despite the fact that Weigley also discussed strategies of shock and terror, such as the air-power theories of Billy Mitchell, as well as some of the nascent strategies of nuclear deterrence developed in the 1950s and 1960s, which he aptly dubbed America's "golden age" of strategic thinking.

Finally, Weigley's analysis—again, partly as a consequence of being conceived of and written as a history of ideas—overlooked how multiple military strategies became nested in the course of a single war or campaign. As battle frontages increased and strategic and operational environments became more complex, commanders employed combinations of strategies. In describing the practice of American military strategy, we would do well to recall Moltke's well-known description of strategy as a "system of expedients."[18] Moltke's principal message was that strategy is more than a disciplined body of concepts. It is also the ad hoc practice of adapting those concepts to changing circumstances. If there is any single phrase that best captures the spirit of American military strategy through its first century, from the Revolutionary War to the Spanish–American War, it is that.

Types of Military Strategies

In 1966, Thomas C. Schelling, the renowned American theorist of coercive diplomacy wrote: "Military strategy can no longer be thought of, as it could for some countries in some areas, as the science of military victory. It is now equally, if not more, the art of coercion, of intimidation and deterrence."[19] Schelling was wrong to think that military strategy—as the art of coercion, intimidation, and deterrence—was somehow new or that these components had not enjoyed parity with the science of military victory. In the American case, military strategy had always been varied. The Civil War and the First and Second World Wars, where by necessity the science of military victory took precedence, were the exceptions, not the rule. This section describes some of the key types of military strategy that appeared in American military practice over the course of more than two centuries.

American military strategy has largely been a combination of Clausewitz's battle-centric approach and the position-centric method of Antoine-Henri, baron de Jomini. While a great deal of overlap exists between them, they are distinguished by the emphasis each places on the principal ways they use to achieve their ends. Until Clausewitz's center-of-gravity concept matured, he tended to see strategy as enemy-oriented, aimed at destroying the core of an opponent's armed forces and at the same time, if possible, their general will to fight. Strategy, therefore, began with the study of the enemy's dispositions—the strengths and weaknesses of his forces in relation to one's own. For Jomini, in contrast, strategy was the "the art of making war upon the map" and began with a thorough terrain analysis of the theater of war, its decisive points, appropriate base areas, zones of operations and probable objectives within them, and their resultant lines of operations.[20] In short, Clausewitz saw war as a way of destroying an opponent's primary means of resistance, the armed forces, whereas Jomini saw war as an instrument for seizing and controlling capital cities, major transportation and communication routes, fortifications, defensive lines, and economic and logistical centers. Destruction of enemy forces was, for him, incidental to achieving control of such key points.

American military strategy has largely been a combination of these two approaches. Throughout most of the nineteenth century, it was more influenced by the system of the Swiss, Jomini, than that of the Prussian, Clausewitz. Nonetheless, American military strategy has not been as binary, confined by annihilation and attrition, as Weigley claimed. In fact, as the following chapters show, Americans also used strategies of graduated pressure, as in the war with Mexico in 1846–48; age-old strategies of divide-and-conquer, as in the Indian wars, the Philippine wars, the Caribbean interventions, and the early operations in Afghanistan; and strategies of decapitation, as with Pershing's expedition into Mexico in 1916 and the fateful Bay of Pigs (Cuba) invasion in 1961; as well as strategies that used military power in a more traditional carrot-and-stick approach, a familiar label describing a broad strategic technique that became something of a pseudoscience during the Cold War and eventually evolved into the concept of coercive diplomacy.

Annihilation

A strategy of annihilation is best defined as an effort to destroy an opponent's physical capacity to fight in a single decisive battle or rapid campaign. Destroying an adversary's main forces can open the road to seizure of his capital and government. Even if sizeable hostile forces remained in the field, an overwhelming victory could generate enough shock to induce an opponent to surrender in order to avoid further losses in what might be a hopeless cause. Rapid exploitation of such a victory is crucial, however—otherwise the enemy could use the time to recover and reorganize. In July 1861, Federal and Confederate forces each expected to achieve such a victory at the Battle of First Manassas, but events took a different turn. Hannibal's campaigns against Rome are classic examples of this strategy, as are some of Napoleon Bonaparte's land campaigns, particularly those of Ulm and Austerlitz (1805), as well as the naval battles at Manila Bay and Santiago Bay during the Spanish–American War (1898).[21] Alfred Thayer Mahan's theories of sea power are based largely on this approach. Hannibal's campaigns, for all their triumphs over Rome's legions, also illustrate the limitations of this strategy because they did not bring about the collapse of Rome's will to resist. A strategy of annihilation is usually chosen when a belligerent wants to avoid a long war. However, that desire also makes it vulnerable to a strategy of exhaustion, which endeavors to win by prolonging the war beyond the other party's breaking point.

Attrition and Exhaustion

As described above, and as President Franklin D. Roosevelt so ably articulated in 1943, a strategy of attrition is the continual destruction of an opponent's fighting power. It can be used offensively or defensively. It typically requires the side using it to possess quantitative superiority, either on hand or as a mobilization potential. Battle need not be avoided under a strategy of attrition. On the contrary, it is usually sought because all exchanges, save a decisive loss, favor the side with material superiority. It is thus most effective when the side using it is not constrained by time. A strategy of exhaustion is for the most part a defensive strategy, and it can be effective against a foe possessing numerical superiority. Under a strategy of exhaustion, one usually avoids fighting battles unless conditions are clearly favorable. The basic idea is to chip away at an opponent's morale by fighting minor engagements, often in the form of guerrilla-style operations, which avoid the enemy's main strength and minimize the risk of major losses. A strategy of exhaustion can also be used in a more conventional sense, as Frederick the Great's campaigns during the Seven Years' War illustrate, by fighting major battles designed to inflict enough casualties to weaken an opponent's resolve and possibly force a change in policies.[22] This type of strategy is vulnerable to enemies with enough skill to restrict the movement of guerrilla forces or to bring about a decisive battle. It also requires time, which may not be available politically or otherwise.

Decapitation

A strategy of decapitation calls for capturing or killing a hostile group's key leaders, frequently referred to in contemporary operations as high-value targets (HVTs). The goal is to neutralize the leadership of a group. That can be done either by separating the leaders from the group and signaling that only they will be punished or by eliminating them altogether so as to reduce the group's effectiveness and possibly deter others from taking charge. The United States used this approach against Francisco "Pancho" Villa in 1916 unsuccessfully and against Manuel Noriega in 1989 successfully. Strategies of decapitation are appealing as counterterrorism measures, especially in situations where eliminating the group completely is considered difficult or risky. The development of drones and other twenty-first-century technologies have facilitated its use, but they also have given rise to a number of legal and ethical concerns, particularly with regard to the involvement of intelligence agencies such as the Central Intelligence Agency (CIA).[23] However, this approach is vulnerable against foes with resilient leadership networks capable of making the costs of periodically "mowing the lawn" greater than the benefits.

Coercive Diplomacy

Put simply, coercive diplomacy is the process of threatening to use military power, backed up if necessary by its actual use in limited ways, to compel an adversary to comply with one's aims.[24] Some interpretations claim that coercive diplomacy is an alternative to war and thus ceases the moment war begins. The point of such claims is to show that military power can be used to compel a desired outcome without having to resort to war itself. Thus coercive diplomacy sees the use of military force, more than war or the clash of arms itself, as a way of continuing policy by other means. However, when one considers that campaigns against the Plains Indians were fought with long periods of negotiations broken by brief but intense periods of fighting, these interpretations become legalistic, even nonsensical. The techniques of coercive diplomacy or Thomas Schelling–like "compellence" were frequently practiced in spirit, if not in name. In any case, this approach is vulnerable to a stubborn or aggressive adversary capable of countering one's use of force with his own, which, even if not necessarily proportionate, can cause us an unacceptable level of harm.

Terror and Intimidation

There is some confusion between terrorism as a tactic and terror as a strategy. Terrorist groups can be said to employ tactics of terror—bombing specific political, cultural, or military targets—in an overall strategy of terror designed to shape public opinion and force governments to alter their policies. The basic idea is to frighten or intimidate people into taking a desired action. Similarly, the fundamental principles underpinning air power's strategic bombing theories had to do with instilling terror in the populace. For Giulio Douhet and Mitchell, for instance, the "real objectives" of war were a nation's "vital centers," and bombing them, it was believed, would cripple industry, terrorize the populace, and "bring about quick decisions."[25] More recent versions of this approach can be found in the air-power theories of Col. John Warden, which were applied in the Gulf War, and the so-called shock-and-awe campaign of the Iraq War. These approaches involve synchronized precision strikes purportedly aimed at inducing a condition called "strategic paralysis," similar in concept to decapitation, which is then supposed to cause the enemy's military and political systems to collapse. This strategic paralysis is mainly rhetorical excess, however. In practical terms, these approaches aim at achieving Schelling-like compellence through fear and intimidation.

Deterrence

A strategy of deterrence presupposes one's opponent is a rational actor at some level, respects the use of force, and is therefore able to be dissuaded from taking a particular action. Strategies of deterrence nearly evolved into a science during the Cold War, but they are as old as antiquity. Indeed, Weigley duly noted their use in America's naval operations during much of the early nineteenth century "to ward off combat by persuading prospective enemies that descents upon the American coast would be more costly than they could be worth."[26] Weigley also quite appropriately linked deterrence to strategies of denial, such as the tradition of pairing coastal artillery and gunboats for coastal defense.

In the twenty-first century, denial strategies are frequently used in the realm of cyberspace. In that domain they are more offensive in nature. Attacks are launched for the express purpose of neutralizing specific cyber capabilities, whether these have to do with critical infrastructure (as with the Stuxnet attack against Iran's nuclear centrifuges), intelligence gathering, or the disruption of basic services. Cyberspace has clearly become a new military domain with tactical, operational, and strategic significance. Cyberwarfare is not likely to change the fundamental principles of warfare, but it is becoming increasingly difficult to conceive of a situation in which a major military operation would be launched without including some sort of cyber operation as well. Certainly the protection of cyber assets has become a prerequisite for any military operation. Since this domain of warfare is still developing rapidly and since the patterns that might be derived from it would be too embryonic, cyber operations are not discussed in this book.

American Operational Practice

Just as this book uses the term *military practice* instead of *military art*, so too it prefers the term *operational practice* over *operational art*. Operational practice includes both operational science and operational art. The former pertains to the planning of military operations and campaigns and everything that supports it, such as the staff functions discussed earlier; the broader operational functions of intelligence, deployment, maneuver, sustainment, and command and control; and the development of operational doctrine.[27] Operational art, as with military art, has traditionally been thought of as how operations and campaigns were planned and executed. Again, this will be referred to here as operational practice.

The origins of operational practice are unclear. The prevailing view has been that it began with Napoleon's campaigns, in particular his use of the modern staff system and army corps as maneuver elements. More recently, however, some scholars have tried to push the origins of operational practice to the era of Frederick the Great.[28] Operational practice is seen as providing the "conceptual and physical" link between strategy and tactics in the form of campaigns.[29] Thus as armies grew larger and wars became more global, operational practice, or the "planning and execution of large-scale operations," expanded as well.[30] That much is true. However, the practice has also been attributed to smaller groups, such as terrorist groups like al-Qaeda, which also endeavor to coordinate their activities over broad distances or for sustained periods of time.[31] Therefore, the tendency to associate operational practice only with large-scale operations or campaigns is questionable. Indeed, one thing the following chapters show is that American operational practice, though frequently involving only relatively small forces, often took place over great distances and required substantial logistical planning and preparation.

American operational doctrine throughout the nineteenth century and most of the twentieth century resembled its European counterparts in that it called for conducting offensive operations aimed at defeating an opponent's main force. It was a doctrine that pitted strength against strength, and it was considered valid for operations on land as well as those at sea. Throughout the eighteenth and nineteenth centuries, the United States was actively engaged in projecting power across land and sea, but until the Spanish–American War those projections rarely called for formations larger than a brigade. Due to deficiencies in the operational functions mentioned earlier, a central planning body was established along the lines of the German general staff, the purpose of which was to conduct contingency planning.[32]

By the end of the nineteenth century, operational terminology—such as plan of campaign, theater of operations, and lines of operations—had become elevated to common usage. More importantly, American operational practice had become both the "means and methods" for achieving victory.[33] This doctrinal shift meant that operational practice had essentially taken the place of, or become interchangeable with, the chief components of military strategy. Clausewitz had divided strategy into purpose (the aim one wishes to achieve) and means (the types of military forces needed).

By the beginning of the twentieth century, American operational planning routinely included not only measures to project sizable forces overseas, but also to protect them and their lines of communication and supply, for the duration of a conflict. The US Army officially established the operational "level" of war in the 1980s, and the US Air Force and US Navy did so in the 1990s.[34] This level was associated with corps headquarters and higher, the command echelons at which campaign planning and execution and the design of operations traditionally occurred. It was expected to facilitate the coordination necessary for multinational operations and to aid in connecting "tactical actions and strategic purposes."[35] However, in practice the level acted as both a shield to fend off unwanted political influence and a bridge to connect strategic goals and tactical actions, depending on the individuals involved and the specifics of the situation.[36]

It is also worth noting that while a large portion of American military practice is science, science fails at times. It is important to understand how it fails and why. One of the things Thomas Kuhn's much-cited and much-abused work *The Structure of Scientific Revolutions* tells us is that science often fails to shift in light of new evidence partly because science itself is neither monolithic nor purely objective. It is more like a "ramshackle structure," composed of various subfields and groups, some of which may have vested interests in existing paradigms, and for them the evidence for change never seems quite sufficient.[37] Another reason science sometimes fails is due to the ways in which scientists themselves have been taught, which in turn affects their ability to see the evidence for what it is.

These reasons also explain why operational science sometimes fails. Operational science is not monolithic. The military services have vested interests in maintaining the narratives, if not the paradigms, regarding their roles and missions. They may therefore resist change in one direction while aggressively promoting it in another, regardless of the objective benefits of the change. Moreover, due to the influences of their background and experience, military practitioners are not always able to see strategic and operational situations for what they are. The following chapters lay out the principal patterns in American strategic and operational practice and provide a partial account of why operational practice succeeded or failed.

Notes

1. Clausewitz, *Vom Kriege*, bk. 2, chap. 3, 302, and *On War*, 149; emphasis in the original. Clausewitz said that war, properly understood, was a social activity—an interaction among humans involving competing interests.

2. Strachan, "Meaning of Strategy."

3. Military staff systems have changed over time, but their functions have remained similar. Hittle, *Military Staff*. On the scientific method, see Heilbron, *Oxford Companion*.

4. O'Hanlon, *Science of War*. For a classic treatment, see Fuller, *Foundations of the Science of War*.

5. Milan Vego's "Science vs. the Art of War," covers the attempts to reduce the art of war to so-called scientific theories or formulas, but such efforts are not genuine science.

6. It does also add the clause "supported by their skill, knowledge, and experience." Joint Publication 1-02, Department of Defense *Dictionary of Military and Associated Terms* (available online at www.dtic.mil/doctrine/jel/doddict/data/o/index.html, accessed August 7, 2012) states that operational art is "the cognitive approach by commanders and staffs—supported by their skill, knowledge, experience, creativity, and judgment—to develop strategies, campaigns, and operations to organize and employ military forces by integrating ends, ways, and means." Van Riper, "Foundation of Strategic Thinking," rightly suggests this is more properly "operational design" rather than "operational art." However, doctrine still emphasizes the intangibles of art.

7. For example, *American Military History*, 10–11, quotes Dennis Hart Mahan: "In war, as in every other art based upon settled principles, there are exceptions to all general rules. It is in discovering these cases that the talent of the general is shown."

8. "Generation Kill," 2.

9. See Echevarria, *Clausewitz and Contemporary War*.

10. These definitions differ from those in Murray, *Military Adaptation*, which describes innovation as changes made in peacetime and adaptation as adjustments made in wartime.

11. Weigley, "Normandy to Falaise."

12. On Patton's active cultivation of his personal image, see Showalter, *Patton and Rommel*, esp. 370–74, 422–23. On the seemingly common trait of egocentrism in some of history's more remarkable operational artists, see Brighton, *Patton, Montgomery, Rommel*.

13. MacArthur's approach has been described as representative of the American way of war—the "habit of thinking of war in terms of annihilative victories." Weigley, *American Way of War*, 382.

14. Ibid., xx.

15. Clausewitz, *Vom Kriege*, bk. 3, chap. 1, 345, and *On War*, 177.

16. As Linn suggested, Weigley likely obtained these categories not from reading Delbrück directly, but from Craig's "Delbrück." Weigley was not able to benefit from the Howard and Paret translation of *On War*, which appeared in 1976—after the first edition of *American Way of War*.

17. Liddell Hart, *Strategy of Indirect Approach*. Portions of the book were published in 1929 under the title *Decisive Wars in History: A Study in Strategy*.

18. Moltke, "Über Strategie," and Hughes, *Moltke on the Art of War*, 44–47.

19. Schelling, *Arms and Influence*, 34.

20. Jomini, *Art of War*, 61–62.

21. At Ulm, Napoleon with 200,000 troops was able to encircle a force of 72,000 Austrians under Gen. Karl Mack von Leiberich, capturing 50,000 of them. Six weeks later at Austerlitz, Napoleon with 67,000 troops destroyed a Russo-Austrian army of 85,000 under Gen. Mikhail Kutuzov. Chandler, *Campaigns of Napoleon*, 390–432. As chapter 5 shows, the US Navy destroyed the Spanish squadrons at Manila Bay (May 1898) and Santiago Bay (July 1898) in swift battles of annihilation and ended Spanish naval influence in those areas.

22. Showalter, *Wars of Frederick the Great*.

23. See the forum on drones, "Drones and US Strategy: Costs and Benefits," in *Parameters* 42/43, no. 4/1 (Winter/Spring 2013): 7–33.

24. For a discussion of its fundamentals, see George, *Forceful Persuasion*.

25. Mitchell, *Skyways*, 255–56. Cf. Weigley, *American Way of War*, 234.

26. Weigley, *American Way of War*, 366–67.

27. Moran, "Operational Level." Matheny, *Carrying the War*, xix, offers similar functions.

28. Cf. Krause and Phillips, *Historical Perspectives*, and Telp, *Evolution of Operational Art*.

29. "If *strategy* is the art of war and *tactics* the art of battle, then *operations* is the art of campaigning." English, "Operational Art," 7.

30. Matheny, *Carrying the War*, xiii.

31. Adamsky, "Jihadi Operational Art."

32. *American Military History*, 343–57, and Hewes, *From Root to McNamara*.

33. Kobbe, *Notes*, 17, and Scott, *Military Dictionary*, 574. Cf. Nelson, "Origins of Operational Art," 333–48.

34. Jones, *Development of Air Force*, and Hughes, "Naval Operations." Wass de Czege, "Systemic Operational Design," argues that in the twenty-first century, operational-level planning is needed at battalion command.

35. Swain, "Filling the Void."

36. Cf. Kelly and Brennan, *Alien*; Van Riper, "Foundation of Strategic Thinking"; and Strachan, "Strategy or Alibi?"

37. Kuhn, *Structure of Scientific Revolutions*, 49.

PART II

American Military Practice

4

The Revolutionary War to the Mexican War

War is not, as some seem to suppose, a mere game of chance. Its principles constitute one of the most intricate of modern sciences. The general who rightly understands the art of applying its rules . . . may be morally certain of success.

Henry W. Halleck, Elements of Military Art and Science, *1846*

HENRY WAGER HALLECK, a US Army engineer officer by commission and a lawyer by trade, was prone to seeing the conduct of war as governed by discernible rules. The word *intricate*, under his pen in 1846, meant interwoven and inviolable. That description might well have held true for the engineering and logistical aspects of war but certainly not for the rest. Even then warfare was not the rigid, predictive science Halleck wished it to be. Moreover, at no point in the nineteenth century did Americans fight as if it were. Halleck translated Jomini's *Art of War*, embellished it with specifics relevant to the American experience, published it as *Elements of Military Art and Science*, and in the process earned for himself a reputation as the army's foremost military scientist.[1] However, "Old Brains," as he was called, failed to honor his own critical distinction between science, which "investigates general principles and institutes an analysis of military operations," and art, which is the application of "practical rules for conducting campaigns, sieges, battles, etc."[2] Halleck inverted the two and treated the art itself as a prescribed science. Analysis, so essential to genuine science, was not encouraged when he later commanded the Army of the Ohio in 1862 during the Civil War. For Halleck, once the art was established, the purpose of science was to reaffirm it through historical examples, not to reassess it in light of new evidence or changed circumstances.

Fortunately for American strategic and operational practice in the nineteenth century, reassessments did occur. Many American officers—both before and after 1846—analyzed their situations well enough to make adjustments that helped achieve favorable outcomes in campaigns, sieges, or battles. To be sure, they did not do so as often or as thoroughly as they might have. Nonetheless, as the following chapters show, American military strategy, as put into practice, went beyond Halleck's Jominian definition of "directing masses on decisive points." It was more akin to what Moltke famously referred to as a system of expedients, the success of which depended upon practical logic rather than pure reason.

From the Revolutionary War to the Spanish–American War, American military strategy was, in truth, an ad hoc combination of the Jominian ideal of controlling strategic points, the Clausewitzian use of combats, and the proverbial carrot-and-stick approach long familiar to diplomats. American land operations in the nineteenth century were frequently expeditionary in nature. That was true largely because many of them took place over distances routinely two or three times greater on average than those with which European armies had to reckon. Logistical planning thus became all the more important to American operational practice. Unfortunately, appreciation of that bit of operational science would occur only in fits and starts, until the beginning of the twentieth century when American operational practice truly became established.

The Revolutionary War

For most of the War of Independence, American military leaders practiced a strategy of exhaustion, though they did not refer to it as such. Still, Nathanael Greene came close, stating, "General Washington, as every defender ought, has . . . [been] endeavoring to skirmish with the enemy at all times and avoid a general engagement."[3] Greene himself would follow the same strategy in South Carolina later in the war, writing in 1780, "Everything here depends upon opinion. If you lose the confidence of the people, you lose all support."[4] After their successes in 1775, the Americans in theory ought to have enjoyed all the advantages Clausewitz said were inherent in the nature of the defense: (a) the defender's ability to win by merely surviving, (b) physical advantages in terms of shorter lines of supply and familiarity with the terrain, (c) psychological advantages derived from having been wronged by an act of aggression, which might thus result in outside support, and (d) time.[5]

However, in practice, only the first advantage—needing merely to survive—was truly on the side of the Americans. Independence, finally declared in 1776, was clearly not a limited aim. Yet it was possible to achieve it without conquering Britain, destroying its army or navy, or even inflicting major damage upon them. All the Americans needed to do was wear down whatever military expeditions the Crown sent against them, until the king, distracted by other conflicts and affairs, grew weary of the game. How long that might take was obviously unknown, but what was known was that British political leadership was divided on the issue. Nonetheless, the Continental Congress initially lacked the wherewithal to wage a longish war, and while enthusiasm for independence ran high at the outset, it was not clear how the American population would respond under the full burden of war, including taxation— one of the war's key issues. The colonies also had the advantage of being distant (though eminently accessible by sea) and not vital to the existence of Britain. However, that also made efforts to draw allies to the American cause more difficult, as they stood to gain less by joining compared to what they might lose, and the revolution itself upset the established order.

By comparison, the British, who clearly had the harder task, needed to retake territories they once held and to reestablish imperial control over them. Those territories totaled some 360,000 square miles with a population of about 2.5 million people, most of whom lived within two hundred miles of the coastline. Moreover, imperial control had to be reestablished with a ground force that, at its peak, would number no more than thirty-five thousand troops and that had to operate over lines of communication and supply that were nearly thirty-five-hundred miles long. While these sea routes were vulnerable to storms and raiding, among other things, the difficulties of operating over such distances on land would have been much greater. The breadth of the theater itself was another problem: It was nearly a thousand miles by road from Boston to Charleston, roughly equal to the distance from Madrid to Antwerp. Such distances added to British command and logistical problems, despite the presence of the Royal Navy, which offered superb operational mobility along the North American coastline, with its many inlets and waterways. This mobility was only modestly contested by the fledgling American navy. That situation changed when France and Spain entered the conflict in 1778 and 1779, respectively, but it was still some time before they could bring their considerable naval forces to bear. Tactically, the Americans, especially the local militias, possessed some familiarity with the terrain, which favored defensive operations. However, that advantage was offset by the fact that Loyalists, too, knew the terrain, and by the fact that the Continental Army and Continental Navy had some way to go before they could function as competent instruments of policy. To be sure, not all the American populace was hostile. Some historians estimate that only one-third of it was, but determining the centers of support and their strength and resolve was difficult at best.[6] Despite the conventional wisdom, none of the strategic, tactical, and moral advantages of the defense wholly favored the Americans.

The war could thus be thought of as a race against time for both sides. The idea that time favors only one side or the other is often inaccurate. In this case, each side initially grew stronger as time wore on, maneuvering to strengthen its position while taking as many actions as possible to weaken its opponent. Yet as time increased, so did the risks for each side. The longer the war lasted, the more opportunities the Crown's continental rivals would have to find ways of weakening it in the ongoing struggle for power in Europe. However, a longish war would also draw Congress deeper into debt and other uncharted territories. It did, in fact, run up a large debt during the war by borrowing millions from European nations. Also, its attempt to pay for the war by printing money only led to inflation, adding to the "economic tax" already being paid by farmers and craftsmen forced to leave their livelihoods for prolonged periods of time. In other words, time was not a zero-sum game in this case. Rather, it increased in importance as the war progressed. Especially as the interval between each side's victories grew, victories needed to sustain moral as well as physical support.

The nature of the terrain conspired to make such victories difficult to come by, however. It was characterized by mountain chains and thick forests, broken up by small farms, and by towns connected by narrow roads and waterways. As a result, open-field battles seldom occurred. Fighting was done primarily by infantry, supported by some light artillery, as heavier guns were difficult to move and to keep supplied. Cavalry could not be used in the large numbers to which European armies were accustomed, which meant that many engagements could not be decisive.[7] When open-field battles did occur—as at Brandywine Creek (September 1777) and Cowpens (January 1781)—they paled in comparison to the battles of annihilation that Napoleon would achieve three decades later. Despite the war's many unconventional aspects, it was chiefly a struggle over outposts and fortifications, with a premium placed on operational rather than tactical maneuver. The crucial events of the war were, for instance, sieges, as at Charleston (April–May 1780), Pensacola (March–May 1781), and Yorktown (September–October 1781). These typically came about by means of operational maneuvers that forced an opponent into a confined area and systematically closed all avenues of escape or resupply. For most of the war, in fact, neither side had what it felt were sufficient numbers of troops or supplies.

As mentioned, historians have referred to George Washington as the "American Fabian" because he initially avoided being drawn into pitched battles, despite the fact that Congress repeatedly urged him to do so.[8] Actually, Washington's approach was closer to Frederick the Great's style of *Ermattungsstrategie*: He gave battle when forced to do so, as at Brooklyn Heights

(August 1776), and endeavored to win, not just delay or harass.[9] This approach fit well within the customs and logistical limitations of eighteenth-century warfare. Given the right conditions, Washington might have been able to achieve a decisive battle; however, as historians have pointed out, Congress's expectations were unduly high. The successes enjoyed by American militia units in the battles near Lexington and Concord in April 1775, and again on the heights dominating Boston harbor in June 1775, contributed to these expectations by suggesting that the militia system was sufficient for defending the colonies.[10] Americans could—or so it seemed—rally to the cause as they desired, commit to it for as long as they wanted, fight on their own terms, and return to their families and occupations without having incurred much risk or suffered much disruption. However, the successes of 1775 were the result of specific conditions, such as the advantages of the tactical defense, which offset American deficiencies in maneuver and discipline. British overconfidence and failure to follow basic tactical principles also contributed to that outcome.

Washington, for his part, appreciated these facts. Over time, his forces would improve in quantity and quality, but that was not the situation in 1776 as he took up defensive positions in the heights above New York City to block the British invasion. The ranks of the Continental Army—though twenty thousand strong with 120 guns—were filled by short-term enlistees who lacked the discipline and training necessary to execute difficult battlefield maneuvers, such as frontal assaults, withdrawals under fire, and flanking movements.[11] Moreover, the militias that showed up to fight were shaky at best. Accordingly, Washington stressed simplicity, putting his forces into defensive positions along the Brooklyn Heights in preparation for Gen. William Howe's assault with a combined British and Hessian army of thirty thousand soldiers.

Unfortunately, Washington's positions were amateurishly exposed. Howe managed to find and attack the weak points in the Patriot line, flank it, and drive the Americans back in confusion. The colonists' success at Breed's Hill was not to be repeated in Brooklyn: American losses exceeded two thousand troops, five times the number of British casualties.[12] While the Patriots could accept higher losses, a 5:1 ratio of exchange was severely damaging to morale, and desertions increased. Howe halted his advance, presumably to allow time for negotiations, and he has been justly criticized ever since for holding out too much hope for reconciliation and for exercising too much caution.[13] Time and again Howe outmaneuvered the American Fabian but never quite managed to capture him. At times the British commander, perhaps a victim of wishful thinking, acted as if the American declaration of independence had been nothing more than a tantrum—the product of a radical few and not representative of the sentiments of the colonists in general. If such were true, a firm but restrained show of force might restore the status quo ante. On the other hand, the revolutionaries were highly skeptical of British willingness to honor any long-term agreement.

The Continental Congress was the intellectual center of the rebellion, and Washington's Continental Army, though plagued with manpower and logistical problems, was its physical and psychological core. By late summer 1776, these were the two focal points, the dual center of gravity of Patriot resistance.[14] Destroying Washington's army and arresting the members of Congress would have halted the rebellion, at least for a time, assuming no cause-rallying atrocities had been committed in the process. Instead, Washington, whose operational science had been increasing rapidly during the autumn months, was able to avoid being decisively defeated and launched a brief but war-saving "Christmas campaign" on December 25–26, 1776, and January 2–3, 1777. He raided first Trenton then Princeton, inflicting some fifty casualties on the Hessians and taking a thousand prisoners while, more important, boosting the morale of his soldiers.[15]

American military strategy in 1777 followed the same general pattern: Avoid battle except under favorable circumstances or unless forced. Like most defensive strategies, it was reactive, surrendering the initiative to the foe. In contrast, British strategy shifted in 1777 to one oriented on controlling territory, the express purpose of which was to separate New England, the perceived center of American resistance, from the other colonies.[16] The scheme of maneuver to achieve that separation was to seize control of the Hudson River from three directions: from the north by Gen. John Burgoyne (ten thousand troops), from the west by Col. Barry St. Leger (two thousand), and from the south by Gen. Henry Clinton (three thousand).[17] Once the flame of rebellion was snuffed out in New England, it was thought, the task would be easier elsewhere.

Howe, for his own reasons, did not support the concept of maneuver and instead moved against Philadelphia by sea with thirteen thousand troops. The move forced Washington's army of eleven thousand Continentals and militiamen to attempt to defend the city. Howe outmaneuvered Washington, however, and inflicted a significant defeat on him at Brandywine Creek on September 11, 1777, but again he did not destroy Washington's army. Howe took Philadelphia and some forts along the Delaware River, but he lacked the operational strength to hold the city and pursue Washington. On October 17, Burgoyne was defeated at Saratoga, and St. Leger too was compelled to withdraw. By the end of 1777, the British held Philadelphia and New York, but their attempt to isolate New England had failed completely. Their inability to end the war in 1777 encouraged the French to enter the conflict in 1778, with Spain following one year later. Cooperation among the Americans and the French and Spanish remained fraught with friction for some time, however. Thus the entry of these powerful states into the war did not immediately spell defeat for Britain, but it did mean the Crown now had a more complex strategic situation on its hands. Meanwhile, the fledgling American navy under the command of John Paul Jones conducted guerrilla-style raids and hit-and-run actions in the British Isles. These accomplished more for morale, raising that of the Americans and testing that of the British, than they did in terms of causing physical damage.

In the spring of 1779, Washington ordered a punitive expedition against the Iroquois Confederacy in New York, which was allied with the British and had been raiding American settlements since the war began. He sent Maj. Gen. John Sullivan and four brigades (thirty-five hundred troops, mostly militiamen) northward along the Susquehanna River to the Chemung River valley and called upon him to accomplish the "total destruction and devastation" of the Iroquois tribes in the Finger Lakes region of New York.[18] Administrative and logistical problems delayed the expedition's departure until the end of July, but ironically this might have increased the destructive effect it would have, since the delay carried the campaign into the harvest season. The expedition razed some forty villages and destroyed several thousand acres of crops.[19] As a form of war, it resembled what Clausewitz would later say of medieval conflicts: "waged relatively quickly; not much time wasted in the field; [the] aim was to punish the enemy, not subdue him. When his cattle had been driven off and his castles burned, one could go home."[20] Indeed, Sullivan's troops withdrew after destroying villages, crops, and livestock in a campaign of reprisal, punishing the Iroquois and their allies for conducting raids. Despite the harshness of the rhetoric in Washington's letters to Sullivan, therefore, the expedition was not a campaign of annihilation. It does, however, serve as an example of how rhetoric can be misleading.

American military strategy returned to being a system of expedients thereafter. By comparison, the character of British strategy remained terrain-oriented through the final years of the war. In 1780, the thrust of Britain's military operations shifted from the mid-Atlantic region to the southern colonies. In truth, this terrain-oriented "southern strategy" was driven by a desire to find a firm base of Loyalist support and to use it as a springboard for future operations.[21] The search had little to go on except vague promises and rumors, but support was found and some effective units of Loyalist militia-men were raised. The British won several victories in the spring and summer of 1780, most notably at the siege of Charleston (April 18 to May 12, 1780), where the Americans lost 267 killed and wounded and 6,700 prisoners, and at the Battle of Camden (August 1780), where they lost more than 1,900 troops killed, wounded, or missing. These victories enabled the British to control the southern coast of North America.

However, the victories may also have given the impression that the southern colonies were more vulnerable than they actually were. As Nathanael Greene said, the campaign in the South turned on public opinion and that largely depended upon his ability to stay ahead of the British through good intelligence and logistical planning.[22] The latter depended greatly on Greene's use of a county's system of mills—eighteenth-century economic centers—whereby he could replenish his provisions.[23] The importance of mills also validated what Jomini would later say about strategy being the act of "making war on a map." Greene's movements, as well as those of the British, were largely contingent on the distances and topography between mills.

To be sure, Washington was nominally threatened by Gen. Clinton's army ensconced in New York City and Gen. Charles Cornwallis's army in the South, each comprising ten thousand troops. However, extension of the front by the British gave Washington interior lines, which enabled him to reinforce American efforts in the South, while also stretching British sea lines of communication and rendering them more vulnerable to the French. In January 1781, Gen. Daniel Morgan (one thousand troops) destroyed a British task force under Col. Banastre Tarleton (eleven hundred) at Cowpens.[24] British casualties were 110 killed, 200 wounded, and 529 prisoners. In response, Cornwallis vigorously pursued Morgan. However, the latter's tactics of attrition, combined with strategic consumption, worked to sap British strength. Cornwallis won a Pyrrhic victory at Guilford Courthouse a few months later (March 1781) and advanced into Virginia, establishing a main base of operations around Yorktown. The French fleet scored a victory over the Royal Navy on September 5, 1781, and blocked Cornwallis's army from further reinforcement and supply. A combined American and French force of twenty thousand then besieged Cornwallis's nine thousand in Yorktown until his surrender on October 19, 1781.[25] American forces under Washington returned to the Hudson River valley to contain the remainder of the British army deployed in New York City. The Treaty of Paris was signed two years later, ending the war but not before disquiet arose within the American army's officer ranks in March 1783 over unpaid wages and unfunded pensions.

To the War of 1812

The reasons for the War of 1812 are still obscure. This obscurity is partly explained by the fact that the war is sometimes studied independently of the context of smaller conflicts preceding it. Between 1783 and 1812, the United States would fight several other conflicts—a war against Ohio Indians in the Northwest Territory (1790–95); the suppression of several small uprisings, such as the rebellion in western Pennsylvania (1794) over whiskey taxation; and an undeclared war with France (1798–1801), the so-called Quasi-War, over French piracy of American shipping and political insults (the infamous XYZ affair)—and would engage in several antipiracy actions to halt Algerian (Barbary) pirates from extorting ransom for American hostages. The war against the Ohio Indian tribes finally ended with Maj. Gen. Anthony Wayne's victory at Fallen Timbers (1794) and the Treaty of Greenville (1795), but the US Army had first suffered a humiliating defeat at the Battle of the Wabash on November 4, 1791, at the hands of a confederacy of Miamis, Shawnees, and Buckongahelas.[26] The uprisings were handled by shows of force as when Washington, the hero of the revolution and the country's first president, marched at the head of several thousand militiamen. Washington led the troops as far west as Carlisle, Pennsylvania, whereupon the rebels, hearing of his impending arrival, dispersed. Washington thereafter delegated the handling of the rebellion to Alexander Hamilton, who took the opportunity to escalate matters.[27]

There was actually little that was quasi about America's naval war with France: It was limited, but it was clearly a "commerce war" at sea in the *guerre de course* (privateering) manner. From 1789 to 1798, the tonnage of the American merchant fleet increased more than fourfold (202,000 to 898,000), evidence of a growing economy.[28] However, between 1786 and 1798, the French Navy and associated privateers freely raided that fleet, capturing some 316 American vessels.[29] During the war, the growth in tonnage of the American merchant fleet actually plateaued: 939,000 in 1799 to 948,000 in 1801.[30] By 1800, the value of American vessels lost to the French was estimated at $20 million. The fledgling US Navy, charged with protecting American coasts and commerce by the newly created Department of the Navy, numbered only three frigates (of six planned) in 1798. Nonetheless, by converting captured French ships and by increasing domestic construction, it grew to fifty-six vessels by war's end. This ad hoc fleet managed to defeat French privateers in numerous counterpiracy actions in the Atlantic and Caribbean: 111 French privateers were captured, 4 more were sunk, and 70 American merchant vessels were recaptured.[31] These successes in combination with Napoleon's coup in 1799 brought about a change in French policy, which resulted in the Treaty of Mortefontaine, signed on September 30, 1800. The French agreed to abrogate the 1778 Treaty of Alliance and to recognize American neutrality; both sides also agreed to refrain from seizing each other's merchant vessels, though the French actually continued this activity for some time. The US Navy conducted antipiracy operations until Congress ratified the initial treaty on February 18, 1801, with the final ratification taking place ten months later.

The war with France was not yet officially concluded when the first war with the Barbary pirates got under way. Piracy along the Barbary Coast had been a perennial problem for most European states, which preferred to pay ransoms and tributes to Moroccan and Algerian pashas rather than to divert resources from the continent's recurring power struggles to deal with the issue directly. The newly established United States first suffered from the spoliations of the Barbary pirates in 1784, when one of its ships was captured and ransomed by the pasha of Algiers. This practice of seizing merchant vessels and crews for ransom continued into the next decade. The United States finally bought peace with Algiers in 1796 by agreeing to ransom and tribute totaling 15 percent of the national budget.[32] America's Mediterranean commerce had grown to $11 million by 1800, but this trade was offset by the nearly $2 million in tribute it had paid to the Barbary states to that point.[33] On March 10, 1801, the bashaw of Tripoli, Yusuf Karamanli, made new demands for tribute and, when it was clear they would not be met, declared war on the United States by the customary practice of cutting down the flagpole at the US consulate.[34] On May 20, President Thomas Jefferson sent two-thirds of the US Navy (three frigates and one schooner) to the Barbary Coast for the purpose of protecting US commerce and providing a show of force. The schooner *Enterprise* (twelve guns) defeated the larger corsair *Tripoli* (fourteen guns) on July 24, 1801, but the fleet reverted to patrol duties and did not press its advantage.[35] Two frigates remained on patrol in the Mediterranean while the remainder of the fleet returned to the United States in April 1802 before the sailors' terms of enlistment expired.

The US government was not well served by its choice of naval commander for the second year of the war, Commo. Richard Morris, who was later relieved by Jefferson. The squadron had been reinforced and now had six frigates and one schooner, but most of the year was squandered in inactivity, save for two brief but successful raids. In 1803, Commo. Edward Preble took command of a task force of two frigates, two schooners, and two brigs and sailed against Algiers in October. He brought his ships' sixty guns to bear against the bashaw's fortress, and through a show of force secured a renewal of the peace treaty of 1786 but without tribute. Preble then sailed to Tripoli against Pasha Yusuf but had a frigate captured by Tripolitan corsairs. Deployment of this ship by the Tripolitans would have shifted the balance of power in the war. Fortunately, the frigate was scuttled on February 16, 1804, by Lt. Stephen Decatur and about sixty officers and men during a daring night raid. Preble's squadron was reinforced by four more frigates and moved against Tripoli and Yusuf. At the same time, an advancing land expedition of some 650 irregular fighters under the command of US Army captain William Eaton and Yusuf's brother Hamet was also moving against Tripoli from Derna. Pressured from two directions, Yusuf cut a deal with US forces and ended the war, exchanging American prisoners for $60,000 and agreeing to demand no further tribute from the United States. This round of the Barbary Wars came to an end when Commo. John Rodgers conducted a show of force with five frigates and several brigs in Tunis harbor on August 1, 1805, and demanded, and received, most-favored-nation status from the bey (provincial ruler) of Tunis for the United States.[36]

The next round of the Barbary Wars began as the War of 1812 tied down American warships. The dey (regional or regency ruler) of Algiers captured an American merchant vessel in 1815 and sentenced the crew to hard labor. Once the Treaty of Ghent had been signed, ending the War of 1812, President James Madison asked Congress to declare war on Algiers, which it did on March 3, 1815. In May, Madison sent two squadrons (eight frigates, fifteen schooners) into the Mediterranean under commodores Stephen Decatur and William Bainbridge. Decatur's squadron destroyed the Algerian flagship and captured its escort, and Decatur strong-armed the dey of Algiers into granting the United States most-favored-nation status and returning all prisoners with compensation. His squadron also delivered a show of force at Tunis and Tripoli, exacting cash recompense for captured vessels and reclaiming hostages and prisoners. Bainbridge's squadron then joined Decatur's, and the combined fleets sailed the Mediterranean basin in a further show of force.

Since the War of Independence, the US government had concerned itself with consolidating or expanding its frontiers, as well as earning the respect of Europe's great powers, especially Britain and France. Britain, interested in protecting its economic interests in the West Indies and addressing the threat of French expansion under Napoleon, had become somewhat heavy-handed in its treatment of the former colonies. The relationship between the United States and Great Britain has been likened to a cold war.[37] The Royal Navy's harassment of US shipping and its impressments of American seamen added to latent tensions and suggested American independence was not being taken seriously by the Crown. Between 1803 and 1807, for instance, some 528 American vessels were lost to British seizures, and between

1807 and 1812, when the Crown's policies relaxed somewhat, another 389 vessels were still lost to British—a total of 917 in the span of a decade.[38] In essence, the practice of search and seizure by British ships located near major American ports such as New York City amounted to a naval blockade.

Yet Britain's violation of American maritime rights is not considered the primary cause of the war. Some historians suggest instead that the conflict was at root a civil war, fought between the forces of republican revolution and imperial counterrevolution, to determine the future of North America.[39] It is also true that a number of war hawks saw the British and Loyalist presence among the cities and forts along the St. Lawrence waterways as a threat and agitated for offensive action. If the period leading up to 1812 was a cold war, then the Americans were the ones being strategically contained. The British held territories to the north and south of their former colonies and disrupted American shipping across the Atlantic and with the West Indies, all of which amounted to de facto containment.

When war was declared on June 18, 1812, the principal objective for the Americans was twofold: to settle unfinished business by "liberating" Canada— expelling Loyalists and British subjects—and to secure the Great Lakes and St. Lawrence waterways for the northward expansion of American commerce and settlements. Achieving that goal would have broken Britain's de facto containment. Claims that the American goal was the conquest of Canada are thus somewhat inaccurate; even leading hawks at the time declared that "Canada was not the end but the means."[40] Nonetheless, the conflict was a Clausewitzian war of conquest in character since the United States intended to take, and hold, certain portions of Canadian territory along the vital water-ways. At the same time, the United States was evidently not willing to venture much to gain those territories and was open to trading some of them for concessions.

What is patently clear, however, is that expectations were egregiously high among America's political leaders. Former president Jefferson was not alone in believing that "the acquisition of Canada, this year, as far as the neighborhood of Quebec, will be a mere matter of marching."[41] American military strategy was neither one of annihilation nor one of exhaustion. The wherewithal did not exist for the former, and the latter was not expected to be necessary. America's main military objectives were the major port cities and fortifications along Lake Erie, Lake Ontario, and the St. Lawrence River. However, little analysis had gone into determining which of these were the most important. Nor was the US Army—which numbered fewer than twelve thousand officers and men and was plagued by recruiting, administrative, and logistical problems—adequately organized and prepared for an undertaking of this magnitude. British land forces at the beginning of the war numbered roughly seven thousand regulars, ten thousand militiamen, and thirty-five hundred Native American warriors. The US Navy at the time owned only twenty ships: three forty-four-gun frigates, three thirty-six-gun frigates, and fourteen smaller vessels. In comparison, by September 1812, the Royal Navy would have eleven ships of the line, thirty-four frigates, and three dozen smaller craft operating in the theater.[42] American forces could achieve only local operational superiority and only with significant planning and coordination, neither of which occurred to the degree necessary.

The Americans launched a series of expeditions from August to November of 1812 designed to seize three port towns along the St. Lawrence waterways: Brig. Gen. William Hull (eighteen hundred troops) was to take Sandwich, Maj. Gen. Stephen van Rensselaer (thirty-two hundred) was to seize Queenstown, and Maj. Gen. Henry Dearborn (thirty-five hundred) was to capture Montreal. However, the expeditions lacked determination and were either aborted before they gained any momentum or turned back without achieving anything of note.[43] In the process, the Americans lost the port city of Detroit and failed to retake it after repeated attempts in the winter of 1812–13.

American naval operations, however, fared much better. On September 10, 1813, Commo. Oliver Hazard Perry destroyed a British flotilla in Lake Erie in an action involving 15 vessels, 117 guns, and 1,000 men.[44] Perry's victory enabled the Americans to take control of the lake and to begin a series of joint operations (some with infantry under William H. Harrison, elected president in 1840) that forced the British to withdraw their forces from Detroit and Fort Malden. Another American victory followed at Moravian-town on October 5, 1813, which also broke up the pro-British Indian alliance of northwestern tribes under Tecumseh, though Indian participation on both sides continued.[45] In the meantime, other American seamen conducted a *guerre de course* along the Canadian waterways, inflicting appreciable losses on Britain's merchant fleet.

However, the Americans overlooked the strategic value of the port city of Kingston, which controlled access to both Lake Erie and Lake Ontario. Rather than making it a priority objective, they made only limited efforts to capture it in 1813, all of which failed. Instead, they directed the bulk of their attention against Niagara, Montreal, and York (now Toronto), but each of these attempts failed as well. In the summer of 1814, the Americans launched an offensive along the Niagara River, but at nearly the same time the British, reinforced with veterans from the campaigns against Napoleon, launched an offensive into New York along two axes. The first advanced in the direction of

Niagara, and the second along the Richelieu River toward Lake Champlain. The first advance was checked by Brig. Gen. Jacob Brown at Chippewa (July 5, 1814) and at Lundy's Lane (July 25, 1814). However, these actions proved costly for the Americans and left them without sufficient strength to resume their summer offensive. The second axis withdrew after Commo. Thomas Macdonough destroyed the expedition's accompanying flotilla at Plattsburgh Bay on September 11, 1814.[46]

British blue-water superiority enabled the Royal Navy to conduct a blockade in conjunction with joint raids along the North American coast throughout 1813 and 1814.[47] The most infamous foray, from the American perspective, occurred in August 1814 when the Royal Navy, transporting substantial numbers of infantrymen, entered the Chesapeake Bay and the Potomac River. British infantry disembarked and marched on Washington, burning the White House, the Capitol, and several other prominent government buildings. The motive for these acts is still unclear, though claims surfaced after the fact that they were in retaliation for the earlier American burning of parliamentary buildings in York or for other excesses. In truth, a number of such actions had occurred on both sides. It is still plausible, however, that there were multiple motives, the chief one being to teach the American government a lesson about impertinence.[48] This humiliation was redressed somewhat by Andrew Jackson's victory at New Orleans on January 8, 1815, though it came two weeks after the Treaty of Ghent, which had ended the war.[49] Jackson's force of thirty-two hundred regulars and militiamen caught some five thousand British regulars in a withering crossfire, inflicting nearly two thousand casualties on them.

Jackson used the victory to raise his profile as a military and political leader, which later aided his bid for the presidency. It also helped set the conditions for American expansion into Florida with the First Seminole War (1817–18). That war was followed nearly two decades later by the Second Seminole War (1835), which took place under President Jackson's stern Indian removal policy. Of particular note in this war was the massacre of Maj. Francis Dade's expedition (110 troops) on December 23, 1835. The war also featured efforts by Winfield Scott and Zachary Taylor, among other notable army officers, to subdue the Seminoles. The army's strategy involved searching for and attempting to destroy Indian stores of supplies. One example occurred at the Battle of Lake Okeechobee where Taylor led a force of a thousand troops against a number of Seminoles uncharacteristically occupying a defensive position. Taylor's men suffered 133 casualties but managed to drive off the Seminoles and destroy their provisions. Taylor also tried dividing the area into squares (twenty miles by twenty miles), with a fortification in each (not unlike the contemporary forward operating base, or FOB), for a total of fifty-three forts and conducted active patrolling within the squares. He also built more roads, nearly 850 miles of them, over the course of eight months.[50] Collectively, these measures helped reduce Indian activity, but they resulted in the destruction of few Indian stores. Nonetheless, the constant search-and-destroy operations and active patrolling may have forced the Seminoles to remain on the move and thus reduced their ability to conduct raids and other hostile activities. The situation became something of a stalemate: Both sides were engaged in a war of maneuver with very little hostile activity. While the pressure was relentless, it was not sufficient to force the Seminoles and other tribes to comply with the US government's relocation policies. The US Army departed the area after seven years of debilitating campaigns and intermittent fighting, and the war essentially came to an end.[51]

The Mexican War

The Mexican conflict was a classic Clausewitzian war of negotiated settlement in which one side seized territories from another and used them as bargaining chips. The difference in this case was that the United States intended to keep the territories it captured and to persuade the Mexican government to cede them for monetary compensation. Also, while the war was a limited one for the United States, the Mexicans saw it differently. The United States would eventually have to invade Mexico, defeat the Mexican army, and occupy the country's capital to satisfy President James K. Polk's policy of annexation—a policy of expansion in today's terms. In pursuit of that policy, American military strategy is said to have resembled Thomas Schelling's theory of applying graduated pressure—increasing or decreasing force as necessary to achieve a desired outcome—more than it did the traditional strategies of annihilation or attrition.[52] That interpretation is defensible, even though it may have been influenced by scholars wishing to fit the events of the war into Schelling's theory. The Mexican army was indeed ground to pieces by a process of attrition, but that process was not relentless, nor was the Mexican army's destruction the military aim. From a Jominian perspective, the key strategic points were Mexico's port cities and its capital, all of which were captured in due course.

As discussed in chapter 3, Schelling's theory advocated following a path first of threatening to use force, then of applying it gradually, easing the pressure in the case of compliance, and increasing it in the event of noncompliance. The theory has long been attractive because it suggests policy objectives can be achieved while using only as much military force as necessary. In practice, however, the theory tends to assume an opponent will make rational calculations. It fails to take full account of irrational factors such as national or personal honor and animosity. Polk did, indeed, follow the broad outlines of the theory: He first threatened the use of force, then applied it incrementally in the form of a naval blockade and a limited land incursion, and then added more pressure by ordering his land forces to advance on the Mexican capital, eventually occupying and holding it until the Mexican government agreed to a settlement.[53]

However, due to the Clausewitzian element of enmity and other irrational factors, the war cost the Polk administration more than it anticipated. As Polk would discover, the strategy of graduated pressure has a number of vulnerabilities. The first and most obvious is that an adversary's will to resist is difficult to measure. Second, applying pressure in stages offers a cunning opponent opportunities to buy time, perhaps by feigning a willingness to negotiate, in order to strengthen his defenses, thereby prolonging the war and increasing its costs. Even more important, the strategy is ineffective when an opponent's government is divided internally or is otherwise dysfunctional and therefore is incapable of agreeing to a peace or of controlling its military forces. Polk encountered all of these at one time or another in the course of the war. However, he also added to the war's risks and its eventual costs by not increasing the size and capability of the US Army beforehand or by aligning his general defense policy with his strategy.[54]

Polk's strategy transitioned from theory to practice in March 1846, when he ordered American naval squadrons to concentrate against major Mexican ports along the eastern and western coasts, especially San Francisco and Monterey (in present-day California) and Mazatlán. He also ordered the land forces under Bvt. Brig. Gen. Zachary Taylor (four thousand troops) to cross the Nueces River and occupy defensive positions along the Rio Grande, which provoked the Mexicans into taking action. Taylor's force—four regiments of line infantry, one regiment of dragoons, one battery of horse (or "flying") artillery, and a detachment of heavier guns—constituted about half the strength of the regular army at the time.[55] Many American officers had enough frontier experience to feel comfortable fighting independently in company units or smaller, but they had little knowledge or experience with coordinating the movements and resupply of larger formations. The Mexican army was several times larger than its American counterpart, with about thirty-five thousand officers and men on its lists. It also possessed more cavalry regiments, which in theory gave it a larger mobile arm. However, as a whole, the army's mobility was compromised by a lack of horses, supplies, and quartermaster support; it was also short of arms, ammunition, modern artillery, medical supplies, and training.[56] The terrain in the area of operations was rugged, compartmentalized by ridges, arroyos, and marshes, which meant that even large battles sometimes devolved into a series of small, semi-independent actions. Only a few serviceable roads existed, which made the timely movement of heavy guns and supply trains difficult.

Taylor's forces enjoyed some success in the war's opening battles, Palo Alto and Resaca de la Palma, in early May 1846. They inflicted some 770 casualties on Gen. Mariano Arista's army and forced him to withdraw, while suffering fewer than 190 casualties of their own.[57] However, Taylor had not given enough thought to the possibility of having to pursue Arista and thus had not made preparations for crossing the Rio Grande and continuing operations deeper into Mexico. In June, the Polk administration decided to put more pressure on the Mexican government by expanding the land campaign. It ordered an advance in three columns. The first, under Col. Stephen Kearny (fifteen hundred troops) marched from Fort Leavenworth to Santa Fe, with the ultimate objective of taking San Diego, which it finally did in December 1846, though US naval forces arrived beforehand.[58] The second, under Taylor (six thousand troops), advanced from Matamoras toward Monterrey. The third column, under Brig. Gen. John Wool (twenty-five hundred troops), set out from San Antonio toward Parras, where it linked up with a portion of Kearny's column (nine hundred men under Col. A. W. Doniphan) and later joined Taylor's force, which had occupied defensive positions near Saltillo. In the meantime, the US Navy was also ordered to increase operations and captured the port cities of Santa Barbara, Los Angeles, San Diego, and Tampico.

None of these moves, however, compelled the Mexicans to come to the negotiating table. Instead, the Mexican government launched a counteroffensive in February 1847. Gen. Antonio López de Santa Anna and twenty-five thousand troops advanced on Taylor's forces at Buena Vista and fought a close battle over the course of two days. The Americans were outnumbered 3:1, but their superior artillery proved decisive, breaking up several Mexican infantry and cavalry attacks. The Mexicans sustained more than fifteen hundred casualties, while the Americans suffered some seven hundred killed and wounded. Although the Mexicans withdrew, the strategy of graduated pressure was showing how vulnerable it could be against a determined foe. The American victories were enough, nonetheless, to persuade European powers not to intervene materially in the conflict.

However, some units in Taylor's command committed atrocities while dealing with Mexican guerrillas, which in turn set off a vicious cycle of reprisals.[59] After news of an American massacre of twenty-five Mexican civilians at Agua Nueva in February 1847 appeared in the press, support for the war began to drop precipitously.[60] By the summer of 1847, the war had essentially become a moral liability for Polk. However, an end to the fighting was not yet in sight: The US naval blockade and limited land campaigns thus far had failed to persuade the Mexican government to come to terms. While the public still regarded "Old Rough and Ready" as a war hero, Polk, already rather jealous of his commander's growing popularity, gutted Taylor's command and turned those forces over to Winfield Scott, whom he also disliked but not as much. Polk ordered Scott to increase the pressure on the Mexicans by conducting a more direct campaign against Mexico City.[61] The campaign has since been lauded as an example of the incremental use of force. Indeed, Scott conducted his campaign in stages, periodically halting operations to enable the Mexicans to assess the situation and possibly come to terms.[62] Time and again, however, the Mexicans merely used such respites to rest and refit and to strengthen their positions. Nonetheless, the military strategy underpinning the campaign complemented Polk's diplomatic strategy.

The campaign against Mexico City began on March 9, 1847, when Scott's force of ten thousand landed at Veracruz in what would later be hailed as the US military's first major joint amphibious operation. The Americans laid siege to Veracruz, which fell on March 27, and moved inland on April 8 along the Mexican national highway. Scott's forces engaged in an artillery duel at Cerro Gordo ten days later but eventually forced the Mexicans to withdraw. They took Jalapa the following day and occupied Puebla one month later. Scott halted his forces there for three months to wait for replacements to refill his ranks, which were being depleted by expiring enlistments. The halt also provided an opportunity to give negotiations with the Mexican government another chance, but no agreement was reached.

Scott resumed his measured advance on Mexico City on August 7, 1847, with about ten thousand men, famously abandoning his lines of communication and supply in the process.[63] Over the next two weeks, the Americans won several more victories, albeit costly ones. Their relentless advance drove Santa Anna to ask for another armistice, which he received. Negotiations resumed but, once again, proved fruitless. Scott resumed his offensive on September 8 and orchestrated several successful flanking attacks over difficult terrain at Contreras, Churubusco, and Chapultepec. The success was due largely to reconnaissance and intrepid intelligence gathering by several young officers, among them Capt. Robert E. Lee.[64] For their part, Mexican units typically offered brief but spirited resistance, then withdrew, denying American forces an opportunity to destroy them. As a result, Ulysses S. Grant, one of many junior officers frustrated by such tactics, later remarked, "It is always in order to follow a retreating foe, unless stopped or otherwise directed."[65]

Despite the vexing nature of Mexican resistance, Scott's campaign was successful. Grant aptly summed it up years later: "[Scott] invaded a populous country, penetrating two hundred and sixty miles into the interior, with a force at no time equal to one half of that opposed to him; he was without a base; the enemy was always entrenched, always on the defensive; yet he won every battle, he captured the capital, and conquered the government."[66] Mexico City officially surrendered on September 14, 1847, though ambushes, sniping, and other violence continued for several more days. The Treaty of Guadalupe Hidalgo was not signed until February 2, 1848, and not fully ratified by both sides until May 30, 1848.[67] Despite the treaty's ratification, Scott's army remained in Mexico throughout the autumn and winter of 1848–49, performing occupation duties that included suppressing insurrections and conducting counterguerrilla operations in the Mexican countryside.[68] Casualties from the march on Mexico City, the ensuing counterguerrilla campaign, and disease reduced Scott's force to seven thousand soldiers by June 1849, when it finally reembarked for the United States.

Conclusion

Halleck was certainly correct to write in 1846 that war was not "a mere game of chance." However, it was also far more intricate than he realized. For one thing, it included the Clausewitzian element of enmity, or hostile feelings, which contributed to making American conflicts from the War of Independence to the Mexican War last as long as they did. Enough atrocities were committed in each of these conflicts to tarnish American honor, but they were only one part of a dialectic of dishonorable acts. Second, American military strategies were much more varied than applying the rules of position of which Halleck was so fond. American victories were won not only by applying such rules, but also by grinding down an adversary's military might or by applying relentless pressure against its seat of power or both. Americans rarely put favorable force ratios in the field or at sea during this period, except in the final stages of the Barbary Wars. The new government had dubious taxing authority. Thus, keeping only a smallish standing army and navy made fiscal sense, and paying ransom or tribute became a tolerable practice. The practice changed when the president and Congress realized that paying any amount of tribute meant an almost sure escalation in the price the next time around or whenever America's interests were diverted by another threat. The Barbary menace was finally ended in 1815—not with strategies of annihilation or attrition, but with a show of overwhelming force and a few intrepid commanders. Contrary to Weigley's argument,

Americans clearly knew how to use force in ways beyond annihilation and attrition, the two types of military strategy most commonly practiced in the Civil War. By then, however, Halleck's brand of military science had other problems.

Notes

1. Compare the opposing views of Ambrose, *Halleck*, 7, and Weigley, *History of United States Army*, 151.

2. Halleck, *Elements*, 37.

3. Cf. Weigley, *History of United States Army*, 65. See also Keithly, "Poor, Nasty, and Brutish."

4. Haw, "'Every Thing Here.'"

5. Clausewitz, *Vom Kriege*, bk. 6, chap. 1, 614; bk. 6, chap. 2, 618; bk. 6, chap. 3, 622–23; *On War*, 358, 360, 363, respectively.

6. Patriot and Loyalist support varied by locale but remains difficult to assess. Phillips, *1775*, xix–xx, states that the vanguard of the revolution was the four colonies Massachusetts, Virginia, Connecticut, and South Carolina, and that the leading revolutionary cities were Boston, New York, Philadelphia, and Charleston. Millett, Maslowksi, and Feis, *For the Common Defense*, 49, claim Loyalist support was less than twenty percent overall. However, this percentage increases appreciably if one also considers British colonies in Canada and the Caribbean, where the Crown had stronger bases. O'Shaughnessy, *Empire Divided*.

7. Piecuch, *Cavalry of the American Revolution*, offers details on cavalry equipment, training, and operations.

8. Weigley, *History of the United States Army*, 65. For a brief account of historical interpretations of Washington's generalship, see Palmer, *George Washington's Military Genius*, xi–xv.

9. Showalter, *Wars of Frederick the Great*, esp. 106–7.

10. Militias inflicted heavy casualties on the British, especially at the Battle of Breed's Hill (mistaken for Bunker Hill), where they lost a thousand out of twenty-five hundred effectives and were forced to withdraw.

11. Despite Congress's aversion to the idea of a standing army, it established one (the Continental Army) on June 14, 1775, and the Continental Navy four months later. Both were to suffer from chronic shortages of arms and personnel throughout the conflict.

12. Gruber, "America's First Battle."

13. O'Shaughnessy, *Men Who Lost America*, 96–98.

14. Clausewitz stated that the center of gravity in popular uprisings was the personalities of the leaders and public opinion. *Vom Kriege*, bk. 8, chap. 4; *On War*, 596.

15. *American Military History*, 67–69.

16. Weddle, "'Change,'" discusses the processes and outcomes of the assessment.

17. Griffith, *War for American Independence*, 365–76.

18. Hammond, *Letters and Papers*, vol. 3, 1–5, and Fischer, *Well-Executed Failure*.

19. The Sullivan campaign earned Washington the name among the Iroquois of Caunotaucarious, or "Town Destroyer." Williams, *Year of the Hangman*, x.

20. Clausewitz, *Vom Kriege*, bk. 8, chap. 3B; *On War*, 587.

21. Wilson, *Southern Strategy*.

22. Haw, "'Every Thing Here,'" 212, and Keithly, "Poor, Nasty and Brutish."

23. Babits, "Greene's Strategy," gives an excellent account of the detailed logistical planning involved in eighteenth-century warfare and why Greene was successful at it.

24. Babits, *Devil of a Whipping*.

25. Gruber, "From Cowpens to Yorktown."

26. Sword, *President Washington's Indian War*.

27. Hogeland, *Whiskey Rebellion*, 213, 219–21.

28. Davis and Engerman, *Naval Blockades*, 78.

29. Palmer, *Stoddert's War*, 6.

30. Davis and Engerman, *Naval Blockades*, 78.

31. The US Navy was downsized after the war. Thirteen frigates were retained, six of which remained on active duty while the others were laid up, and twenty-nine other vessels were sold. Dupuy and Baumer, *Little Wars*, 23–25.

32. Lambert, *Barbary Wars*, 82, 200.

33. Dupuy and Baumer, *Little Wars*, 29–30.

34. Lambert, *Barbary* Wars, 125–26.

35. Turner, "President Thomas Jefferson," 162.

36. Dupuy and Baumer, *Little Wars*, 59–60.

37. The causes are discussed in Trautsch, "Causes of the War of 1812"; Stagg, *War of 1812*; and Wood, "War We Lost."

38. Davis and Engerman, *Naval Blockades*, 73–77.

39. Taylor, *Civil War of 1812*.

40. Letter from Henry Clay to Thomas Bodley, December 18, 1813, in Hickey, "1812," 970.

41. Grodzinski, "Opening Shots," 1188. See also Watson, "Trusting," 973, who notes that many Republicans shared Jefferson's "faith that an untrained militia could easily conquer Canada," but they failed to take any steps to improve militia training or administration in order to make it happen.

42. *American Military History*, 123–24. See also Black, "North American Theater," and McCranie, "War of 1812," which describe Britain's other entanglements.

43. Crackel, "Battle of Queenston Heights."

44. Skaggs, *Oliver Hazard Perry*.

45. Bowes, "Transformation."

46. Skaggs, *Thomas Macdonough*.

47. Lambert, *Challenge*.

48. Graves, "Why the White House," argues that even though retaliation was permitted by the laws of war as they were understood at the time, there is no clear answer as to whether the burning of Washington was in response to similar actions committed in Canada or due to British annoyance with American impertinence in starting the war.

49. Lee, "Battles of Plattsburg." The treaty was signed on December 24, 1814, but was not considered to be in effect until ratified by Congress, which did not occur until February 1815.

50. Jones, *Elements of Military Strategy*, 23.

51. Hall, "Dubious Means."

52. Schelling, *Arms and Influence*.

53. Wheelan, *Invading Mexico*, reminds readers that it was Polk's last resort, after having tried buying the territories and inciting a settlers' revolt.

54. Singletary, *Mexican War*, 23–24.

55. Weigley, *History of United States Army*, 171.

56. Vásquez, "War and Peace," 362.

57. Bauer, "Battles on the Rio Grande," 61–63, 73, 78.

58. Groom, *Kearny's March*, is a readable account. Kearny's expedition included the First US Dragoons, one battalion of artillery, one battalion of infantry, and one of Missouri volunteer mounted infantry, pp. 62–63.

59. Levinson, *Wars within War*, 22–23, 65–67, covers Taylor's approach to guerrillas.

60. Greenberg, *Wicked War*, 193–99.

61. Scott was appointed commander of the Veracruz expedition on November 19, 1847. Ibid., 235–36. For more on the relationships between Polk, Taylor, and Scott, see Eisenhower, "Polk and His Generals."

62. Johnson, *Gallant Little Army*, 5.

63. *American Military History*, 176.

64. Johnson, *Gallant Little Army*, 210–26. On the generation of American officers who fought in the Mexican War and the Civil War, see Dugard, *Training Ground*.

65. Grant, *Personal Memoirs*, vol. 1, 63.

66. Ibid., 71.

67. The treaty ceded California and New Mexico to the United States and confirmed that the border of Texas was the Rio Grande. The US government also agreed to pay Mexico $15 million and to assume all claims against the Mexican government by US citizens. Singletary, *Mexican War*, 160–61.

68. Bauer, *Mexican War*, 326–35, and Dawson, "Final Campaign," 95–105.

5

The Civil War
to the Boxer Rebellion

We are not only fighting hostile armies, but a hostile people, and
must make old and young, rich and poor, feel the hard hand of war,
as well as the organized armies.

Gen. William T. Sherman, 1864

GENERAL SHERMAN'S NOW FAMOUS EXPRESSION "hard hand of war" is
likely the most quoted phrase of the American Civil War, and it is insepar-
ably connected to the debate over whether that war was total.[1] Although the
debate will likely continue, the expression itself is useful from another standpoint: It illustrates how broad the gap can be between rhetoric and practice. Sherman's infamous "March to the Sea" may have destroyed Georgia's
economy, taken the war directly to the Southern populace, and endeavored
to make it fear the armies of the North—fear being the "beginning of wisdom" in Sherman's view.[2]

However, it is easy to overlook the conditions that brought the war to
that point: the tremendous loss of life, destruction of property, economic
hardship, and political uncertainty for Lincoln's administration brought on
by three years of war.[3] By 1864, the hand of war had indeed hardened, but
the campaign of 1861 was as American as those of 1864 and 1865. Moreover, Sherman's strategy of attrition was not without its olive branches: The
door to peace remained open, and the way through it was obvious, if still
unattractive to the Confederacy. His devastating campaigns in Georgia and
South Carolina, and Maj. Gen. Philip Sheridan's campaign in the Shenandoah valley before them, were notable for their destructiveness, but they
were not uniquely American in character. Similarities could be found in Europe's Thirty Years' War and in the harsh ways nineteenth-century European
governments dealt with rebellions in general. Nor was it a foreshadowing of

how Americans would approach the use of force thereafter, as the Spanish–American War and operations in the Philippines and Asia would attest.

The world wars of the twentieth century were products of the industrial age, with opponents waging their own versions of total war and applying tiered strategies of annihilation and attrition. The hard hand of war, thus, had Japanese, German, Russian, and British features as well.

The Civil War

When hostilities commenced on April 12, 1861, most of the US Army was engaged in performing frontier duties. It was deployed in 198 company-size detachments, over 90 percent of which were stationed west of the Mississippi River.[4] The army had fought more than twenty-two distinct Indian wars in the 1850s but had neither conducted nor trained for large-scale operations since Winfield Scott's 1847 campaign in Mexico. This deficiency became evident in the first months of the war, as both sides struggled to adjust to the difficulties of maneuvering and supplying large bodies of troops. However, serious deficiencies were also evident in the crucial functions of intelligence, logistics, engineering, and fire and movement for any military operation involving formations larger than a regiment (slightly more than a thousand officers and men at full strength).

Although Scott was nearly seventy-five years old, his professional opinion still mattered. His basic strategy for subduing the rebellion, which was derided in the press as "Scott's Great Snake" or "the Anaconda Plan," was sound in concept, but it did assume a longish war. That assumption rendered it especially vulnerable to criticism in the press. Also, Union forces were initially woefully short in terms of the eighty-five thousand troops and twenty naval vessels Scott believed it would require. The plan called for the economic and military strangulation of the Confederacy by capturing key forts along the Mississippi River valley and by establishing a blockade of the thirty-five hundred miles of southern coast in order to cut its overseas commerce and deprive the rebels of vital war materials. Northern military strategy would also see Ulysses S. Grant and William T. Sherman introduce successful variations of Scott's overall concept in the form of operational raiding and psychological warfare.[5] These were expedients driven more by circumstances than by professional instruction, military theories, or doctrine.

Although Scott's plan was sound in concept, President Lincoln added his own variations by pushing early for direct offensives on Richmond, only a hundred miles south of Washington. He was right to do so. As events were to show, Lincoln was wrong in the types of generals he initially selected (five within twenty-four months) to lead those offensives, but political realities justified his persistent urging to take the war to the enemy and by as direct a route as possible.[6] Some historians suggest that the war was destined to be long, bloody, and bitter. But that is not true. Had the North scored a decisive victory by means of a battle of annihilation at First Manassas in the summer of 1861 and marched directly on to Richmond, the war might have ended quickly. Both sides shared the same expectation: The war would be short. A decisive battle at the outset would have met nearly everyone's expectation, although another war might have erupted a few years later because the political differences between the North and South ran too deep to be solved by diplomacy alone. Nonetheless, the longer the war, the greater the political strain on Lincoln's administration. He won the electoral vote in 1860 but not the popular vote, and the election results precipitated South Carolina's secession in December and the others that followed.[7]

The Northern states possessed clear advantages in manpower (3.5:1) and in industrial capacities (50:1), which gave them the edge in a protracted struggle. However, these advantages were offset by a number of practical conditions.[8] With regard to manpower, for instance, strategic consumption in the form of protecting lines of communication and supply usually meant the North could rarely achieve more than a ratio of 1.5:1 on the battlefield.[9] Complicating the situation was the fact that short enlistment terms required constant nurturing of public support and afforded only limited windows of opportunity for major military actions. In theory, the South had what Clausewitz described as the defense's principal advantage: It could win by merely surviving. However, Scott's Anaconda Plan offset this advantage somewhat by making mere survival more difficult.

The military strategy followed by the South, albeit inconsistently, was that of exhaustion—attempting to break the North's will to fight by making any incursion as costly as possible, perhaps attracting some European allies along the way, until the North finally wearied of the struggle or lost confidence in its ability to win. In contrast, the approach the North actually pursued, of which Scott's plan was the intellectual basis, was that of attrition—eroding the South's military and economic wherewithal to make war. What the North lacked initially but needed in order to carry out the strategy was (1) the ability to win battles more often than not and (2) the ability to exploit them aggressively. It would not have these key prerequisites until the final two years of the war. At that stage, the strategy of attrition was applied in earnest. Time was not, therefore, on the side of the defender in this conflict, but it was also not entirely on the side of the attacker. In the end, the war would not be as brief as Lincoln desired, but it would be short enough for him to manage the strain to his political base.

The campaign season of 1861 saw both sides commit the same types of operational failures. Officers had little experience moving large bodies of troops and often misunderstood or overreacted to their orders or to the few intelligence reports they received. Operational science of the sort Halleck described was nonexistent, despite his claims to the contrary, and thus operational practice suffered. Units were committed piecemeal into battle, rather than as part of a coordinated effort; battles were engaged with the intent of pinning down and destroying an opponent, but they were seldom planned with the phases—approach, assault, and pursuit—necessary to realize such intentions. Instead, engagements frequently unfolded as ad hoc affairs, with the operative principle being to mass one's combat power at the decisive point more quickly than one's foe. Security and reconnaissance were inconsistent, which gave the element of surprise greater impact than it otherwise would have had. Unity of effort also proved difficult to achieve across the broader tactical frontages required by rifled cannon and muskets, which meant that supporting attacks often took place beyond the range of tactical communications. Cooperation between artillery and infantry left much to be desired. The troops, predominantly short-term volunteers, were hastily trained and lacked the discipline and psychological stamina necessary to execute complex maneuvers under fire, but officers and men were generally brave on both sides. However, only a few of the former veterans of the detested Mexican War had seen organized offensive and defensive operations on a scale above regimental command. As historians have remarked, a number of "hardened veterans" occupied Federal and Confederate ranks by the end of the war.[10] Nonetheless, that was not true during the first two years of the conflict. Each side learned how to wage modern war at about the same rate, but that process was at times offset by a relatively high rate of attrition across all ranks—through combat losses, disease, or expiration of service terms.

Between 1861 and 1863, the war's major campaigns followed two parallel courses. In the East, the fighting took place in the valleys and waterways between and around Washington and Richmond. In the West, the struggle was for control of the Mississippi River valley from Louisiana to Kentucky and the major transportation hubs at Grand Junction–Corinth, Nashville, and Chattanooga. Combined, these two campaign areas formed a theater of operations approximately 650 miles wide and 1,300 miles long, divided by a formidable but not impassable mountain range. The war's opening campaign saw a clash between Union Brigadier General Irvin McDowell (thirty-five thousand troops) and Confederate brigadier general P. T. G. Beauregard (thirty-two thousand troops) at Manassas junction on July 21, 1861, though inexperience with high-level command and maneuver prevented either side from bringing much more than half its troops into contact at any one time. Union forces were thrown back in confusion, suffering twenty-seven hundred casualties to two thousand losses for the Confederates.[11] The clash destroyed Federal hopes of a short war and inspired Lincoln to call for a revamping of the means for recruiting volunteers and to extend the term of enlistment to three years.

As the armies of both sides reorganized for the next campaign season, the US Navy assembled some two hundred ships to strengthen its ability to enforce the blockade of key Southern ports. There was to be no major battle at sea between the North and South during the war. However, naval engagements did take place in coastal waters, inlets, and harbors, and joint army-navy operations occurred on the major rivers inland, such as Brig. Gen. Ulysses S. Grant's assault on Fort Henry and Fort Donelson in early February 1862, which also employed a number of armored gunboats under the command of Flag Officer Andrew Foote. Federal army and naval forces also conducted crucial joint operations at New Orleans (April 1862), Mobile (August 1864), Savannah (December 1864), Charleston (February 1865), and Wilmington (February 1865), which either destroyed or reduced harbor defenses and permitted the capture of these vital port cities.[12]

The campaigns of 1862 and 1863 were conducted on a scale three or four times greater than that of the campaign of 1861. Confederate forces purportedly had the advantage of interior lines, which ought to have enabled them to move troops and supplies expeditiously from one part of the theater of operations to the other. In reality, the Appalachian mountain range, situated in the upper middle of the theater, made such moves difficult. Also, Confederate railroad gauges were not fully standardized, which meant that troops sometimes had to be detrained and reboarded, which invariably impeded the relocation of men and materiel. The Confederacy was also denied the use of coastal waterways to move troops and supplies across the theater due to the Federal blockade. These facts made the task of defense much more difficult for the South. In truth, the Confederacy's difficulties in transferring troops from one threatened sector to another were about the same as those faced by the Union with its exterior lines.

In the West, Grant took Henry and Donelson in February 1862, and Capt. David Farragut took New Orleans in April 1862. By midsummer Federal troops held strongholds all along the Mississippi River except at Vicksburg and Port Hudson. The Confederates launched a strong counterattack up the

Tennessee River valley but were checked at Shiloh (April 6, 1862) with heavy losses to both sides: The North lost thirteen thousand troops, or 20 percent of its strength; the South suffered eleven thousand casualties, or 28 percent of its effectives.[13] With the blockade continuing to tighten and strong Union forces now positioned in western Tennessee and northern Virginia, the South attempted to change the strategic situation by launching a series of counter-offensives. The first of these, led by Gen. Braxton Bragg, advanced northward from Chattanooga in an effort to drive Union forces out of Tennessee and draw Kentucky into the Confederacy. The second, led by Gen. Robert E. Lee, invaded Maryland and attempted to draw Gen. George McClellan into a de-cisive battle. Lee had already achieved timely, if costly, successes in defend-ing Richmond against McClellan's Army of the Potomac (May–July 1862) and in defeating Maj. Gen. John Pope's Army of Virginia at the Second Battle of Manassas (August 1862). He also deserved some credit for facilitating Lt. Gen. Thomas "Stonewall" Jackson's string of victories in the Shenandoah valley between the end of March and the beginning of June 1862.

Despite some initial successes, both of these counteroffensives stalled—Lee's at Antietam on September 17, 1862, and Bragg's at Perryville on Octo-ber 7, 1862. Not only had the counteroffensives failed to draw more domestic and international support for the Southern cause—they actually strength-ened doubts about the Confederacy's ability to prevail. Even with the level of operational incompetence demonstrated by the North, the South's attacks could not achieve anything of note. They scored too few tactical successes to weaken Lincoln's position politically, which was under constant attack from critics such as the Copperheads, who persistently agitated for peace. The Confederate offensives also never seriously weakened Lincoln's popular-ity with the troops, which told in his favor in the 1864 election.[14] In short, the counteroffensives spent valuable resources in men and materiel, resources the South would find ever more difficult to replace, but never struck at the heart of Union resolve and achieved little more than a few tactical victories. Lee's losses at Antietam were over ten thousand, or about 30 percent of his forces engaged; McClellan's casualties were over twelve thousand, or 25 per-cent of his forces.[15] Again, Lee was less able to afford such a high rate of loss. The North's strategy of attrition was working but at a perilously slow pace.

The fact that Lee was forced to quit the battlefield enabled Lincoln to make use of the fight politically. A tactical draw became a strategic victory with the announcement of the Emancipation Proclamation on September 22, 1862, which went into effect three months later. It demonstrated yet another way in which war can serve as an instrument of policy, an instrument Lincoln clearly knew how to use. Bragg lost only three thousand men at Perryville and would continue to inflict heavy casualties and confusion on Union forces in subsequent battles throughout the autumn of 1862, but the South's high-water mark in the West had been reached. Only the North's command failures at corps and army levels prevented Antietam and Perryville from being operationally decisive. This ineptness was evident again at the Battle of Fredericksburg on December 13, 1862, where Lee defeated Maj. Gen. Ambrose Burnside, who lost twelve thousand casualties compared to Lee's fifty-three hundred and withdrew into winter quarters. The lack of aggressiveness on the part of Union generals also continued to frustrate Lincoln, who believed, justifiably, that many opportunities to end the war sooner rather than later had been allowed to slip by.

In the West, Grant renewed his campaign against Vicksburg, finally taking it on July 4, 1863. Port Hudson fell four days later. The two victories gave the Union control of the Mississippi River. Union forces under Maj. Gen. William Rosecrans (eighty-four thousand troops) pushed from Murfreesboro toward Chattanooga in August and September, attempting to engage Bragg (forty-five thousand troops) in a decisive battle. However, Bragg checked the Union advance at Chickamauga, with heavy losses on both sides. Rosecrans withdrew into Chattanooga and allowed himself to be besieged there. Lincoln sent reinforcements and, more important, relieved Rosecrans, replacing him with Grant, who lost no time in launching a counterattack in late November that drove the Confederates back.

In the east, Lee (sixty thousand men) defeated a Union army under Maj. Gen. Joseph Hooker (one-hundred thirty-four thousand) at the battle of Chancellorsville in the first week of May, but again his casualties were high: thirteen thousand compared to seventeen thousand for the Union, or a ratio of 22 percent to 13 percent. In addition, Lee's casualties also included the loss of the irreplaceable Jackson. Lee tried one more time to score a major material and psychological victory over the North by invading Maryland and Pennsylvania in the summer of 1863. Such a victory, it was hoped, would secure recognition of the Confederacy by European powers. However, Lee (seventy-five thousand) was turned back at Gettysburg by Union forces (ninety thousand) under Maj. Gen. George Meade after three days of fighting, July 1–3, 1863. Confederate casualties were twenty-eight thousand compared to twenty-three thousand for the Union, or a ratio of 37 percent to 25 percent.[16] Again, an invasion of the North had achieved little but had cost dearly. Still, at this rate of attrition, the war could last several more years.

As if to make good on that possibility, in March 1864, the Confederate government in Richmond ordered all guerrilla units (save two battalions in Virginia) to disband and to transfer into conventional army ranks.[17] Consequently, by the spring of 1864, the North had to do more than inflict a higher rate of casualties on the South—it needed to destroy Southern armies and corps as fighting organizations. To do that it had to maneuver relentlessly against Confederate formations, force them to fight under unfavorable conditions, and exploit each success before the rebels could regroup. Tactical lethality was less a problem in this war than the inability to exploit success operationally.

The campaigns in 1864 and 1865 thus saw renewed Union offensives in the East and West. The campaign in the East was designed to deprive Lee of room to maneuver and further wear down his army. It involved Sheridan's devastation of the Shenandoah valley in September and October 1864. Lee would remain a tough quarry, scoring minor victories against superior Union forces throughout the autumn and winter of 1864–65. However, Grant was relentless and used his numerical advantage to good effect. Moreover, his operational science was such that he rarely made the same mistake twice. He eventually cornered Lee at Appomattox, Virginia, forcing his surrender on April 9, 1865. The latter Union offensive pushed toward Atlanta, which fell to Sherman on September 1–2, 1864. On November 15, 1864, Sherman began to move along a sixty-mile front from Atlanta to Savannah with sixty-two thousand men, destroying tons of crops and thousands of livestock along the way. Sherman's controversial march was not only an effort at economic warfare designed to break the South's ability to feed itself—it also inflicted a huge psychological blow by demonstrating the impotence of the Confederacy: The South might have commanders and forces nimble enough to elude Federal armies for some time, but it was no longer truly able to defend its citizens and territory. Sherman reached Savannah on December 21, 1864, then headed northward to Columbia, arriving on February 17, 1865. He finally cornered Johnston near Raleigh, North Carolina, and forced his surrender on April 26, 1865.[18]

There was talk among some Confederate leaders of continuing to resist by means of guerrilla warfare. However, the guerrilla campaigns had been something of a double-edged sword for both sides. Raids by irregulars had given rise to brutal and indiscriminate reprisals, and a vicious cycle of acrimony took hold with little of military value to show for it beyond basic harassment of communications and supply. Lee and Confederate president Jefferson Davis advised against it, seeing no real "prospect by that means," and Grant offered a period of amnesty in May and June 1865, guaranteeing the safety of any group willing to come in from the hills and lay down its arms.[19]

Years of occupation and reconstruction were to follow for the US Army as the hard hand of war transitioned to the marginally softer hand of peace. The army was quickly downsized from nearly 1 million troops in April 1865, to one-hundred eighty-three thousand by November 10, 1865, to about twenty-five thousand at the end of 1866, then increased again to a postwar peak of fifty-seven thousand in 1867.[20] Some twenty thousand of these troops, augmented by various militia units, were assigned to reconstruction duties in the South from 1867 to 1875. These duties were not those of a typical occupation force. The troops remained largely confined to their barracks, posts, or forts and were not quartered among the population. They were deployed mainly to supervise elections and quell disorders.

The Wars against the Plains Indians

Weigley inaccurately claimed the US Army employed a strategy of annihilation against the Plains Indians. Its approach was actually a harsh form of coercive diplomacy—with a heavy reliance on military force. The basic idea was to compel the tribes to relocate by negotiating with them or to deal a severe blow to them militarily if they refused. The military component of the strategy consisted of doing what armed forces have traditionally done in war—that is, attempt to destroy an opponent's wherewithal to subsist and to fight.

Some scholars have described this as a logistics-based strategy, but it was more than that.[21] Much of the material destroyed would have contributed more to the survival of noncombatants than to the war effort directly. This strategy did not discriminate between war material and an individual's basic livelihood. It was an amalgamation of attrition, exhaustion, terror, and divide-and-conquer—all aimed at breaking the Indians' will to resist. The Plains Indian Wars resembled medieval warfare without the presence of castles and manors to provide protection. The Indians were nomadic or semi-nomadic, which was both an advantage and a disadvantage for them. From the standpoint of the army, the campaigns had much in common with Sullivan's 1779 expedition with its intention not only to punish, but to dispossess. There are obvious parallels between these campaigns and the "hard hand of war" Sherman practiced in 1864. However, his rhetoric obscures the fact that the fighting on the northern and southern plains was intermittent, interrupted by negotiations and renegotiations to the extent that drawing a precise distinction between war and diplomacy is artificial.

While war was a way of life for the Plains Indians—a means to acquire wealth and status—it was also highly individualistic, centering on personal feats of bravery and skill. In short, it was the antithesis of fighting in disciplined, organized formations and thus was asymmetrical from the outset. From 1865 to 1890, the US Army and its irregular scouts and auxiliaries are said to have fought more than a thousand engagements against the Plains Indians.[22] The army's regulars found most of these encounters frustrating, as Plains warriors rarely held ground or fought pitched battles, preferring instead to attack from ambush or by raid, then withdraw. Aside from several notable massacres—such as the ambush of Capt. William Fetterman's command on December 21, 1866, and the annihilation of Lt. Col. George Custer's command on June 24, 1876—most of the thousand or so engagements that occurred with the Plains Indians were little more than brief skirmishes resulting in few casualties on either side.[23] All told, the Plains tribes are believed to have killed 919 US soldiers between 1865 and 1898, or fewer than 28 per year.[24]

Most of the frontier violence came not from such brief skirmishes, but from raids against unprotected villages, atrocities committed against immigrant workers or migrants, forced relocations under difficult conditions, and ongoing intertribal warfare. Examples include the Snake Indian attack on the Ward party (1854), which resulted in the deaths of nineteen migrants; the Mountain Meadows Massacre (1857), in which a group of Mormons and Indians killed one hundred migrants; the Shoshone assault on the Otter–Van Orman train (1860), in which thirty-two migrants were killed; and Col. Christopher "Kit" Carson's forcible relocation of Navajo Indians to the Bosque Redondo Reservation (1864), which reportedly resulted in scores of Navajo deaths.[25] Intertribal warfare sometimes involved extreme measures: Defeated enemy noncombatants, including women and children, were usually slain or taken into captivity, and ponies, livestock, and food stores were often stolen, killed, or destroyed, which in turn meant severe hardships, even death, for survivors. Such brutal measures have been described by some Western scholars as a form of total war.[26]

US Army units were required to protect settlers, trading outposts, stagecoach and telegraph stations, and mining towns in far-flung areas across the western frontier. The problem was that semi-nomadic tribes of the plains were elusive—mobile, unencumbered by weighty provisions and supply lines, and depending on the situation, able to live off the land. Conventional practices of fixing and destroying an opponent did not work, as Plains warriors, fighting as individuals or in small numbers, simply refused to be fixed. This problem was all the more acute since army units were seriously undermanned. For example, the Military Division of the Missouri, one of two major theaters of operation west of the Mississippi River, had a security ratio of one soldier for every hundred square miles of territory. Moreover, communication among such widely dispersed detachments was difficult because the telegraph was not yet well established throughout the western territories. Courier was thus the primary means of relaying news and orders. Also, operational and tactical intelligence varied in quality and quantity, depending on the reliability of Indian scouts and reports from auxiliaries and local settlers. In addition, the army had no official doctrine for Indian fighting, though it had a foundation of practices and principles from which it could draw and, with some modification, apply.[27]

As discussed, the army's military strategy derived not only from its experiences in the Civil War, as Weigley claimed, but also from its ingrained appreciation of the importance of supplies and logistics, the fundamental wherewithal any friend or foe must have to survive and fight.[28] It was also a strategy familiar to the Indians themselves: Raiding and stealing horses, supplies, and other possessions was a typical way of strengthening oneself at the expense of one's opponent. The success of the strategy depended on finding and destroying the Indians' material capacity to resist and giving relentless pursuit so they had no opportunity to reconstitute it. Without the basics of food, shelter, clothing, and ponies or horses for transportation, neither Indians nor settlers could survive for long in the hostile environment that was the frontier. This was particularly true during the winters, as the temperatures often dropped below zero degrees Fahrenheit. Once their wherewithal was destroyed or taken, the Indians were left with the choice of complying with US relocation policies or perishing. It was pure operational science. It was also a cruel and brutal form of ethnic cleansing.[29]

The army columns that carried out the strategy were typically equipped as self-sufficient expeditions, with a mix of pack horses and mules to allow them to operate over hundreds of miles of rough terrain for long periods of time and in most kinds of weather. However, that also meant they were weighed down with baggage and supplies, which compromised their mobility compared to the renegade bands or hostile tribes they pursued. They could not match the mobility of Indian war parties, but they could keep pace with the noncombatants. Moreover, the lack of mobility of army columns was offset somewhat by their operational range. The columns would maneuver in much the same way a conventional unit would conduct a movement to contact: Scouting parties would be deployed well forward, followed by light detachments (cavalry) at the front and along the flanks, with heavy elements (infantry and supply wagons) in the rear. An example of such an expedition was Maj. Gen. Winfield Hancock's command (fourteen hundred troops), which set out in April 1867 toward Pawnee Fork, Wyoming, in response to complaints of Cheyenne raiding parties. The Cheyennes responded by sending a "negotiating party" to meet Hancock, the real purpose of which was to stall for time to enable the village to evacuate before the expedition arrived.

The solution to this sort of elusiveness was to converge on an area with multiple columns. This technique did not evolve merely as a way of adapting to the superior mobility of the Indians, as has been suggested: It was standard military practice, traceable in military theory at least to the writings of Jomini. He had expounded upon its advantages and disadvantages, noting that "concentric operations" were useful in two situations: to concentrate one's forces before they engage the enemy and "when they direct to the same end the efforts of two [or more] armies which are in no danger of being beaten separately by a stronger enemy."[30] Halleck, too, wrote of converging lines of operations, describing them as "preferable, under most circumstances, to diverging lines," though "care should be taken" that they not permit one's "own forces [to] be destroyed in detail, before they can affect a junction."[31] Scott had also tried to put it into practice in the Second Seminole War, but the terrain was not conducive to it, and his numbers were too few to carry it out effectively.

Depending on the scale, this technique could be used either as a tactic or as a larger operational maneuver. An example of the former is Custer's attempt to employ it at Little Big Horn in 1876, which also exposed the vulnerability that Jomini and Halleck both noted: The Sioux were able to mass against one element first, then the other.[32] An example of its use as an operational maneuver occurred two years earlier when the army employed five converging columns—Col. Nelson Miles (twelve companies) from Kansas, Lt. Col. Davidson (eight companies) from Fort Sill, Col. Ranald Mackenzie (twelve companies) from central Texas, Maj. William Price (four companies) from the New Mexico territory, and Lt. Col. George Buell (eight companies) from eastern Texas—to subdue Comanche and Kiowa tribes in the Red River valley of the Texas Panhandle.[33] In practice, as converging columns closed within range, an officer could demand the Indians' surrender, open fire, or charge the encampment ("pitch into" in Custer's words), destroying arms, shelters, food stores, and ponies, and scattering the warriors and noncombatants.[34] During the campaign of 1874, few Comanches and Kiowas were actually killed in such assaults; however, the loss of their shelters and food stores broke their will to resist, particularly after months of intensive hunting and severe drought had diminished the buffalo herd.[35]

This harsh form of coercive diplomacy was effective, but it was neither humanitarian nor efficient. Noncombatants were often slain in the panic and melees caused by the assaults, and noncombatant casualties only added to the bitterness of the wars. They also attracted public criticism and political scrutiny and stained the army's honor. Had it not been for the fact that the Indians had to contend with a harsh climate and rival tribes, this composite strategy might not have worked. The harshness of the climate created vulnerabilities that could be exploited, and intertribal conflicts meant it was never difficult to recruit warriors from one tribe to fight another. And the Indians' individualistic style of war could not stand up to the army's collective cohesion and firepower. Ambushes and raids were insufficient to defend villages and encampments against coordinated assaults.[36]

The Spanish–American War

The Spanish–American War may well have validated the theories of Alfred Thayer Mahan and shaped the US Navy's "public and political image" in key respects, as Weigley and others have claimed.[37] However, it also brought to light the key deficiency in Mahan's theories—namely, his assumption that command of the seas was not only necessary but sufficient to secure victory. Mahan's ideas rested on four fundamental assumptions: Competition among nations was perpetual, the chief arena for that competition in the modern era was the seas, a large navy of capital ships was the best tool for securing sea lines of communication, and diplomacy worked best when it followed a successful decision at sea.[38] To be sure, the naval battles at Manila Bay (May 1, 1898) and Santiago Bay (July 3, 1898) were decisive in the Mahanian sense, eliminating Spanish naval power in both the Philippines and Cuba. Yet, protecting American economic interests and establishing some degree of stability in each of those areas would also require projecting troops ashore, as per Julian Corbett's theories on sea power published a decade later.[39] Indeed, each of the American naval commanders, Commo. George Dewey in the Philippines and Rear Adm. William Sampson in the Caribbean, initially found his ability to influence the situations in his respective theaters hampered by the lack of US ground troops.

At the outbreak of war, Spanish regular and volunteer ground forces totaled about two hundred thousand in Cuba, another fifteen thousand in Puerto Rico, and nearly forty-five thousand in the Philippines.[40] Those troops stationed in Cuba and the Philippines had been fighting guerrillas since 1895 and 1896, respectively. The Spanish Navy had undergone some modernization in the 1890s, but when the war began, it had only one modern battleship, five armored cruisers, and a few destroyers and smaller vessels. Four of the armored cruisers and two of the destroyers were located in Santiago Bay. The Spanish squadron in the Philippines had some forty vessels, but none of these could compete with modern warships.[41] In addition, the government in Madrid gave little in the way of instructions to its commanders in the Philippines and Cuba. Evidently, the only consistent signal from the Spanish head of state was that its commanders should seek decisive battles, notwithstanding the odds against success. Pundits such as Fred T. Jane (editor of the annual series *Jane's Fighting Ships* and later *Jane's All the World's Aircraft*) advised Madrid to bombard major cities along the US coast to make the Americans regret intervening and to use that as leverage for obtaining favorable terms.[42] Others suggested that the Spanish squadrons should disperse among the islands of the Caribbean and the Philippines and wage a *guerre de course*, raiding American maritime transportation, similar in style to the approach advocated by the French Jeune École (Young School). However, Madrid chose none of these options and elected instead to proceed as if it saw war as an honorable way to rid itself of territories that had become political and fiscal liabilities.

Despite several years of rising tensions between Spain and the United States before 1898, the American military was not ready for war when it came.[43] The regular army numbered fewer than 28,000 officers and men, and these had not trained for operations involving formations larger than a regiment. Between April 1 and August 1, 1898, it doubled in size—to 56,000 personnel—and volunteers brought the total number of troops to 272,000. However, ammunition, equipment, and training remained inadequate for such a rapid increase.[44] The US Navy was somewhat better off, as it had begun to benefit from a modernization program launched in the mid-1880s. By 1898, it had four, modern, first-class battleships, two, second-class battleships (including the USS *Maine*), two armored cruisers, and a few light cruisers. In addition, 60 percent of President William McKinley's "Fifty Million Dollar Bill," signed into law on March 9, 1898, went to the navy, enabling it to procure 131 more vessels of various capacities before war's end.[45]

Both the US Army and the US Navy began developing wartime scenarios and contingency plans in the 1880s, though no formal body yet existed to oversee the development of strategy and war planning. In the 1890s, the navy and its newly established war college at Newport, Rhode Island, developed several such plans for the possibility of a war with Spain. Interest increased as the insurrection in Cuba grew and tensions between Washington and Madrid heightened.[46] These plans were light on the political dimensions of the conflict, especially with regard to what US political objectives might be, though in truth, the White House was also hard-pressed to provide clear policy guidance at this time. In any case, it is often unnecessary for military planning to wait for political guidance. Planners can begin weighing purely military factors, such as numbers of capital ships, their operational ranges and carrying capacities, the location of coaling stations, and likely courses of action based on fleet or flotilla dispositions.[47] Some of the plans advocated a *guerre de course*, but most called for blockading a key port city such as Havana, preparatory to a decisive naval battle in the Caribbean. Contingencies for ground operations mainly involved landing expeditionary forces to secure Havana or other strategically important cities and supporting indigenous guerrilla groups with arms and ammunition. These broad outlines, as it turned out, were not too far from the course the war would actually take.

However, these plans assumed that there would be enough time for a blockade to take effect and that indigenous guerrilla forces would generally act in accordance with Washington's wishes rather than their own. In fact, McKinley initially desired to have the situation resolved swiftly (speed is, of course, always relative). His war aims for the Philippines began to expand with the increasing success of American military operations. As historians have pointed out, he did not desire war, but he was enough of a politician to seize opportunities when they presented themselves.[48] Moreover, after the capture of Manila, the interests of the Filipino guerrillas quickly diverged from those of the White House, requiring more US ground forces to be deployed into the theater in order to enhance the reach of US policy.

The US Navy, for its part, promptly established powerful blockades in each theater of operations, but it did so as part of a larger strategy of annihilation aimed at destroying Spanish naval might. In contrast, the US Army carried out operations oriented on terrain, Jominian-style, taking and controlling key ports and cities in each area, which were to provide the White House with leverage in the ensuing negotiations. Dewey's Asiatic Squadron (seven warships), for instance, handily destroyed the Spanish fleet in Manila Bay on May 1, 1898—despite the fact that the Spaniards had more warships and were purportedly supported by coastal batteries and underwater mines.[49] His operational science—extensive intelligence-gathering efforts and his subsequent analysis of the situation and the capabilities of the Spanish squadron—showed that there was actually little risk to his forces. As it turned out, his faster ships were able to make several devastating runs at the Spanish squadron while evading most of its return fire. Likewise, on July 3, US naval forces under Commo. Winfield Schley destroyed the Spanish flotilla in Santiago Bay (four cruisers, two destroyers) as it attempted to slip through the blockade and make a run for the open seas.[50]

Although Dewey had defeated the Spanish squadron at Manila, he could not take the city without a sizable and disciplined ground force. Filipino insurgents in the area could conduct limited guerrilla operations and hold a tentative defensive perimeter but could not accomplish much more than that. Unfortunately, VIII Corps (with fifteen thousand troops), commanded by Maj. Gen. Wesley Merritt, would not arrive until the end of July, and it was not ready to launch an assault on Manila, defended by twelve thousand Spanish regulars and volunteers, until mid-August.[51] Both sides had agreed in advance that the defenders would offer only token resistance, largely to satisfy Spanish honor; however, some Filipino guerrillas (to whom the Spaniards refused to surrender) also took part in the assault, and the violence escalated rapidly, resulting in several unnecessary casualties, including 17 American soldiers killed and 105 wounded.[52] These losses were all the more regrettable because, unbeknownst to either side, Spain and the United States had already signed a peace protocol the day before.

As mentioned, Filipino and American interests were diverging. The Filipinos were fighting for their independence—not just from Spain, but from all foreign powers. In contrast, the Americans were attempting to assume control of the Philippines. President McKinley had decided to exploit the initial successes of the US military. This decision occurred not only because Manila and its surrounding islands offered valuable bases for protecting growing American interests in Asia and the Pacific, but also to keep other foreign powers, such as Germany, from taking possession of them. That fateful decision would inspire the insurrectionists to turn fully against American forces in the months ahead.

In the Caribbean theater, the Spanish decision to make a dash for the open seas rather than remain in Santiago Bay was due only partially to the effects of the blockade. It was also the result of the pressure that Maj. Gen. William Shafter's V Corps (seventeen thousand troops) brought against the city of Santiago, particularly once the canal leading from the reservoir to the north was cut. Shafter's corps began arriving on June 22 at the smaller city of Daiquiri, some twelve miles to the east of Santiago. The journey had been an odyssey of frustrating delays and mishaps. The port of Tampa had not been reconnoitered properly, and it lacked the capacity to handle the flow of troops and supplies earmarked for Cuba. Central control was nonexistent, and embarkation was disorganized, as was the subsequent disembarkation.[53] Nonetheless, Shafter managed to get all of his men ashore by June 24. Fearing the deleterious effects of tropical diseases such as yellow fever and malaria, he lost little time in marching on Santiago. Two divisions (eight thousand men) moved directly on Santiago, and a third division (sixty-five hundred) advanced on El Caney, located to the northeast. Gen. Calixto García's force of four thousand insurgents supported the Americans with critical intelligence about Spanish dispositions and the local environs.

On July 1, Shafter's corps, enjoying an overwhelming local superiority over Spanish forces on El Caney and San Juan Hill, drove the defenders from the heights but only with great difficulty. Few American commanders had conducted operations on this scale before, and as a result, attacks were carried out piecemeal and without proper coordination among adjacent units or with supporting fires.[54] Had it not been for the initiative of individual field commanders such as Theodore Roosevelt, the assaults would likely have failed. As it was, taking El Caney cost the Americans 81 killed and 360 wounded, while Spanish casualties were about 370.[55] The famed assault on San Juan Hill cost the Americans a further 124 dead and 820 wounded, compared to 350 Spanish losses.[56] Lack of experience in coordinating large formations and conducting reconnaissance and security missions had proven costly for the Americans again.

The Americans were also unprepared for the effects of the tropical climate. As a result, the number of casualties from sickness began to grow faster than those due to battle. By July 3, Shafter's total casualties numbered nearly seventeen hundred, or slightly more than 10 percent of his original invasion force. He requested permission to withdraw to defensive positions located on higher ground and above the "malaria line," but this move was vetoed by Secretary of War Russell A. Alger, who failed to appreciate the seriousness of the situation. Fortunately, the Spanish forces were not fully committed to defending Cuba and fell back in the face of renewed American attacks. Civilian refugees and retreating Spanish troops doubled the population of Santiago, and with the city's fresh water supply now cut by Shafter's forces, conditions for the inhabitants steadily worsened. The Spanish commander finally agreed to lay down his arms on July 16, and most of the twenty thousand troops defending Santiago and its environs surrendered, though some reverted to guerrilla tactics and continued to resist.

As historians have noted, the surrender of Santiago came none too soon, as more than three thousand of Shafter's troops fell ill with malaria, yellow fever, or typhoid during the following week.[57] By July 28, the number of sick in V Corps reached four thousand, rendering Shafter's command practically combat ineffective. In early August, his troops were finally withdrawn to the United States to convalesce, but V Corps's medical crisis had far-reaching effects. Charges of neglect and incompetence were leveled against many of its commanders.

True to some of the assumptions underpinning the war plans developed in the years before the conflict, the destruction of the Spanish fleet at Santiago Bay made the defense of Puerto Rico untenable. Gen. Nelson Miles landed a force of three thousand troops at Guánica, Puerto Rico, on July 25, and after receiving additional reinforcements within the fortnight, began occupying the island against only light resistance. Major combat operations finally ended when the peace protocol went into effect on August 13. However, the Treaty of Paris, which concluded the war, was not signed until December 10, 1898, four months later.

The Philippine Insurrection

America's "splendid little war" with Spain lasted just over eight months. However, its aftermath in the Philippines developed into an insurrection between Filipinos and Americans that continued for more than three years and cost the United States over seven thousand casualties and $400 million ($320 billion in 2012 dollars).[58] At the time, the Philippines comprised some seven thousand islands, with a population of more than 7 million people divided among various political, religious, and linguistic groups.[59] At the outset of the fighting, which began in early February 1899, the strength of the Filipino army was estimated at between fifteen thousand and forty thousand men, mostly light infantry, under the direction of Emilio Aguinaldo. US forces at the time consisted of VIII Corps, under the command of Maj. Gen. Elwell Otis. Some eleven thousand of his twenty thousand troops were in defensive positions around Manila.[60]

Operating under strict orders from Washington to establish American authority over the area, Otis rejected Aguinaldo's entreaties for a cease-fire and launched a concerted offensive that drove the Filipino army from its positions surrounding Manila with heavy losses. Aguinaldo's efforts to resist the American advance with conventional tactics crumbled against the superior firepower and discipline of US forces. Washington escalated its efforts, sending additional regular and volunteer regiments (thirty-five thousand men) in July and establishing over fifty bases or stations in Luzon. These bases would increase exponentially over the coming months. During this period, US forces were primarily employing a Jominian terrain-oriented strategy by capturing key villages and locales in Luzon and areas adjacent to Manila, thereby denying them to the resistance and disrupting its ability to move and communicate. To a lesser degree, they were also using a Clausewitzian enemy-oriented strategy, hunting Aguinaldo and other resistance leaders.

The cumulative successes of this dual strategy, combined with Aguinaldo's near capture in November 1899, forced him to change his approach. He shifted from conventional to guerrilla-style tactics similar to those he had employed against the Spanish army a few years earlier. The restrictive terrain of the Philippine archipelago—rugged mountains, thick jungles, deep marshes, and tall grasslands—was ideal for such a campaign. Filipino resistance became decentralized: Small groups of regulars and militiamen hid among the native population and struck at US forces by means of small-scale ambushes and raids. As a result of this shift in methods, Aguinaldo's forces became more difficult to find and thus were able to grow in number. Some US estimates put insurrectionist forces between eighty thousand and one hundred thousand fighters by mid-1900. Aguinaldo's strategy had become one of exhaustion: He was attempting to wear down Washington's resolve and perhaps buy enough time for a favorable change of leadership in the White House as a result of the 1900 elections.

One US Army officer at the time described American strategy as breaking rebel resistance by means of a "wearing-out policy"—that is, "pounding away until the bandit chiefs get tired of living in the far distant mountains, and the people, wearying of their importunate demands for money and their impotent military efforts, withdraw their material and moral support for them."[61] Much has been made about the similarities between this approach and the strategies applied during the wars against the Plains Indians, as well as some phases of the Civil War. In truth, there were many similarities, as all of these campaigns were, at root, little more than the continuation of a stern form of diplomacy—of carrots and sticks—by other means. Military force was used in both capacities, as a stick for "pounding away" at undesirable behavior but also as a carrot, to protect and reward desirable behavior. There were obviously other important carrots as well, such as the building of schools—more than a thousand of them—and other infrastructure. By the turn of the century, the US military had several viable traditions from which it could draw, even if these had not been thoroughly incorporated into official doctrine.

Yet there were also key differences. The Philippine conflict was a war of national liberation, and Aguinaldo was its center of gravity. When he was captured in March 1901 by Brig. Gen. Frederick Funston and then persuaded to swear allegiance to the United States, the back of the resistance was broken.[62] It was not Aguinaldo's removal per se that proved decisive but rather the fact that, after his capture, he publicly announced his support for the US government, and his views still held sway. Had he been killed instead of publicly converted, it is likely that he would have become a martyr for the insurrection, an outcome that might well have inspired further resistance. American forces began to withdraw a few months later, though military operations continued for many months in southern Luzon and Samar Island until other principal insurgent leaders, such as Miguel Malvar, surrendered in the spring of 1902. President Roosevelt declared the Philippine Insurrection ended on July 4, 1902, ignoring the risks inherent in unilateral statements of this sort.[63]

In actuality, US forces faced several more years of brutal fighting in the Philippines: against the Moros in the southern islands (1902–13) and the Pulahanes in the northern areas (1902–7).[64] American troops launched numerous punitive expeditions to prevent bandits and rebels from raiding the countryside and terrorizing the population, activities that threatened the fragile postwar stability of the Philippines. The typical expedition or task force consisted of several companies of infantry, a squadron or two of cavalry (mounted or dismounted), a battery of artillery, and a few units of Filipino scouts and constabularies, all supported by mule trains. The artillery was necessary, even in the restrictive terrain of volcanic islands, for reducing the *cottas*, or fortified hamlets. Although US forces generally pursued only key bandit leaders or chieftains such as the Moro outlaw Yusop Jikiri and the Pulahan Ruperto Ríos, and their followers, these groups remained difficult to corner. US military strategy was more productive once it shifted from pursuing bandit leaders to destroying the *cottas*, which systematically eliminated the outlaws' operating bases. This change was made more effective by including broader pacification efforts, such as building roads, clinics, and schools. In short, US military strategy during this period was rarely about the use of force, or sticks, alone.

The Boxer Rebellion

The Philippine Insurrection was not yet over before other American troops were sent to China as part of a larger international rescue effort. The mission of this multinational relief force (mainly comprising British, German, Russian, French, American, Austrian, Italian, and Japanese troops) was to liberate foreign delegates and citizens who had become trapped inside the Legation Quarter of the city of Peking (as Beijing was then called) during the Boxer Rebellion. The mission called for a series of combat operations along a relatively narrow 130-mile-long corridor running from the port city of Taku to Peking, with some detachments detailed along the way to defend key towns and railroad junctions and to keep open lines of communication and supply. Relief forces consisted primarily of naval, marine, and army units with supporting artillery from the main foreign contingents trapped in Peking. The Boxer militia consisted of poorly armed bands of young men. After June 17, 1900, several semiregular Chinese army units (thirty to fifty thousand troops) began actively opposing the allied rescue effort. The Chinese regulars were much better trained and equipped than the Boxer militia, but they were not equal in discipline, morale, or firepower to the allied forces. The first relief attempt, of twenty-one hundred men under the command of British admiral Sir Edward Seymour, took place between June 10 and 22. However, it had to turn back due to destroyed railroad lines after penetrating only as far as Anping, some thirty miles southeast of Peking.[65]

The second attempt took place between August 5 and 14 under the command of British lieutenant general Sir Alfred Gaselee, who had a force of twenty thousand troops (including two thousand Americans under Maj. Gen. Adna Chaffee).[66] Instead of using the railroads, Gaselee's force followed the Peiho River, which was easier to secure and also served well as the expedition's line of communication and supply. The relief operation followed a consistent pattern: "move to contact" until Chinese resistance is encountered, then establish a base of fire with supporting artillery, maneuver to a flank, or conduct a frontal assault. In the actions at Taku and Tientsin, however, the maneuvers were not against enemy flanks but against forts or city walls that had to be breached or scaled. The key to allied success lay simply in applying accepted tactical principles: mutually supporting fire and movement and disciplined execution under fire. The different languages, modes of operation, and political agendas of the allied forces led to considerable miscommunication and misunderstanding, as well as several friendly-fire incidents and other forms of Clausewitzian friction. However, the level of experience of most of the commanders involved, especially in the case of General Chaffee and US Army colonel Aaron S. Daggett (Fourteenth Regiment) for the Americans, plus the initiative and bravery of individual troops, provided sufficient "lubricant" to enable the expedition to overcome Chinese resistance.

As an example of extending the reach of policy, each member nation of the relief expedition sent its military forces with an eye not only to rescuing its beleaguered diplomats and civilians, but also for the purposes of increasing its influence over the Chinese government. The size of each military contingent was an important factor in determining which nation's views would hold the most sway in the various committees established after the fighting to manage the national zones. In the period of stability operations that followed, the Americans were able to draw upon their by-now considerable experiences from the Civil War, the Plains Indian Wars, and the Philippine Insurrection. They set up military courts to administer justice until Chinese judicial and police systems could be reestablished, rebuilt schools and hospitals, and restored basic civil functions.[67] The conduct of authorities in the French, German, and Russian zones especially was brutal and counterproductive by comparison.

Conclusion

As this chapter has shown, the hard hand of war was not the only one Americans employed when waging war in the late nineteenth century. The rhetoric that ran high in the later stages of the Civil War and in the long campaigns against the Plains Indians obscured the basic system of threats and promises at work in both cases. That system also carried over into the Philippine campaigns and the Peking relief expedition, whereas the US occupation of the Caribbean islands of Cuba and Puerto Rico was more political from the start. The art of the general, in other words, had at times to become the art of the diplomat or peace broker. Defeating hostile factions was seldom enough to secure the aims of policy. Military commanders needed not only increased cultural awareness to secure those aims, but also a functional knowledge of human nature, problematic as the term might be.

As before, US military forces from the Civil War to the very beginning of the twentieth century used a blend of Jominian- and Clausewitzian-style strategies to defeat their foes. Key terrain in the form of cities, harbors, rivers, railways, and production centers was identified in prewar planning and either seized or destroyed. At times, this terrain-oriented strategy facilitated the subsequent destruction of hostile forces by making them accept battle under unfavorable conditions. At other times, the hostile forces were destroyed while trying to defend key terrain. By the Spanish–American War, the US Navy, the beneficiary of a modernization program and improvements in prewar planning, was able to achieve battles of annihilation at sea, albeit against a less powerful and less committed foe.

By comparison, US land forces consistently demonstrated their proficiency with minor tactics and company- or battalion-size expeditions. However, they were routinely unprepared to conduct operations requiring regiments or larger formations to act in concert. It was not just the perennially small size of the US Army or US Marine Corps that contributed to this difficulty, but their numbers in relation to the vastness of the areas they were required to control. The practice of augmenting US regular forces with irregulars remained in vogue throughout the nineteenth century but brought with it additional problems of organizational and institutional friction due to the propensity for interests to diverge. Such divergences occurred, for instance, when the US Army worked with local "deputies," volunteers, and Native American scouts in the Plains Indian Wars, as well as with Filipino guerrillas and other auxiliaries in the Pacific. The practice added a layer of complexity to each operation and increased its military as well as its political challenges.

Notes

1. Cf. Neely, "Was the Civil War a Total War?"; Hagerman, "Union Generalship"; and McPherson, "From Limited War."

2. Sherman is reported to have destroyed three hundred miles of railroad, numerous bridges, and telegraph lines; seized five thousand horses, four thousand mules, and thirteen thousand head of cattle; and confiscated 9.5 million

pounds of corn and 10.5 million pounds of fodder. Jones and Hattaway, *How the North Won.*

3. Murray, "American Civil War," describes the most important events.

4. This percentage amounted to a ratio of one soldier for every 129 square miles west of the Mississippi River. See Robertson, "First Bull Run," 81.

5. Maslowski, "To the Edge." Also helpful are Stoker, *Grand Design*; Brooks, *How America Fought*; and Hattaway and Jones, *How the North Won.*

6. See Helfers, "Five Generals."

7. Rodgers, "Saving the Republic," and McPherson, *Battle Cry of Freedom*, 232.

8. For more detail, see Stoker, *Grand Design*, 23–25, and Maslowski, "To the Edge."

9. Murray, "American Civil War."

10. Luvaas, *Military Legacy*, 228.

11. *American Military History*, 201.

12. McPherson, *War on the Waters*, and Symonds, *Civil War at Sea.*

13. *American Military History*, 215.

14. Weigley, *Great Civil War*, 382.

15. Murfin, *Gleam of Bayonets.*

16. Weigley, *Great Civil War*, 253–54.

17. Sutherland, "Union's Counterguerrilla War," 169.

18. Glatthaar, "Termination of the Civil War."

19. Sutherland, "Union's Guerrilla War," 169, and Feis, "Jefferson Davis."

20. Newell and Shrader, "US Army's Transition," esp. 875.

21. For the logistics-based argument, see Jones, *Elements of Military Strategy*, 25–32.

22. *American Military History*, 318. Weigley, *History of the United States Army*, 267, puts the number at 943 engagements between 1865 and 1898. The US Army's authorized strength was 27,442 officers and men in 1876, but it rarely had more than 25,000 officers and men on the rolls until the Spanish–American War. These forces were assigned to some 255 forts, usually manned by units no larger than a company.

23. McGinnis, *Counting Coup.*

24. More than a third of this number fell in the Fetterman and Custer massacres. Bellesiles, "Western Violence," 166.

25. Ibid., 165.

26. Utley, "Total War," 399–414.

27. Birtle, *U.S. Army Counterinsurgency.*

28. The classic treatment of how this appreciation evolved within the US Army is Huston, *Sinews of War.*

29. Utley, "Total War," 399ff, rejects the genocide argument. Both ethnic cleansing and genocide are brutal and reprehensible, but despite the rhetoric of Sherman and others, US policy was closer to ethnic cleansing, driving a society from its land, rather than genocide, attempting to eliminate a people.

30. Jomini, *Art of War*, 115.

31. Halleck, *Elements*, 53.

32. Yenne, *Indian Wars*, 189–206, provides a detailed account of the battle. See also Jones, *Elements of Military Strategy*, 27–29.

33. Hutton, *Phil Sheridan*, 248–49. See also Trudeau, "Battle for the West. "

34. Donovan, *Terrible Glory*, 212.

35. Hämäläinen, *Comanche Empire*, 339–40.

36. McGinnis, "When Courage," esp. 457.

37. Weigley, *American Way of War*, 183–91.

38. Crowl, "Alfred Thayer Mahan."

39. Although published in 1911, Corbett's theories were being taught to British naval officers well before then. See Lambert, "Naval War Course," and Corbett, *Some Principles*.

40. Nofi, *Spanish–American War*, 57–58.

41. Trask, *War with Spain*, 68–70.

42. O'Toole, *Spanish War*, 35–36.

43. For more on the tensions, see Offner, *Unwanted War*.

44. Nofi, *Spanish–American War*, 100.

45. Tucker, *Encyclopedia*, 214–15. For comparison, $50 million in 1898 was equivalent to $40 billion in 2012. Rockoff, *America's Economic Way*, 57.

46. Ross, *American War Plans*, 6–16, and Trask, *War with Spain*, 73–75.

47. Hayes, "War Plans," provides an excellent summary of how logistical and technological factors influenced planning.

48. Linn, *Philippine War*, 3.

49. Freidel, *Splendid Little War*, 26. Several newer battleships and cruisers were positioned in a defensive posture closer to Spain.

50. Nofi, *Spanish–American War*, 185.

51. Merritt's corps had thirteen thousand volunteers and two thousand regular troops. *American Military History*, 336.

52. O'Toole, *Spanish War*, 168–71.

53. Theodore Roosevelt's report to the secretary of war, dated September 10, 1898, details some of the inefficiencies and has become a classic. See Roosevelt, *Rough Riders*, appendix B. V Corps consisted of eighteen regular and two volunteer infantry regiments, ten regular and two volunteer dismounted cavalry squadrons, one mounted cavalry squadron, six artillery batteries, and one Gatling gun company. *American Military History*, 328.

54. Cosmas, "San Juan Hill," 115.

55. Freidel, *Splendid Little War*, 106.

56. The numbers vary. O'Toole, *Spanish War*, 322, puts the total casualties for the actions on July 1 at 205 killed and 1,180 wounded for the Americans and 215 killed and 376 wounded for the Spaniards.

57. Nofi, *Spanish–American War*, 211–13.

58. Linn, *Philippine War*, 15.

59. Birtle, *U.S. Army Counterinsurgency*, 108.

60. Linn, *Philippine War*, 42.

61. Col. William Birkhimer, quoted in Birtle, *U.S. Army Counterinsurgency*, 113–14.

62. Cosmas, "Daring Raid," provides a lively account of the capture.

63. Linn, *Philippine War*.

64. For a summary, see Herbert, *Small Wars*.

65. Fleming, *Siege of Peking*.

66. Leonhard, *China Relief Expedition*, 37–38.

67. Birtle, *U.S. Army Counterinsurgency*, 148–50.

6

The Caribbean Wars
to the Korean War

War is an art and as such not susceptible of explanation by fixed
formula.
George S. Patton Jr., "Success in War," 1931

Plans are worthless, but planning is everything.
*Dwight D. Eisenhower, "Remarks to the National
Defense Executive Reserve Conference," 1957*

BY THE MIDDLE OF THE TWENTIETH CENTURY, American military practice
drew from at least two articles of faith. The first was captured in George S.
Patton Jr.'s statement that war is an art and not reducible to a formula. The
second was reflected in President Dwight D. Eisenhower's pointed remark
about the relative value of plans and planning.[1] Both statements were contradictory. War has always been more than an art, and Patton, despite his
claims, repeatedly reduced it to a simple formula or secret of success—in
this case, the warrior's determination to "conquer or perish."[2] As America's
interventions in the Caribbean and Mexico showed, Patton's formula still
worked under the right conditions. Bold action by small but determined
forces could carry the day. In fact, more Medals of Honor were awarded, per
capita, for such actions in the Philippines, China, and Mexico than in either
world war.[3] In Eisenhower's eyes, war planning was a continuous process, an
operational science, and he considered it more valuable than the product, the
war plan, which rarely survived contact with the enemy. However, by 1957,
war plans and campaign plans had grown important in a sense altogether
obscured by Eisenhower's well-traveled comment.[4] For better or worse, the
war plan—not strategy—did the real bridging between policy aims and the
use of force to achieve those aims.[5] The purpose of the war plan was to identify the "devil in the details," to analyze the situation, and to establish specific
military objectives, as well as tasks and subtasks pursuant to accomplishing
the lofty aims of policy.

By way of illustration, a major campaign plan such as Operation Overlord linked the mission, derived from the governing strategy of the war, to the forces available to accomplish it, their logistical requirements, and the timing and sequencing of supporting and follow-on operations. In a word, the war plan became the practical face of strategy. Without it, no strategy could be put into effect. The rub was not whether a given plan might be flawed or outdated—it invariably would be in some way. Rather, it was to arrive at a consensus on actual policy aims so the branches and sequels of the plan could be worked. It was partly for this reason that Gen. Colin Powell and Defense Secretary Caspar Weinberger later articulated the Powell-Weinberger doctrine, which made "clear" policy goals a prerequisite for undertaking military action.[6] Without such guidance, military planners were apt to set about pursuing military victory directly. Contrary to conventional wisdom, military strategy did not disappear in the twentieth century. Instead it became embedded in the "concept of maneuver"—the heart of the war plan.

The Caribbean Wars

The Boxer Rebellion had only recently concluded and the campaigns in the Philippines were still under way when the United States sent military forces into Panama (1903), Cuba (1906–9), and Nicaragua (1909–12). These were followed later by a similar pattern of interventions in Haiti (1915–34) and the Dominican Republic (1916–24).[7] From an operational standpoint, these interventions fell into two broad categories: a swift, Patton-like show of force intended to preempt a counterrevolution (as in Panama) or to stabilize a political crisis (as in Cuba) or counterguerrilla missions designed to put down rebels or bandits who had already gained control of certain areas (as in Nicaragua, Haiti, and the Dominican Republic). In each type of intervention, only small numbers of trained US troops were used, though these were often supported by significant offshore firepower or supplemented with sundry indigenous paramilitary or police units. The traditional maxim of using a 3:1 force ratio for offensive operations was almost never used. The US Marine Corps battalion that made initial contact with Colombian forces at the outset of the Panamanian Revolution, for instance, faced odds of 1:1 at best. However, this amount of force, backed up by the guns of the USS *Nashville*, proved sufficient under the circumstances, as Colombian forces were neither well trained nor well led. The US intervention in Panama was successful. A marine expeditionary force of fourteen hundred troops was established in January 1904 "to protect" the new Panamanian government and to oversee construction of the canal, completed in 1914. The need to protect the canal was to shape US policy in the region for several more decades.

The US intervention in Cuba took place in response to a revolt launched in early August 1906 by the Liberal Party in response to rigged election results. By late August, more than fifteen thousand rebels had joined the Liberal cause.[8] President Theodore Roosevelt sent troops to Cuba in September to protect American citizens and US economic interests: "Our business is to establish peace and order . . . start the new government, and then leave the island."[9] US forces met no resistance, as both sides desired American intervention to mediate the conflict. However, US efforts were unsuccessful, and Cuba's president, Tomás Estrada Palma, resigned, and the Cuban congress dissolved. By early October, US Army and Marine Corps forces (sixty-six hundred troops) had occupied Cuba and were carrying out stability operations: establishing outposts to protect key transportation networks, training the Cuban army and rural guard, and constructing roads and other infrastructure. US troops suffered no combat casualties, but about 10 percent succumbed to tropical diseases such as malaria. American forces withdrew in 1909, having restored the government but returned again in 1912 and later during the so-called Sugar Wars (1914–22).[10]

The US intervention in Nicaragua began in December 1909, as President William H. Taft ordered the navy to increase its offshore presence (to two gunboats and four cruisers) after two Americans were captured and executed for allegedly participating in a coup against Nicaraguan president José Zelaya. Not only had US security interests increased due to the need to protect the Panama Canal, they also grew because the persistent political and economic instability of many of the Latin American republics threatened foreign investments and businesses. Taft's policy of trading "dollars for bullets"—a form of dollar diplomacy—was an attempt to influence Latin American political affairs by using US economic power rather than military force. However, it is largely seen now as having contributed to political dependence and instability within Latin American countries. US political pressure led to Zelaya's resignation, but conservative factions tried, unsuccessfully, to overthrow Zelaya's successor, Adolfo Díaz.

Civil war erupted again in August 1912, and US marines and sailors were sent to evacuate American citizens from the cities of Managua and Granada and to secure the railroad line between Managua and Corinto. The Managua phase of the operation was successful, but the force sent to relieve Granada ran into a sizeable number of rebels. Again, direct action by US infantry supported by artillery proved sufficient to drive the poorly armed and poorly led rebels from their positions.[11] As a result, Granada was relieved on September 22. Other engagements took place in the ensuing weeks, but all followed the same basic pattern: a strong show of force, sometimes accompanied by a ruse; a movement to contact; and a coordinated assault liberally supported by firepower. On October 4, a task force of US marines and sailors (450 men) defeated a rebel force of 800 near Masaya and broke the back of the rebellion.[12] In November 1912, US forces began withdrawing. However, a detachment of 105 marines remained to assist federal troops in maintaining stability for Nicaragua's population of 460,000.[13]

The US intervention in Haiti began in August 1915 after a bloody coup—one of seven between 1908 and 1915—toppled the regime of President Vilbrun Sam. The situation was chaotic with US citizens threatened by local chieftains controlling groups of armed *cacos* (peasants turned bandits and mercenaries). The purpose of the intervention, as President Woodrow Wilson declared, was "to assist, in a friendly way, the establishment of order and the administration of a government which will safeguard the rights of the people of Haiti as well as protect the rights of foreigners doing business in Haiti."[14] The First Cacos War, which lasted from August 1915 to September 1916, occurred as American military forces, mostly marines and sailors, intervened in Haiti to restore order and protect US citizens. *Caco* tactics generally consisted of intimidation and ambush. US troops occasionally fought outnumbered at odds of 1:10 in ambush situations. Aggressive action and liberal doses of firepower proved effective against the *cacos*, who lacked the training and discipline to withstand determined assaults by trained regulars. The marines also tried a "cash-for-guns" program and granting amnesty to rebels who agreed not to take up arms again, but these measures were only temporarily successful. Strategies of decapitation proved moderately effective, as the deaths of *caco* leaders Charlemagne Péralte (October 1919) and Benoît Batraville (May 1920) illustrate. No rebel leaders of similar ability were able to replace them; hence, their groups disintegrated, hastening the conclusion of the Second Cacos War (1918–20). Large-scale search-and-destroy operations were not effective in achieving decapitation, as the hostile bands had time to melt away. Instead, smaller reconnaissance parties proved better at locating and destroying rebel bases and tracking down and capturing hostile leaders. US troops eventually withdrew in 1934, after transferring security responsibilities to the Haitian gendarmerie, which they had trained.[15]

The goal of the American intervention in the Dominican Republic was, as President Wilson declared, "to guide San Domingo out of its difficulties" by restoring order and protecting US economic interests.[16] Protecting US economic interests essentially meant safeguarding Santo Domingo's custom-houses—customs fees being the country's principal source of revenue. The United States was using this revenue to pay down the Dominican Republic's substantial debt. However, the customhouses were favorite targets of revolutionary chiefs, who used the revenue to pay for their armies as well as line their own pockets. In April 1916, Gen. Desiderio Arias attempted just such a revolution against President Juan Jiménez. By early May, Arias had managed to seize most of the city. President Wilson responded by sending three hundred American troops to protect the US legation in the capital. They arrived on May 5. A second wave of US military personnel landed ten days later and began more extensive operations. In June, US forces conducted landings at Monte Cristi and Porta Plata, and then marched on the city of Santiago from the north and northwest.[17] Arias's forces were defeated at Las Trincheras Ridge (June 27), Guayacanes (July 3), and the Fortaleza at San Francisco de Macorís (November 29). American military strategy was largely terrain-oriented, the aim being to seize the capital and port cities, especially the customhouses in each. Defeating Arias thus remained secondary to protecting US economic interests. Wilson imposed a military government on the Dominican Republic in late November, and US forces subsequently shifted to occupation duty. The last US troops withdrew in 1924, after having established a government capable of maintaining order and stability.

Throughout these interventions, the US military had the capability to put troops ashore nearly anywhere in the Caribbean within about two weeks' time. However, US forces maintained a small footprint in most cases, for both domestic and international reasons. This low profile usually meant soldiers, sailors, and marines had to resort not only to firepower, but also to unorthodox measures ("be innovative and adaptive" in today's terms) to overcome rebel groups and hostile militias and to restore order. Some of these measures included using bribes or commandeering vehicles, private equipment, or other property. While US troops managed to defeat larger bands of outlaws and mercenaries by acting aggressively, American personnel still had to remain in country for lengthy periods in order to maintain stability and to train indigenous security forces. The occupation of Haiti tied down a number of marines for nineteen years. The occupation of the Dominican Republic lasted eight years, and those of Cuba and Nicaragua four years each. Despite how swift and impressive the initial successes were in each case, US interests could only be protected or advanced through prolonged periods of military occupation. However, that bit of operational science took some time to work its way into American operational practice.

The Mexican Interventions

In mid-April 1914, President Wilson ordered US troops to occupy Veracruz, Mexico's largest port and the gateway to Mexico City. He did so for several reasons, the most immediate of which was to redress an affront caused by Mexican forces under President Victoriano Huerta during the Tampico affair two weeks earlier.[18] On April 21, 1914, a detachment of nearly eight hundred marines and sailors went ashore at Veracruz, seized its customhouse, and began occupying the city. Mexican regulars withdrew as US troops disembarked, but cadets from the military academy in Veracruz resisted, along with a portion of the civilian population. Both sides suffered heavy losses in several days of street fighting. American casualties were 19 killed and 72 wounded, while Mexican losses were as high as 120 killed and 200 wounded.[19] On April 30, 1914, Brig. Gen. Frederick Funston arrived with a brigade of infantry and assumed control of the city. Huerta resigned as president in mid-July and left the country. The American brigade departed Veracruz on November 23 and turned the city over to a new Mexican government under President Venustiano Carranza.

Five months later, Wilson ordered Brig. Gen. John J. Pershing to launch a punitive expedition in pursuit of Pancho Villa in retaliation for his cross-border raid at Columbus, New Mexico, which resulted in the deaths of 18 Americans.[20] Pershing's force, which at its height numbered twelve thousand troops, was organized into two cavalry brigades, each with three regiments (two cavalry, one artillery), and one infantry brigade, with two infantry regiments, support troops, Indian scouts, eight airplanes, and motorized vehicles. It was a well-balanced task force by any standard. The expedition was, however, hampered by two major problems. The first was that its mission was too ambitious—to capture or kill Villa and disperse his band. As stated, it meant that Villa could draw the Americans into Mexico as deeply as he wished, thus prolonging the campaign and increasing its costs. Without Villa's capture and the decimation of his band, the mission would be a failure. Hence, Pershing's task was subsequently revised to "pursuit and dispersion of the band or bands that attacked Columbus."[21] The military strategy had thus gone from decapitation, as required by the mission, to a form of search and disrupt. The mission was still open-ended, but it allowed the task force commander to exercise his judgment in determining when the objective had been accomplished.

The second problem was that the expedition had to operate in an area of approximately sixteen hundred square miles, and its logistical support had to cross some four hundred miles of rough terrain with few serviceable roads. The Mexican landscape had not changed much since the war of 1846–48 except that some of the towns and cities were larger, and several of them were now connected by railroads. The United States and Mexico had signed an agreement permitting reciprocal actions, which allowed the Americans to cross the border in pursuit of bandits or outlaws. However, the Mexicans did not consider it applicable to Villa's raid. Consequently, the Mexican government and populace viewed the expedition with hostility and offered it no real assistance or logistical support, including use of the country's railroads. Despite the odds against success, Pershing managed to capture or kill some of Villa's men, engaging some at Guerrero, Ojos Azules, San Geronimo, and Namiquipa, and others in various smaller skirmishes. However, American soldiers and Mexican *federales* clashed at Parral on April 12, 1916, with casualties on both sides, and again at Carrizal on June 1916, with much heavier losses to each party.[22] Pershing's operations were severely restricted thereafter with even scouting being prohibited. The expedition finally withdrew in February 1917 without having captured Villa, though Patton had managed to shoot one of Villa's lieutenants. The recent war against Spain ought to have underscored the importance of logistics for such far-ranging operations. However, Pershing's after-action report noted that requirements for communication and resupply had not been properly anticipated.[23]

The First World War

When Congress declared war on Germany and Austria-Hungary two months later in April 1917, the army had roughly 108,000 officers and men. The navy had a similar number to crew three hundred ships, about 10 percent of which were battleships, and the marine corps had about eleven thousand personnel under arms.[24] By August 1918, the American Expeditionary Force (AEF) listed 2 million soldiers in its ranks and had deployed over a distance of three thousand miles. It had also fought successful actions at Cantigny in May, Château-Thierry and Belleau Wood in June, and participated in the Saint-Mihiel and Meuse–Argonne offensives in September 1918.[25] The Saint-Mihiel offensive involved nine US and five French divisions supported by 3,000 guns, 270 tanks, and 1,500 aircraft, while the Meuse–Argonne offensive employed fifty-two American divisions, ten of which were assigned to French and British armies, and was supported by 2,700 guns, 200 tanks, and 1,000 planes.[26] By the armistice, the AEF had advanced approximately 34 miles, occupied 580 square miles of territory, and had suffered about 320,000 casualties (16 percent), of which over 50,000 were killed in action.[27]

While these operations were successful, the AEF proved to be deficient in the areas of higher-level coordination of fire and movement; timely issuance of orders, communication, and coordination with adjacent units and higher headquarters; and logistics—in short, operational science.[28] The AEF's lack of experience was clearly a factor in its performance, particularly at higher levels: Its headquarters had only three months' practice maneuvering formations larger than a division by the time the armistice took effect on November 11, 1918. Consequently, its adaptations were still very much a work in progress. Although American officers lacked higher-level command experience, they were not unfamiliar with the principal ideas underpinning industrial-age warfare: use of direct and indirect firepower to facilitate forward movement and concentration of all available firepower at the decisive point to weaken the enemy before the final assault. However, just like European armies, the AEF had to adapt its prewar tactics to the actual conditions of trench warfare in 1917, which demanded greater materiel preparation and much tighter coordination between infantry and artillery formations. By most historical accounts, the adaptations went rapidly, if unevenly, with front-line units—perhaps not surprisingly—making the adjustments faster than higher-command echelons.[29]

Russian and Siberian Expeditions, 1917–20

The Great War was not yet over before President Wilson committed American forces again, albeit reluctantly, to participate in the multinational Russian and Siberian expeditions. The political objectives for these interventions were vague at best. Wilson evidently felt obliged to "fall in" with the wishes of America's French and British allies, even though the prospects for accomplishing anything militarily were as remote as St. Petersburg and Vladivostok.[30] Each of these was the equivalent of a Clausewitzian war of half-measures, an enterprise in which one or more parties participates not so much for the sake of the ultimate outcome as to honor alliance or treaty obligations.[31] In that sense, both expeditions were successful—but only to a point. The American forces, after all, were not given the latitude to operate as the allied commanders desired. The Yanks were present but not committed to their allies' goals, which in any case were likely too ambitious.

The first, or North Russia, expedition began in September 1918 with the arrival of fifty-five hundred US troops, under the command of Col. George Stewart, in the city of Archangel to support British and other allied forces that had conducted a forced entry into the area one month earlier. The mission was to defend Archangel and the military supplies stored there and to open and maintain lines of communication with the Czech Legion (fifty thousand troops), which was holding positions along the Trans-Siberian Railroad. However, the British commander launched an aggressive reconnaissance in force, advancing some four hundred miles toward Moscow in an effort that would have been bold—had he been the vanguard of a larger force. He was not. Two battalions of Stewart's contingent took part in the advance but were initially deployed piecemeal in support of the British-led offensive. The Red Army counterattacked in November 1918 and drove the expedition back. American troops fought notable defensive actions along the Dvina River, particularly at the village of Tulgas.[32]

The second, or Siberian, expedition also began in September 1918, with ten thousand US troops arriving in Vladivostok under the command of Maj. Gen. William Graves. These soldiers were part of a larger multinational force with a large Japanese contingent. The mission of this expedition was also to defend military supplies and to secure a line of communication with the Czech Legion. Graves's troops did not participate in any major offensive operations, but they conducted successful stability, support, and counter-guerrilla operations in the vicinity of Vladivostok. The expedition eventually withdrew, with the last American troops departing in June 1920 as the White Army began to collapse.

The interwar period also saw additional US interventions in Panama (1918–20), Nicaragua (1926–33), Germany (1918–23), and China (1912–38).[33] These were largely protection missions, intended to provide security for US citizens and property, to enforce treaty terms, or to stabilize tense situations. Usually the mere presence of force and the attendant threat of its use sufficed to accomplish these missions and preserve peace. The notable exception to this rule was Nicaragua. A coup led by a Conservative Party faction under Emiliano Chamorro Vargas seized power in 1925. The United States refused to recognize him, however, and violence escalated as the Liberal Party attempted to take back the government. In the summer of 1926, American troops were sent to the city of Bluefields to protect US citizens and economic interests. Chamorro eventually resigned, and a Nicaraguan congress selected Adolfo Díaz to serve as president until new elections in 1928. Liberal forces agreed to disarm, except for Augusto C. Sandino, who withdrew into the mountains with a small band of fighters. Sandino's forces increased over time, and on July 16, 1927, he launched an attack against marines and Nicaraguan national guardsmen in Ocotal but was driven back with heavy casualties by accurate small-arms fire and the timely arrival of five US fighter-bombers.[34] Thereafter, Sandino withdrew into the jungles and mountains and resorted to hit-and-run tactics. His small guerrilla bands, the Sandinistas, remained elusive, but

US forces, which at their peak numbered nearly five thousand troops, were able to secure the major cities and towns in the western part of Nicaragua and supervise the elections of 1928, 1930, and 1932. The last marines and sailors were withdrawn in January 1933 as the Great Depression and a reassessment of the costs of the intervention led to a consolidation of US interests. The second intervention in Nicaragua had lasted six years, involved some 150 combat actions, and cost 136 American lives.[35]

While the US military was performing its protection missions and demobilizing from the Great War, significant self-analysis went into extracting lessons from the experiences of the AEF.[36] Many of these were debated in the pages of professional journals, and some were incorporated into the military education programs at US staff and war colleges. American operational doctrine was revised and updated in the interwar years. Schools of thought developed around similarities in battlefield experiences, and each offered distinct (and often competing) recommendations for doctrinal change. The *Field Service Regulations* (1923), for instance, emphasized the decisive nature of offensive operations, while the *Manual for Commanders of Large Units* (1930) stressed the power of the defensive and infantry-artillery cooperation.[37] In the meantime, the US Army's manual *General Tactical Functions of Larger Units* (1926) identified five main components or phases of operations, which further refined operational science: "mobilization, concentration, advance, occupation of positions, and combat." It also reaffirmed the primacy of tactics: "Where tactical and strategic considerations conflict, tactical considerations must govern. The gaining of decision in combat is of primary importance."[38] Clausewitzian concepts such as center of gravity and culmination point, which were drawn from the mechanical sciences, appeared more frequently in US military theory and doctrine.[39] The center of gravity was defined as the enemy's main fighting force, while the culminating point was defined as the condition caused by the "inevitable process of weakening" that takes place during a campaign and after which the chances of success declined for the attacker.[40] These concepts joined many time-honored Jominian theories, such as lines of operation and decisive points. Operational science thus reflected a more balanced mix of Jominian and Clausewitzian theories.

Despite some evidence of reform, American operational science remained imperfect. The scientific method produces a way forward through the process of elimination, but it does not necessarily eliminate subjective interpretations. One could argue, for instance, that Mahan's theories of sea power were a rationale for a blue-water navy in search of historical evidence, rather than the rationale itself emerging from the evidence. That resulted in a somewhat narrow body of sea-power theory centered on winning decisive naval battles. Julian Corbett's reaction to Mahan's theories demonstrates that operational science, like science in general, can be self-correcting. The ability to project power ashore was the key that Mahan, in his efforts to establish a rationale for a blue-water navy, overlooked. In fact, the US Navy found that the doctrines of Mahan were not entirely sufficient for the operational tasks it had to perform during the First World War. It had been built and trained for the mission of defeating another navy, and that was its operational purpose, but it found itself hunting German U-boats instead. This required mental reorientation on the part of US naval officers, as well as the construction of many more destroyers. When the navy entered the war, it had 70 destroyers, only 44 of which were modern. By war's end, it had 248 destroyers, 60 large subchasers, and 116 small ones built or being built.[41] Within eighteen months, the navy had essentially changed the entire balance of its force structure from one designed to defeat a surface enemy to one capable of neutralizing a subsurface threat.

Scientific analysis likely impaired the appreciation of air power, however. That was due in part to the fact that air-power theorists often made bold, unverifiable claims. While the US Army's George C. Marshall and the US Navy's William A. Moffett were receptive to exploring the capabilities of air power, enthusiasts such as US Army aviator Billy Mitchell tended to make assertions regarding the revolutionary potential of the air arm that were, of course, unverifiable because the historical evidence for them did not yet exist.[42] Enthusiasts also tended to dismiss potential problems. US military observers who witnessed the Battle of Britain in 1940, for instance, claimed that while British and German bombers clearly proved susceptible to fighters, American bombers were much better armed, would be flying at a higher altitude, and thus would not be as vulnerable.[43] The rhetoric that went into obtaining respect and recognition for the air arm, in other words, created expectations that would prove impossible to meet. Sober analysis of the uses of air power in the First World War revealed three key lessons: Air superiority had to be established before other air operations could take place, long-range bombing held promise but was not particularly accurate, and aircraft had vital reconnaissance and close-air-support (attack) roles to play in surface operations.[44] Each of these evolved into major roles and missions—pursuit, bombardment, and attack—which, in turn, led to the development of different aircraft designs. By the attack on Pearl Harbor, American operational practice in the air had settled on a number of nested, yet vulnerable, assumptions: A nation's vital areas could be identified and hit from high altitude; once hit, they could be destroyed, and if destroyed, the result would be the collapse of the enemy's will to resist; and fighters need not escort long-range, high-altitude bombers.[45]

The problem of selective scientific analysis returned for the US Navy. Despite its experience with submarine chasing in the Great War, the navy reaffirmed the validity of Mahan's basic concept that the primary objective of operations at sea was the "destruction of the enemy's main force."[46] The operational value of the submarine was not lost on the Americans. However, ethical, legal, and technical issues slowed its integration. The submarine was considered by many to be unethical for a variety of reasons, not least of which was that submarines were too small to take on crews and passengers of the vessels they torpedoed, nor were their own crews large enough to take control of vessels willing to surrender as an alternative to being sunk. Waging war directly on commerce—the deliberate sinking of merchant vessels—was not lawful. Technological issues with range, depth, speed, and torpedo development also had to be resolved, but fiscal restraints essentially slowed technological progress. These issues notwithstanding, American political and military leaders did not want to give up the submarine, particularly as long as the Japanese continued to add them to their own inventory. Still, the constraints were such that US operational planners considered submarines suitable for two missions only: coastal protection and fleet operations (attacks against warships). Submarines were to attack only heavy warships, such as battleships and aircraft carriers.[47]

Rhetorically, the battleship remained the US Navy's capital ship going into the war.[48] However, operational planners realized the navy would have to take its air support with it or forfeit its freedom of maneuver. Preconflict war games revealed key differences in the dynamics of engagements between battleships and aircraft carriers. In the former, fire occurred in streams that could be adjusted as the battle progressed; in the latter, firepower was delivered in pulses, as aircraft needed time to return to ship, rearm, refuel, and relaunch. This difference was key information for operational planners, who had to ensure enough carriers were present in any major operation so that a canopy of air protection was always present. The games also showed, beyond question, that an opponent's aircraft carriers must always be the first target in any strike and must be rendered combat ineffective as soon as possible in order to establish air superiority.[49] Newer battleships were now several orders of magnitude faster and more powerful than their predecessors in the Great War. However, in operational planning and execution, aircraft carriers had become the actual gauge of a fleet's power.

American operational practice at sea also further explored the dimension of amphibious operations. As mentioned, American experience with amphibious operations began well before the Great War. The unopposed landing of US troops at Veracruz in 1847 was touted as the first such operation in American military history.[50] Yet, as earlier chapters have shown, amphibious operations also occurred in the War of 1812. Landings at Santiago, Cuba, and Manila also served as key examples in the *Tentative Manual for Landing Operations* (1934–35), which outlined the essential, if still rough, principles for amphibious operations.[51] Unfortunately, the United States, like most countries, had little in the way of fiscal resources to dedicate to the development of amphibious concepts and technologies in the interwar years.

The US military's "small wars" doctrine—its collective corpus of accepted practices—also took a step forward during this period. The marine corps's *Small Wars Manual*, first published in 1935 and revised in 1940, is the best-known example. However, the army's Training Regulation 15-70, *Field Service Regulations: Special Operations* (1922), formally addressed the issue of "minor warfare," which was defined not according to the scale of the conflict, but rather as combat between regular and irregular forces.[52] In addition, instructors at the Infantry School and elsewhere incorporated some of the principles learned from past US interventions, as well as those published by the British, especially Charles Callwell, and others. Although this instruction clearly underscored the value of "carrots" in combating irregular forces, it also noted that the preferred method was to preempt the problem altogether by sending in enough force to defeat an opponent completely—materially and psychologically—before an insurrection could take root.

The Second World War

Contrary to the received wisdom, it is not clear that American operational practice in the Second World War changed as a result of its growing materiel preponderance, especially since that predominance was not evident in the initial years of the war. Certainly the disparity between Allied (particularly American) and Axis production figures and population bases meant that the latter could not afford to suffer losses at a rate higher than that of the Allies. However, it was not until 1943 that American production figures surpassed those of the Axis by an appreciable margin: forty-seven thousand American planes to twenty-seven thousand Axis aircraft, twenty-four thousand American tanks to eleven thousand Axis, six American heavy guns for every one produced by the Axis. By war's end, the United States was launching sixteen warships for every one built by Japan.[53]

Nonetheless, the operational doctrine the US military had going into the war was essentially the same as when the war ended, save for minor adaptations. In 1936, for instance, American operational theory reaffirmed that the first law of strategy was still what it had been for nearly a century: "Be stronger at the decisive point."[54] American operational doctrine, moreover, mimicked many of the theories and concepts found in European doctrines and was influenced by British, French, and German prewar debates over the use of mechanized formations, particularly with respect to the use of "wide envelopment" and "penetration and encirclement" of enemy forces. Even in the Pacific theater, operational practice rested on a few key principles, such as concentrating combat power to capture key operational infrastructure (airfields and road and rail junctions) and to neutralize critical fighting formations. In short, the same modern maneuver principles in vogue in Europe were applied in a theater characterized by vast expanses of water and scattered islands of volcanic rock, instead of contiguous land borders and extensive road and rail networks.

Admittedly, the sheer volume of materiel production made it possible for American operational practice to learn through the scientific process of trial and error, a luxury few nations could afford. That helped offset the fact that prewar planning exercises and maneuvers in the United States had not prepared enough American commanders and staffs to handle division, corps, and army formations.[55] The battle at Kasserine Pass in February 1943 illustrates the point. Elements of II Corps were driven back fifty miles by a portion of Rommel's Panzer Army Africa with losses of two hundred tanks, three thousand men killed and wounded, and thirty-seven hundred prisoners.[56] After-action analyses concluded that the US Army's "basic principles" were sound but that better all-arms coordination and cooperation was needed in execution.[57] For instance, the practice of pooling tank, tank destroyer, and antiaircraft battalions at division level hindered "coordinated team play" (cohesion and efficiency) and operational responsiveness.[58] On-call artillery was also too slow, and communication problems existed between ground forces and aircraft, which resulted in air-ground operations being disjointed and the loss of air superiority over the battle area.

Some of the fixes were put in place immediately—others were facilitated by improving the leadership of II Corps with an aggressive commander, Patton, and by gaining more experience with operational-level actions. The application of operational science, though never perfect, became more evident by the beginning of the Sicily Campaign in July 1943, five months later. By the end of the six-week campaign, commanders and staffs of the Seventh Army had gained additional operational experience, which further improved their operational science, particularly with regard to amphibious operations and air-ground coordination, though the latter was still deficient. By the Italy

Campaign, operational-level maneuver had crystallized into a discernible pattern: Air cover facilitated the forward movement of ground forces, which resulted in the capture of airfields, which in turn enabled air cover to be extended, which again facilitated the forward movement of ground forces, and so on. Amphibious "hooks," as at Salerno and Anzio, were also attempted with heavy naval gunfire and air strikes in support, to outflank German defensive lines. These attempts were not as fruitful as hoped due to difficult terrain and Allied command failures.[59] Nonetheless, it was clear that the coordination of fire and movement had evolved from a tactical to an operational function and required expert planning and orchestration at corps and army headquarters.

This coordination was even more evident by the invasion of Normandy on June 6, 1944. Some four thousand ships and landing vessels transported nearly one-hundred seventy-six thousand troops and materiel across the English Channel; six hundred Allied warships, twenty-five hundred heavy bombers, and seven thousand fighters were in support. By the conclusion of the first day, five divisions were ashore, and three airborne divisions had been dropped further inland. Within a month, the total number of troops ashore had grown to one million, with one-hundred fifty thousand vehicles.[60] Operational science was clearly fundamental to American operational practice.

That was no less true in the Pacific theater and was perhaps even more so given that the distances involved were much greater. The Allied strategy of a two-pronged advance (Gen. Douglas MacArthur from the south through the Philippines and Adm. Chester Nimitz across the Central Pacific from Hawaii) toward Japan had to cover 14,200 miles of archipelagos. The international and interservice cooperation necessary to enable a campaign of that magnitude to succeed had evolved iteratively. However, getting combat power to a theater was only half the battle; the other half was interdicting the flow of an opponent's materiel. In that regard, the US submarine force succeeded. It severely constricted the flow of Japanese shipping. Three hundred American submarines sank over 4,779,900 tons of merchant shipping and 540,192 tons of warships during the conflict, for a total of 54.6 percent of all Japanese tonnage.[61] Aerial interdiction was also enormously effective. These successes reveal just how interconnected military operations—and their attendant functions—had become. Operational success or failure in one dimension, in other words, clearly influenced the probability of success in others.

Postwar operational assessments also examined why Allied strategic bombing campaigns had failed to break the will of the Axis. Expectations before the war were that air power would be able to cripple an opponent's psychological center of gravity in record time, thus obviating the need for costly surface campaigns. The United States Strategic Bombing Survey conducted after the war provided only enough evidence to conclude that bombing major population and industrial centers may have been necessary, but it was not sufficient.[62] To be sure, the destructive power of modern bombers was unparalleled. The bombing of Hamburg in 1943 caused 90,000 casualties over four months, the bombing of Dresden in 1945 resulted in 80,000 casualties in three months, and the Tokyo raids caused 125,000 casualties in the month of May 1945.[63] Yet, rather than forcing their governments to surrender, civilian populations appear to have adapted to the changed conditions, learned to live with danger, and responded with calls for retaliation. Arguably the psychological centers of gravity of the Axis powers were strengthened rather than weakened. Also, the prewar assumption that the relationship between a public and its political leadership functioned the same in democracies as in autocracies was considered flawed.

The strategic bombing campaigns of the Allies might well have diverted considerable enemy fighter aircraft and antiaircraft resources from possible use on other fronts, thereby ceding control of the air in those sectors and facilitating the advance of Allied surface forces.[64] Yet, it is difficult to know the extent to which Axis production figures were, in fact, diminished by Allied bombing. German wartime production actually increased during the period of the bombing, due in part to the fact that Germany converted to a full wartime economy only after 1943, though it resorted to extreme measures in the process.[65] The controversy has continued to the present, with historical evidence, imperfect as it is, subjectively reinterpreted each time the question of the effectiveness of strategic bombing is raised.

The Korean War

American operational doctrine changed little between 1945 and 1950. The key operational principles were still those of maneuver warfare, with air-ground cooperation considered essential for operational success. The real difference was not in doctrine or concepts, but in the ability to put them into practice. Combat readiness was low overall, and the practice of carrying out air-ground cooperation had deteriorated.[66] Most of the equipment—save for some improved tanks and artillery pieces, and jet aircraft—was of World War II vintage but serviceable. Demobilization left the US Army with only ten understrength divisions, many of which had only two of their three authorized combat elements and were without their full complement of armor.[67]

These shortfalls created serious difficulties for US units operating in the mountains and valleys of Korea according to a doctrine that placed a premium on mobility. Gaps or exposed flanks were to be expected in maneuver warfare, but a unit's mobility and organic firepower would enable it to counterattack or seal off enemy flanking movements or penetrations. However, in the restrictive terrain of Korea, American units, lacking some of their organic maneuver and firepower assets, found themselves at a disadvantage against North Korean and Chinese envelopment and infiltration tactics designed to exploit gaps. As a result, as one astute officer noted, "infiltrating enemy units frequently occupied positions to the Americans' rear, striking command posts, support units or artillery positions."[68] It was an environment conducive to the use of small guerrilla units as well, which mounted raids throughout American rear areas, sometimes creating the impression that enemy forces were much more numerous than they actually were. In a word, this was a failure of operational science.

The doctrine of the newly created US Air Force differed little from that used by the US Army Air Corps in the Second World War. USAF leaders entered the conflict with the general scheme of first achieving air superiority, then conducting bombing campaigns against major economic and military targets so as to break the enemy's will and capacity to resist.[69] The high expectations of air power that characterized the war against the Axis were still present in 1950.

The Eighth Army's decision to fall back on Pusan in the wake of the initial North Korean invasion on June 25, 1950, was also driven by what military professionals would call the most important element in operational science—logistics. With the capacity to discharge only fourteen thousand tons per day, Pusan was the only port left to Gen. MacArthur that was capable of receiving modern military forces in sufficient quantities to influence the outcome of the war.[70] It was not a matter of intuition, but simple arithmetic: Moving forces from Japan, where four US infantry divisions were on occupation duty, to Pusan required sixteen sailing days.

As mentioned earlier, the landing at Inchon on September 15, 1950, has been touted as an example of operational art par excellence. Even President Truman referred to it as "a brilliant maneuver."[71] However, it could not have happened without the preparatory work of a considerable amount of operational science. Planning and coordination, though done in record time, had to be thorough: Due to extreme tidal conditions, the landing could only occur on September 15, October 11, or November 3, and launching it on September 15, the date actually selected, meant it would have to take place in two stages, early morning and early evening.[72] Sea walls, instead of sloping beaches, had to be overcome, and the Han River had to be crossed before the city of Seoul itself could be taken. Units had to be drawn and marshaled from locations in South Korea, Japan, the United States, and the Mediterranean.

Some 230 ships and 30 tank-landing ships (LSTs) were assembled for the operation, and air strikes had to be conducted well in advance to neutralize targets inland. While other port areas, such as Kunsan, would have presented fewer difficulties, none offered a payoff on the scale that Inchon promised: The area was only lightly defended, and North Korean communication and supply lines ran through the road and rail networks in and around Seoul. A strike there, if successful, would deal a catastrophic blow to the communist advance.

Despite the difficulties, the landing at Inchon was successfully accomplished on September 15, 1950, by X Corps, consisting of the First Marine Division and the Seventh Infantry Division, supported by the First Marine Air Wing. By September 26, X Corps had recaptured most of Seoul and cut the major north–south transportation routes. The North Korean withdrawal from the Pusan perimeter, which had begun on the 23rd, quickly became a rout. Although the Joint Chiefs of Staff had considered Operation Chromite unduly risky and historians have since called it a gamble, the experience of the officers involved in planning and executing it, many of them veterans of the Second World War, made it a calculated risk. In short, intelligence collection and staff work made the probability of success higher than the chance of failure, and the potential payoff made the enterprise worth the wager.

If the landing at Inchon was indeed brilliant, the ensuing phase of exploitation and pursuit was quite the opposite. MacArthur's plan called for X Corps to withdraw from Seoul and conduct an amphibious operation on the eastern coast of Korea, while the exhausted Eighth Army was to continue the main attack northward but without an opportunity to reorganize and refit properly.[73] MacArthur had thus violated the military principles of simplicity, objective, maneuver, and unity of command. Although US units and forces of the United Nations (UN) advanced northward toward the Manchurian border at a pace of ten miles per day, the North Korean army had not been completely destroyed because valuable time had been lost and because the logistical situation had become unnecessarily complicated.[74] The advances of the Eighth Army and X Corps were first stopped, then completely turned back by Chinese counteroffensives in October and December 1950. UN forces withdrew to a defensive line about forty miles south of Seoul, and elements of X Corps had to be extracted amphibiously from ports along the east coast. While MacArthur continued to pursue the goal of complete military victory, the extent of the Chinese intervention had actually made that impossible—unless further escalation were undertaken by the United States and its allies, a course of action President Truman and British Prime Minister Clement Atlee explicitly rejected in early December 1950.[75]

MacArthur's style of operational practice could not work as long as there was what he referred to as a "privileged sanctuary" from which the enemy could launch air strikes or marshal ground forces, as was the case with the air bases and staging areas that existed north of the Yalu River. US military commanders had not confronted the problem of an enemy sanctuary during the Second World War, and it required some adjustment for operational planners. Limited victories could still be achieved against Chinese and North Korean incursions, but carrying the war across the border into Manchuria, as MacArthur wanted, even if it did not involve resorting to nuclear weapons, would have required escalation on a scale that UN forces simply could not carry out and that the American public was not likely to support.[76] UN forces would never be strong enough or have sufficient mobility in the restrictive terrain of Korea to accomplish more than blunting and rolling back communist offensives. MacArthur's refusal to accept the political and military realities of the situation and the constraints imposed by Washington led to his removal in April 1951, and it assured that his storied legacy would add further credence to the view that military thinking is dangerously narrow and inflexible.

After the series of major offensives and counteroffensives that marked the first year of the war, the conflict settled into a pattern of attrition from the summer of 1951 to the signing of the armistice in 1953. Each side used limited ground offensives (though UN forces also launched extensive bombing campaigns) to acquire defensible terrain around the Thirty-Eighth Parallel and to settle the issue of repatriation of prisoners of war.[77] UN operations were joint throughout, with naval forces keeping the land and air forces supplied and projecting power ashore through amphibious landings, blockades, air interdiction missions from carriers, and coastal bombardments. The doctrines of Mahan were thus less applicable than those of Corbett. Air operations were initially hampered by a shortage of airfields capable of handling jet aircraft and large bombers. Most sorties, therefore, had to come from Japan until suitable airfields could be established in Korea. Despite inadequate doctrine, air–ground cooperation gradually improved for UN forces, with close air support and air interdiction proving effective against communist combat and combat support units. The USAF achieved air superiority over most of the Korean Peninsula, except for "MiG Alley," where enemy fighters could loiter at higher altitudes than US-made F-86A Sabres and in superior numbers. US pilots had to develop innovative techniques to combat the MiG-15, the superior operational ceiling, climb, and dive capabilities of which came as a surprise to the West. Nonetheless, US pilots were able to achieve ten enemy kills for every friendly aircraft lost.

Even while the Korean conflict was still under way, considerable analytical effort went into coming to terms with Maoist-style peoples' war and the North Korean and Chinese use of guerrillas, which was extensive. X Corps, for instance, reported 109 guerrilla attacks in its sector during November 1950, or an average of three and a half per day.[78] The light weapons and field rations of the North Korean and Chinese forces were ideal for guerrilla operations, and often whole battalions and regiments were dissolved into guerrilla formations as part of an offensive or when bypassed or surrounded by UN forces. The Tenth Special Forces Group, stood up at Fort Bragg in 1952, took on the mission of focusing on unconventional warfare, and the US Army produced several doctrinal publications at the height of the conflict, which it updated after the war.[79] Numerous articles and books also appeared discussing irregular warfare, the techniques of insurrection, and guerrilla tactics, and how to counter them.[80] The US military's doctrinal publications were revised and updated throughout the 1960s, particularly as the roles and responsibilities of the US Special Forces were expanded.[81] The doctrine clearly had gaps, and there was some confusion over the differences between irregular, unconventional, and guerrilla warfare. In addition, some of the methods outlined in the doctrine were heavy on offensive action, though they were far less aggressive than the techniques of Che Guevara or Ho Chi Minh.[82] Regardless, knowledge of insurgency/counterinsurgency techniques clearly existed and was being cultivated in some commands. The doctrinal foundation was thus established for the expansion of the US military through the addition of the Special Forces, which would be trained to deal with small-level actions and insurgencies, especially in Latin America and Africa, which Secretary of Defense Robert McNamara famously referred to as the "Third World's brushfire wars."[83] However, it had to compete with efforts to develop doctrine for fighting on an "atomic" battlefield, with chemical and biological agents used to enhance the destructive effects, and to test new divisional organizations, such as the Pentomic Division and the Reorganization Objectives Army Division, or ROAD.[84]

Conclusion

Contrary to Patton's wishes, the American way of war in the early twentieth century followed at least a few fixed rules. US troops combined bold, aggressive action and, when necessary, firepower against much larger bands of *cacos* and rebels. They were deployed in the Caribbean much like a quick-response force, relocating from one crisis to another in support of American interests. US forces were used because they were available, and they were available because they were used. Famous soldiers, such as the marine Smedley Butler, acquired not only proficiency in counterguerrilla actions, but a veritable dexterity. Their repeated deployments created a sixth sense for dealing with crisis situations. Unfortunately, it also led, as in Butler's case, to cynicism about war's other nature—as a "racket."[85] Butler's cynicism resulted in part from the fact that the responsiveness and effectiveness of US forces led to repeated deployments, the point of which seemed more economic than political or military in nature. Just as the Spanish conquistadors were co-opted into supporting one tribe against another in an ongoing civil war, so too US forces not only intervened on behalf of American interests, but also found themselves influenced or exploited by one side or the other. After the actions were concluded and the medals awarded, prolonged occupations remained. The legacy of the Banana Wars was that a great deal of time and effort can be required to extend the reach of US policy.

In contrast, defeating skilled and disciplined adversaries in the world wars and the Korean War required extensive planning and a proficiency at conducting maneuver—fire and movement—on an operational as well as a strategic scale. American logistical planning was not unique in having to take into account the wherewithal needed to support millions of troops over lengthy supply lines and broad frontages extending thousands of miles. The operational pattern of leapfrogging air cover and surface forces to facilitate forward movement was an example of sound operational science driven by an analysis of technological and geographic conditions. Indeed, by mid-century operational science had nearly displaced operational art, and this was just as true for the American way of war as it was for those of its allies and adversaries.

When Eisenhower made his famous comment about war planning in 1957, he would have been justified in adding a corollary: Amateurs strategize while professionals plan. Strategy is implicit in the war plan, though critics often treat them as separate items. An education in strategy is as essential as instruction in planning, because the war plan does not always put into effect the most appropriate military strategy. The science is not foolproof. Nor does it automatically link military strategy to a larger national or grand strategy. Doing so requires a conscious effort. This truth has been a source of frustration for scholars and practitioners alike for some time and for similar reasons. Both want to see military actions contribute to a larger purpose; both want to hold the hands of policy to that purpose. In any case, war in this period was clearly an instrument of policy, as Clausewitz duly described. However, as civilian strategists and military practitioners came to realize, policy is well advised—but never wholly obliged—to use its tool according to sound principles of strategic and operational practice.[86]

Notes

1. The actual quote is "I tell this story to illustrate the truth of the statement I heard long ago in the Army: Plans are worthless, but planning is everything." See also Gaddis, *Strategies of Containment*, 171.

2. Cf. Linn, *Echo of Battle*, 137. To be sure, Patton also appreciated the importance of planning.

3. The official totals for all services are Philippines, 86; Boxer Rebellion, 59; Mexican Campaign, 56; Caribbean (collectively), 13; World War I, 124; and World War II, 464; Center of Military History, Medal of Honor Recipients. To be sure, the standards for awarding the medal changed over time, but heroic actions occurred in small wars and were recognized.

4. See the excellent series by Stephen T. Ross: *American War Plans, 1890–1939*; *American War Plans, 1941–1945*; and *American War Plans, 1945–1950*.

5. Gray, *Strategy Bridge*, properly argues that strategy serves as the bridge between policy and military action.

6. Roth, *Sacred Honor*, 102.

7. Scheina, *Latin America's Wars*.

8. Pedraja, *Wars of Latin America*, 107–10.

9. Roosevelt ordered the second occupation of Cuba in September 1906; the first occurred from 1899 to 1902. Collins, *America's Small Wars*, 99. By 1906, Americans had invested a total of $159.5 million in Cuba, most of it in sugar, tobacco, and cattle, but only 30 of 181 sugar mills were American-owned. Hitchman, "US Control."

10. Millett, *Politics of Intervention*. By 1914, Americans had over $200 million invested in Cuba. Hitchman, "US Control," 105.

11. Langley, *Banana Wars*, 65.

12. Herbert, *Small Wars*.

13. Langley and Schoonover, *Banana Men*, 12.

14. Cf. Calhoun, *Uses of Force*, 20.

15. Schmidt, *United States' Occupation of Haiti*, 207–13.

16. Calhoun, *Uses of Force*, 26.

17. Scheina, *Latin America's Wars*, 49–51, and Collins, *America's Small Wars*, 107–8.

18. Calhoun, *Uses of Force*, 36–38, and Quirk, *Matter of Honor*. The affront in question referred to the Mexican refusal to fire a twenty-one-gun salute in apology for having wrongfully arrested nine US sailors on April 9, 1914.

19. Eisenhower, *Intervention!*, 120–22.

20. Between July 1915 and June 1916, thirty-eight cross-border raids occurred, resulting in the deaths of thirty-seven Americans.

21. Calhoun, *Uses of Force*, 42.

22. Two US troopers were reported as casualties at Parral, with forty-two Mexicans killed or wounded. Seven US soldiers were killed and eleven wounded at Carrizal. Gustavson, "Carrizal 1916," proposes a different account. Seven US soldiers were killed and eleven wounded at Carrizal.

23. Pershing, *Punitive Expedition*, 34–36.

24. Ross, *American War Plans, 1890–1939*, 25–27; Nenninger, "American Military Effectiveness"; and Trask, "Entry of the USA."

25. Grotelueschen, *AEF Way of War*, and Millett, "Cantigny," 149–85.

26. Approximately fifteen thousand German prisoners were captured at a cost of seven thousand Allied casualties. *American Military History*, 398–99.

27. Trask, "Entry of USA," 43. American casualties by the time of the armistice were about 320,710 overall. *American Military History*, 403, and Coffman, "Meuse–Argonne Offensive."

28. Millett, "Cantigny," 180–81.

29. Grotelueschen, *AEF Way of War*, 6–8, and Nenninger, "American Military Effectiveness," 141.

30. Recollection of US Secretary of War, Newton Baker, quoted in Calhoun, *Uses of Force*, 115.

31. Clausewitz, *Vom Kriege*, bk. 8, chap. 6A, 987–88; *On War*, 603–4. The debate continues as to the motives and value of the interventions. Cf. Melton, *Between War and Peace*; Richard, "'Shadow of a Plan'"; and Long, "American Intervention." As early as 1939, military authors used these cases to warn against mission creep and misuse of resources. See Dupuy, *Perish by the Sword*.

32. For contrasting views of the American effort, compare Birtle, *U.S. Army Counterinsurgency*, 210–26, and Boot, *Savage Wars*, 216–20.

33. Other interventions in Haiti (1915–34) and the Dominican Republic (1916–24) were already well under way before American "doughboys" departed for Europe.

34. Musicant, *Banana Wars*, 313–15.

35. Ibid., 360–61. Sandino was killed on February 21, 1934, by a Nicaraguan firing squad.

36. During the 1920s and 1930s, the active strength of the army declined from 2 million officers and men to approximately 135,000. No new battleships were built until 1937, but sixteen armored cruisers were constructed, and two older battleships were converted into aircraft carriers. Spector, "Military Effectiveness," 72.

37. As the commandant of the US Army War College noted in 1938, the *Manual for Commanders of Large Units* was essentially a translation of the French army's *Instruction provisoire du 6 Octobre 1921 sur l'emploi tactique des grandes unites* (1921) [*Provisional Instruction on the Tactical Employment of Large Units*]. Odom, *After the Trenches*.

38. General Service Schools, *General Tactical Functions*, 1–2. Cf. Nelson, "Origins of Operational Art," 340.

39. Naylor, *Principles of Strategy*. Cf. Matheny, *Carrying the War*, 50–53.

40. Naylor, *Principles of Strategy*, 49, 106.

41. Nenninger, "American Military Effectiveness," 129.

42. Murray, "Strategic Bombing," 107.

43. Ibid., 126; Muller, "Close Air Support"; and Biddle, *Rhetoric and Reality*.

44. Murray, "Strategic Bombing," 115, 123–25, and Meilinger, *Paths of Heaven*.

45. Murray, "Strategic Bombing," 127.

46. Herwig, "Innovation Ignored, 254.

47. Ibid., 255–56.

48. Till, "Adopting the Aircraft Carrier."

49. Watts and Murray, "Military Innovation in Peacetime," 399–400.

50. Bauer, *Surfboats and Horse Marines*.

51. Millett, "Assault from the Sea."

52. Birtle, *U.S. Army Counterinsurgency*, 249–50.

53. Clifford, "World War II," 846.

54. *Principles of Strategy*, 37.

55. Blumenson, "Kasserine Pass," 229, noted that "by 1939, the army had virtually forgotten how to conduct training on a broad scale. Very few officers could handle organizations larger than a battalion." At the outbreak of World War II, the United States had some seventeen army divisions rated as combat-ready, along with another twenty in various states of mobilization.

56. Blumenson, *Patton*, 181.

57. War Department, "Training Lessons," 1.

58. Harmon, "Notes on Combat Experience," 3, and Hart, *How the Allies Won*, 281.

59. Italy proved not to be the "soft underbelly," and the Italian campaign cost the Allies 320,000 casualties (114,000 American) by the end of the war. Botjer, *Sideshow War*, and Graham, *Tug of War*.

60. Keegan, *Six Armies*.

61. Herwig, "Innovation Ignored," 253.

62. United States Strategic Bombing Survey, Summary Report (European War), September 30, 1945, and Summary Report (Pacific War), July 1, 1946.

63. Overy, *Air War*, and *Why the Allies Won*.

64. Tooze, *Wages of Destruction*, 627, and Rostow, *Concept and Controversy*, 39–41. See also ibid.

65. Rockoff, *America's Economic Way*, 206.

66. This was true despite the fact that many Second World War veterans remained in service. Training was not as consistent or intense as it had been in the years before 1945. Flint, "Task Force Smith."

67. Each division had an authorized peacetime strength of 12,500 personnel, but this was only 66 percent of its wartime strength. By 1950, the US Army

had demobilized from eight million men and eighty-nine divisions to fewer than 600,000 men and ten divisions. *American Military History*, 540–42.

68. Doughty, *Evolution of US Army Tactical Doctrine*, 3.

69. Crane, *American Airpower Strategy*, 7.

70. Flint, *Confrontation in Asia*, 12–13.

71. Fehrenbach, *This Kind of War*, 160.

72. Futrell, *United States Air Force in Korea*, 147.

73. Flint, *Confrontation in Asia*, 24–30.

74. Milkowski, "After Inch'on."

75. Schnabel, *Policy and Direction*, 292–93.

76. Presidents Truman and Eisenhower considered using nuclear weapons more than once, whereas MacArthur did not consider using them. James and Wells, *Re-fighting the Last War*, 206, 237.

77. Crane, "Coercion through Air Pressure."

78. Appleman, *South to the Naktong*, 726.

79. Kelly, *US Army Special Forces*; *FM 31-20: Operations against Guerrilla Forces* (February 1951); *FM 31-21: Organization and Conduct of Guerrilla Warfare* (October 1951; updated 1955 and 1958); and *FM 31-15: Operations against Airborne Attack, Guerrilla Action, and Infiltration* (January 1953).

80. Many of the articles were reprinted in Osanka, *Modern Guerrilla Warfare*.

81. *FM 31-15: Operations against Irregular Forces* (May 1961); *FM 31-16: Counter-guerrilla Operations* (February 1963; updated March 1967); *FM 31-22: U.S. Army Counterinsurgency Forces* (November 1963); *FM 31-73: Advisor Handbook for Counterinsurgencies* (April 1965); and *FM 31-73: Advisor Handbook for Stability Operations* (October 1967).

82. Doughty, *Evolution of Tactical Doctrine*, 25–29, and Krepenevich, *Army and Vietnam*.

83. "Armed Forces."

84. *FM 100-5: Field Service Regulations*.

85. See the classic Butler, *War Is a Racket*. Butler was a veteran of the Spanish–American War, the Philippine Insurrection, the Boxer Rebellion, most of the Caribbean wars, the Mexican interventions, and the First World War. He was awarded the Medal of Honor twice: in the Veracruz operation (1914) and the intervention in Haiti (1915).

86. For an example of this frustration from the standpoint of contemporary British strategy, see Strachan, "British National Strategy."

7

The Guatemalan Coup
to the War on Terrorism

We will do what must be done. And we will do only what must
be done.

President Lyndon B. Johnson, 1965

PRESIDENT JOHNSON'S PROMISE, delivered in a message concerning ap-
propriations for the Vietnam War, was intended to reassure Congress and
the American people that US involvement in Southeast Asia would remain
precise and focused. It was a promise that would prove almost impossible
to keep. The idea of doing "what must be done" invited mission creep of
which the Vietnam War had plenty. At the same time, the idea of doing "only"
what must be done implied an unwillingness to commit fully. The tensions
between the two were never completely reconciled. Yet Johnson's remark is
noteworthy, as it succinctly captures the political logic that would underpin
US military interventions for decades with but few exceptions. Beginning
with President John F. Kennedy's doctrine of "flexible response," which sought
to provide more nuclear and conventional military options for responding to
crises than Eisenhower's all-or-nothing strategy of "massive retaliation," US
policy would try to walk the fine line between doing too little and doing too
much.[1] It would have been difficult to walk that line even without the threat
of nuclear escalation, but that threat put further pressure on the need for
precise measures. As one of Defense Secretary McNamara's aides wrote in
1964, "Our military forces must be used in a measured, limited, controlled
and deliberate way, as an instrument to carry out our foreign policy."[2] The
call was very Clausewitzian on the surface, implying that American military
forces were foremost an instrument of US policy, but the remark was simply
too naive for the state of American operational practice at the time.

It was a peculiar irony of the policy of flexible response that it actually resulted in reduced flexibility for American conventional forces. It did, however,
make greater use of some types of special military forces and CIA personnel.[3] Their operations, which were generally covert or clandestine in nature,
increased in frequency.[4] Yet the logic of precision—of doing just enough—
outlasted the collapse of the Soviet Union and the end of the Cold War, perhaps out of habit. By then, the operational practice of American conventional
forces had been refined enough that the logic became somewhat easier to
sustain.

The Guatemalan Coup

The invasion of Cuba in 1961 might have been an anomaly were it not for the
fact that a number of similar interventions, such as President Eisenhower's
overthrow of the Guatemalan government in 1954, Operation PBSuccess,
had taken place beforehand.[5] Its objective was to depose Guatemalan president Jacobo Árbenz and his communist allies and replace him with Col. Castillo Armas. The US intention was to isolate Guatemala diplomatically, economically, and militarily, then have the CIA assist a small land invasion by
Castillo's forces aimed at taking key towns and military posts and ultimately
seizing the capital. The invasion took place on June 18, 1954, with four columns (480 personnel) crossing the border into Guatemala from Honduras.
Two of the columns were soundly defeated within the first three days, and
desertions began to occur among the other two. Elsewhere, Castillo's ranks
were swelling with recruits from the peasantry, but these did little to increase
his actual combat power. The peasants generally stayed away from the fighting and merely consumed his supplies. The Guatemalan military had little
doubt about its ability to defeat Castillo's small army. However, the general
sense was that if Castillo's invasion failed, the United States would use it as
a pretext to intervene with even greater force, remove Árbenz, and punish
those who had supported him. In response, the Guatemalan army delivered
an ultimatum to Árbenz: "If you don't resign, the Army will march on the
capital and depose you."[6] He resigned on June 27.

The operation was planned as a coup, and in concept it was essentially a
military strategy of decapitation. US psychological operations and rumors of
intervention drove a wedge between the Guatemalan army and its political
leadership; the former turned on the latter to avoid greater harm to itself. The
primary cause of Árbenz's fall was thus the belief that the United States was
directly involved in the operation from the outset, which gave the psychological operations (psyops) campaign credibility. Unfortunately, the lessons

US policymakers drew from the operation overlooked that key ingredient. They believed that rebel military pressure, plus token US air support, and the psyops campaign had provided a compelling formula. In actuality, the rebel force, which employed conventional rather than guerrilla tactics, had been decimated during its assaults; the air attacks came after the army's ultimatum to Árbenz and caused only limited physical damage; and the psyops campaign had weakened the resolve of the Guatemalan military but had little impact on the general population.[7] Operation PBSuccess achieved its objectives, but the science underpinning it had been misunderstood.[8] The covert nature of the operation fooled no one; in fact, knowledge that the United States backed the overthrow of Árbenz was crucial to its success. The covert nature of this operation differed markedly from Eisenhower's open show of force in Lebanon from July to October 1958, Operation Blue Bat. Some fifteen thousand US troops were deployed on short notice to nip a rebellion in the bud and to restore political stability, which they rapidly accomplished through aggressive patrolling and overflights.[9]

The Cuban Invasion

Three years later, in April 1961, President Kennedy gave approval for an invasion of Cuba. A force was to land at Playa Girón (Giron Beach) on the Bahía de Cochinos (Bay of Pigs). The goal was regime change, which was to be achieved by a military strategy of decapitation—specifically, toppling the Castro regime by drawing popular support away from it preparatory to an assault on Havana. The mission teetered between a covert and an overt operation for some time. When it was launched in mid-April 1961, it was a dysfunctional combination of both, and its failed execution belied the hours spent planning it, most of which occurred under the Eisenhower administration. The operation's chances of success had been dubious from the start, due largely to its bifurcated nature. On the one hand, it was imperative that the operation retain a small footprint in order to maintain secrecy and what White House officials called "plausible deniability," though both of these aims had been compromised early on. On the other hand, an amphibious assault against a modern, semiprofessional military armed with tanks, field artillery, aircraft (six B-26 bombers, four T-33 fighters, and a few Sea Fury fighters), and antiaircraft weapons required extensive cross-service coordination, logistical support, and, above all, air cover.[10] Castro's army—though uneven in experience, training, and loyalty—totaled nearly thirty thousand troops and could draw from some two hundred thousand more (untested) militiamen. Against this force, the United States—perhaps encouraged by knowledge that some hundred thousand exiles had already fled Cuba in the first year of Castro's reign—landed a CIA-led task force (Brigade 2506) of mostly Cuban exiles numbering fourteen hundred personnel, supported by a platoon of tanks, sixteen B-26 bombers, and sixteen transport aircraft.[11]

Air strikes were launched on April 15, 1961, two days before the operation, and they succeeded in destroying between 30 and 50 percent of Castro's air force. However, follow-up strikes were scaled down or canceled altogether to maintain the illusion that the United States was not involved. The remainder of Castro's air force counterattacked on April 17 while Brigade 2506 was disembarking, and elements of the Cuban army, reinforced with tanks and artillery, converged on the landing beaches. By April 19, the invasion force had been defeated, and the larger uprising it was supposed to have inspired never gathered momentum. Officially the operation failed due to lack of air support and the inability to conduct resupply, but the deeper reason was that its conflicted character was never reconciled. Had it been resolved in favor of an overt operation, then American air assets and other support could have participated freely. Obviously, the Kennedy administration would have had to accept the risks and criticisms that would have come with such a larger campaign. Had it been resolved in the direction of a covert operation, with more Guevara-style *focoist* groups inserted at key locations within Cuba, the approach would have come with different risks. One of these was whether it could have kept pace with and ultimately undermined Castro's efforts to strengthen his influence over the populace through propaganda and by increasing the size of his regular army and militia. In the end, the invasion was an overt operation carried out as a covert one, unsuccessfully. Brigade 2506 lost 114 troops killed and another 1,214 wounded and captured (1,179 of whom were later returned to the United States), while Castro's forces suffered about 1,800 casualties, 178 of which were believed to have been killed.[12]

If the operation's hybrid nature doomed it, other attempts to carry out covert interventions—such as Kennedy's intervention in British Guiana (1963), Johnson's use of military force to support a successful coup in Brazil (1964), his invasion of the Dominican Republic the following year (1965), and Nixon's intervention in Chile (1970) in an attempt to prevent the inauguration of Marxist leader Salvador Allende—fared differently.[13] Defeat may well be an "orphan" while victory may have "many fathers," as Kennedy remarked after the Bay of Pigs failure; however, defeat can also sire offspring of its own. Kennedy could not allow a "second Cuba" to develop in British Guiana and thus ordered the removal of its leftist prime minister Cheddi Jagan.[14] The removal was achieved through joint US–UK instigation of a general strike and an alteration of British Guiana's election system. In 1964, the United

States dispatched a carrier battle group to Brazil and pledged to support Gen. Humberto de Alencar Castelo Branco in an attempted overthrow of left-leaning president João Goulart.[15] The coup succeeded on April 4, 1964, without bloodshed and well before US forces arrived. In 1965, the Johnson administration, fearing a replication of Castro's victory in Cuba, sent twenty-three thousand troops to the Dominican Republic to support loyalist forces against a revolutionary movement. American troops succeeded in quelling the violence and in evacuating US citizens and other foreign nationals. In 1970, Nixon's attempts to block Allende's inauguration through sanctions and an attempted coup failed. In 1973, a military coup under Gen. Augusto Pinochet succeeded, during which Allende died.

All but one of these interventions thus accomplished its objectives at minimal cost to the United States and avoided further damage to its credibility. However, in each case the longer-term consequences have been both considerable and controversial. The parties the United States chose to support sometimes became repressive dictatorships, as in the cases of Castelo Branco and Pinochet, or led to further instability and violence. When US military force was used in these cases, it was neither overwhelming nor decisive, but rather enough to signal American political resolve. An operational science, closer in form to what was used at the beginning of the twentieth century, was being employed again to send the message that the United States would not retreat from protecting its interests.

The Vietnam War

American operational practice faced two problems in Vietnam, both similar in nature to those it confronted in Korea. The first was that the conflict was in reality a war within a war. The military strategies and operational methods employed in Southeast Asia were influenced by the circumstances of the Cold War and the evolving US and NATO strategy of containment. As some historians have pointed out, Vietnam was viewed by the Kennedy and Johnson administrations as a "test case" for the strategy of flexible response.[16] It was thus only one, albeit the largest, of several peripheral conflicts taking place globally between the United States and the Soviet Union while a nuclear arms race was also under way. Consequently, US military actions were considered not only within the context of the geopolitical situation in Southeast Asia or how they might affect American domestic politics, but also with respect to how they might be perceived in Moscow or Beijing. Of particular concern was whether Washington could demonstrate the firmness of its resolve to both Moscow and Beijing. A corollary concern was whether military force could be applied in precise and measured ways so as to achieve the aims of a flexible policy.

The second problem for American military practice was that, for much of the war, the North Vietnamese Army (NVA) and Viet Cong guerrillas were able to use sanctuaries in Cambodia and Laos, which extended the operational front by more than a thousand miles along South Vietnam's western border. These sanctuaries enabled NVA and Viet Cong forces to move north-south along the Ho Chi Minh Trail system, assemble, and attack into the northern mountainous regions, the central plateau, and the Saigon and Mekong areas. American, South Vietnamese, and allied forces could move rapidly along east-west and coastal road networks and conduct air-mobile operations and amphibious landings. As a result, both sides were usually able to achieve local superiority when executing offensive operations. The US military presence grew slowly in the early 1960s from 700 military advisers at the beginning of 1960 to 24,000 troops by 1964, then more rapidly between 1965 and 1968, when the number of US personnel rose to 536,000.[17] This period also saw the standing up of 800,000 South Vietnamese troops and security personnel, as well as the participation of 68,000 allied soldiers.[18] Although the strength of enemy forces within South Vietnam was estimated at 283,000 in 1966, it was always difficult to ascertain, not only because the nature of the terrain hindered detection efforts, but also because local, provincial, and main-force Viet Cong units were essentially drawn from and could return to the civilian population.[19] The withdrawal of US forces began in 1969 at a rate of about 14,000 troops per month until the final evacuation of the US embassy in Saigon in April 1975. Nonetheless, for the critical years of 1965 to 1968, American forces and their allies likely had significant numerical superiority. Given that possibility, the crude strategy of attrition that Secretary of Defense Robert McNamara tried to follow, seemingly independently, with body counts and other quantitative metrics is somewhat easier to understand. It was, nonetheless, a perversion of operational science.

American operational practice employed many of the maneuver-oriented concepts used in the Second World War and the Korean conflict, such as the core principle of concentrating overwhelming force at decisive points. However, one key addition was the concept of air mobility, enabled by the increased use of helicopters. Air mobility permitted combat power to be concentrated, or extracted, more quickly than was possible through surface maneuver alone. Vertical envelopment thus inserted a new dimension of combat operations between those dimensions hitherto associated with air power and land power. The operational approach adopted by the US Military Assistance Command (MACV) was essentially that of a mobile defense, divided among four corps tactical zones and combined with extensive counterforce operations. Specific objectives would change in the course of the conflict, but the chief purpose of ground operations in South Vietnam was to eliminate the direct threat that the NVA and Viet Cong posed to the government in Saigon. Early tactical victories by US forces, such as in the Ia Drang Valley in 1965, may well have encouraged American leadership to adhere too long to its search-and-destroy tactics. However, by late 1967, "pacification" measures had also begun.[20] These measures included the Civil Operations and Rural Development Support (CORDS) program designed to "win hearts and minds" (an unfortunate phrase in many respects) by increasing support for the Saigon government, establishing better security, and thereby separating insurgent forces from their base of support.[21] The CORDS program, in particular, met with some success, creating village home guards, provincial militias, and people's self-defense forces—a combined strength of nearly half a million people under arms by 1970—all of which greatly increased the ability of villagers to defend themselves against Viet Cong terrorist attacks.[22] Many of these forces, in fact, contributed to the defeat of the Viet Cong during Hanoi's Tet Offensive, launched on January 31, 1968.[23]

Although the Tet Offensive came as a shock to Washington and Saigon—with some eighty thousand NVA and, primarily, Viet Cong attacking thirty-six provincial capitals, five autonomous cities, and two dozen airfields and bases—it was decisively defeated by combined air, ground, naval, paramilitary, and police actions. These forces inflicted over fifty thousand casualties on the enemy and essentially eliminated the Viet Cong as an effective fighting force.[24] The collective results of the offensive showed that CORDS and other programs were paying off, but the fact that it had taken place at all, and had achieved surprise, undermined public confidence in the Pentagon and the White House. McNamara and MACV commander Gen. William Westmoreland were both replaced within the year. Nixon's Vietnamization program was subsequently put into effect, the principal aim of which was to de-Americanize the conflict by replacing US troops with South Vietnamese soldiers. Unfortunately, corruption within the South Vietnamese government and military structure likely doomed this effort from the start. American military withdrawals began in earnest in the summer of 1969, though these did not prevent the Nixon administration from launching major offensives into Cambodia and Laos in the spring and summer of 1970 to reduce enemy sanctuaries.[25] These actions captured or destroyed several thousand tons of ammunition and supplies but came at a high cost politically. The American public saw the strikes as a deliberate expansion of the war at a time when US troops were said to be withdrawing.

Extensive bombing campaigns, such as Rolling Thunder (1965–68) and Linebacker I and II (1972), were carried out by the US Air Force and US Navy. In 1963, approximately 63,000 tons of bombs were dropped on Hanoi; by 1967, the total of bombs dropped had risen to 226,000 tons; and by 1968, nearly 2,380 sorties had been flown by B-52 bombers and a total of 643,000 tons of bombs had been dropped. The objectives of the bombing campaigns varied from attempting to bring Hanoi to the negotiating table to interdiction of major NVA offensives, such as the 1972 Easter Offensive.[26] Controversy still remains as to whether an American victory, or at least an earlier settlement, might have been achieved had the Johnson administration not insisted on employing a gradualist approach.[27] It is not clear, however, that the North Vietnamese would have responded any differently to massive bombings than the Japanese or the Germans (or the British) had in the Second World War. The bombing surveys from that war, though examples of flawed operational science, provide no evidence that such an approach would have worked three decades later, even with more destructive munitions.

Since the North Vietnamese had little in the way of a conventional navy, US naval operations consisted largely of interdiction of enemy seaborne infiltration efforts and of power projection ashore in support of land and air operations. Corbett once again proved more relevant than Mahan. River patrols and raids were conducted in the waterways of the Mekong Delta to interdict the movement of Viet Cong and NVA troops and supplies. Air strikes launched from carriers conducted continuous bombing of logistical facilities and such road and rail networks as existed. Close-air-support missions were flown with navy and marine corps aircraft, and naval gunfire disrupted enemy offensive operations, most notably the Tet and Easter Offensives. Amphibious forces were often used as floating reserves just off the shores of South Vietnam, particularly in the areas near the demilitarized zone.[28]

Much criticism has been directed at how the US military managed the war—particularly at its reliance on firepower. However, American operational practice maximized the strengths of US forces while minimizing their weaknesses. The US military clearly had advantages in strategic and operational mobility and firepower. However, as a conscript force subject to one-year tours and encumbered with heavy equipment and support requirements, it lacked the elite training and tactical mobility necessary to outpace the lightly armed guerrilla forces of its opponent, particularly in restrictive terrain. As many analysts noted, enemy forces often proved more difficult to "find and fix" than originally assumed. However, whenever enemy tactics shifted from guerrilla operations to large-scale conventional assaults, as in 1968 and 1972, that problem essentially vanished. Pacification programs and counterinsurgency techniques were controversial from the start and fraught with friction in implementation, but they gave the enemy a second, and not inconsequential, set of problems to solve.[29] Even if communist forces avoided destruction by declining combat, they could lose the war if they gave up the ability to intimidate and coerce the civilian population. American use of aerial bombing was plagued by several faulty assumptions, the most important of which were that Hanoi's behavior could be influenced by factors similar in nature to those that might affect US actions (also known as mirror-imaging) and that the United States could deliver the requisite intensity of "pain" through bombing and sustain it as long as necessary. The difficulty of arriving at a negotiated settlement shows that such assumptions were misplaced.

After the Vietnam conflict, US military writers began to think more systematically about the problem of fighting outnumbered and winning. Battles such as Khe Sanh (January–April 1968) were viewed as examples in which the coordination of air and artillery fires enabled well-trained troops to hold out against superior numbers of enemy forces. The Yom Kippur War of October 1973 provided further evidence of the increased destructiveness of modern firepower. A consistent theme running through the doctrinal literature at the time was that modern weaponry had raised the "lethality" of the battlefield to "unprecedented" levels.[30] The professional catchphrase became "If it can be seen, it can be hit; if it can be hit, it can be killed." The challenge the Warsaw Pact posed for NATO forces not only served to reinforce this perception—it made destroying enemy forces more important than taking and holding terrain. However, that conclusion ran counter to classic counterinsurgency doctrine, which rhetorically at least put enemy destruction second to securing key areas and protecting the population.

The need to fight outnumbered and win also underpinned the notable debate that occurred between the "maneuverist" and "attritionist" schools of thought within the US military during the 1970s and 1980s.[31] As the US and other NATO nations turned their attention to deterrence, and to the mission of defeating the Warsaw Pact should deterrence fail, their focus shifted to the likelihood of fighting from a position of overall material inferiority. Estimates of opposing forces varied depending on planning assumptions; however, the consensus was that NATO would be outnumbered 1.4 or 2.4 to 1.[32] Thus NATO forces would have to find ways to achieve local superiority when (and where) it mattered most—that is, at operationally decisive points. Each time they did so, however, they would reduce their ability to achieve it elsewhere. Accordingly, local superiority became the proverbial ace in the hole to be played wisely—to win a campaign, not just a battle.

This train of logic made the concept of center of gravity appealing to maneuverists. For them, NATO forces had little choice but to find ways to maximize the effects of firepower, shock, and maneuver to inflict as telling a blow as possible on the enemy. If opposing forces could be pushed beyond their psychological breaking points, a series of cascading effects might be set in motion. For attritionists, the destructive effect of modern munitions, which included weapons of mass destruction, was too great to achieve that kind of maneuver. In their view, any conflict under modern conditions would quickly devolve into an attritional contest, and operational planning had to proceed not on the hope of achieving the psychological collapse of hostile forces, but on the prospect of reducing or eliminating their ability to shoot, move, and communicate. "Active defense," the concept applied to NATO forces in Europe, was one expression of this line of argument. It both influenced and was informed by the renewed debate over whether war was an art or a science. Maneuverists argued for the former and claimed for themselves the title of artists, while attritionists were left pointing to the importance of weapons of mass destruction and logistics. However, the debate suffered from an unclear understanding of the differences between art and science (discussed in chapter 3).

By comparison, the virtue of the 1982 version of the US Army's operations manual, *FM 100-5*, which introduced the AirLand Battle concept, was that it took both sides of the debate into account. It did not overlook the role of weapons of mass destruction, but it did reinforce the importance of operational maneuver.[33] This point was made even clearer in the 1986 edition of *FM 100-5*, which stated that the "essence of operational art" was "the identification of the enemy's operational center of gravity and the concentration of superior combat power against that point to achieve decisive success."[34] The chief means to that end was the synchronization of mobility and firepower, not only across the forward line of friendly troops, as the active defense concept of the 1976 version of *FM 100-5* did, but also throughout the depth of the battle area. The idea of the "deep attack" was clearly not new, as it had existed in Soviet doctrine for some time. However, what was new for American operational practice, and what some have called revolutionary, was the idea of conceiving the entire depth of an opponent's attacking formations as one "integrated" battle.[35] The operational level of war, though controversial for its potential to filter or even block the influence of policy, was instituted by the United States and other NATO members in part as a conceptual framework for integrating different national doctrines and command-and-control procedures into a unifying effort.[36] The task of stopping the Warsaw Pact would be vastly more difficult if a host of individual national corps and divisions were attempting it, rather than a single alliance following a common doctrine.

Post-Vietnam Interventions

If the desire to maintain a small footprint for the US invasion of Cuba undermined its potential for success, several other attempts to do so in the post-Vietnam era fared better. American interventions in El Salvador (1979–91) and Colombia (1978–2011) have rightly been classified as "minimalist."[37] The US intervention in El Salvador (fifty-five advisers, $6 billion) did not bring about victory for the Salvadoran armed forces, but it prevented their defeat at the hands of a group of "Marxist" revolutionaries. Similarly, US assistance to Colombia (eight hundred soldiers, six hundred contractors, $7 billion) since 2000 ultimately coincided with the success of President Álvaro Uribe's new strategy, which reduced the size and influence of the Revolutionary Armed Forces of Colombia (FARC). These successes suggested that walking the line between doing enough and doing too much was not entirely impossible. With lowered expectations, American operational practice could accomplish some policy objectives with small numbers of US military personnel, trained contractors, and monetary assistance.

The post-Vietnam era also saw American operational practitioners make increasing references to "come-as-you-are wars," or what some analysts later called "no notice, no plan" operations. The operation in Grenada (1983) was one such come-as-you-are war for which no real contingency plan existed.[38] From October 25 to November 2, 1983, a joint force of army rangers, navy SEALs, marines, and paratroopers conducted a series of airborne and amphibious assaults to rescue nearly seven hundred American and other civilians.[39] The operation took place with little planning and coordination and incomplete combat intelligence; however, these shortfalls only underscored the importance of operational science. Planning—analysis of the mission, gathering intelligence, and development and selection of courses of action— became even more important in the absence of contingency plans.[40]

In contrast, the planning for Operation Just Cause in Panama (December 1989) began some twenty-two months before the actual commitment of troops. Combat intelligence was much more detailed, though far from perfect, and the forces scheduled to participate were able to rehearse their roles some weeks beforehand.[41] In a joint operation that lasted eleven days, a US force comprising twenty-eight thousand troops (rangers, airborne troops, light infantry, SEALs, and marines) overcame approximately fifteen thousand Panamanian Defense Forces (PDF) troops and captured dictator Manuel

Noriega.[42] In many ways, Just Cause benefited from the after-action reviews conducted for previous operations, such as Eagle Claw (the 1980 Iran hostage rescue attempt) and the intervention in Grenada.

The after-action analyses of US operations in Somalia (1992–94) were extensive, despite the small size of the forces involved.[43] One reason for this attention was the relatively high casualties—nineteen killed and ninety-one wounded—most of which came from Task Force Ranger's battle in the middle of Mogadishu on the night of October 3–4, 1993.[44] The joint special operations force had the mission of capturing Somali warlord Mohamed Farah Aideed, who was disrupting the humanitarian assistance operations within the city and its surroundings. The task force's casualties were considered avoidable— had the armor and other support requested for the quick-reaction force been provided. However, Defense Secretary Les Aspin, who stepped down in the aftermath of the failed operation, denied the request.[45]

Many of the lessons that came out of the operations in Somalia were applicable to peacekeeping and peace-enforcement missions in general. The first of these was that military forces were not the best tools for peacekeeping operations but were usually the only ones available. Second, unity of effort in such operations is a luxury, not a norm. While coordinating the efforts of allies and coalition partners is difficult as a rule, peacekeeping operations involve a number of players for whom even the appearance of cooperation with the military is anathema. Third, open and continuous communication with the public is essential, whereas in conventional operations it is usually best to conceal one's intentions from the public as long as possible. Fourth, a clear exit strategy connected to the mandate is critical, as peacekeeping operations can evolve into open-ended nation-building exercises, which can prove extremely costly and for which few allies or coalition partners will sign on. Finally, in peacekeeping operations, legitimacy, restraint, and perseverance were considered important enough to enshrine as principles.[46]

In the early 1990s, the US military developed a body of doctrine referred to, somewhat unfortunately, as military operations other than war, or MOOTW.[47] These operations included missions ranging from show of force to humanitarian assistance. The phrase was unfortunate because it implied that such operations were outside war and, by extension, less important than war. These "lesser-includeds" could be trained for as the need arose. Obviously, shows of force and humanitarian assistance are nothing if not the continuation of policy by other means. They are, in short, Clausewitzian in every respect, and they involve taking some political risk while also putting national prestige on the line. Such operations are, in other words, important from a psychological and moral standpoint, even if their political stakes do not involve regime change. As of 2012, the number of UN peacekeeping operations conducted since 1948 was sixty-six, with forty-nine initiated since the end of the Cold War and seventeen still under way.[48]

The Gulf War

American operational practice in Operation Desert Storm was both bifurcated and contentious, reflecting the divergent influences of contemporary air-power and land-power theories. The former held that simultaneous attacks against the vital points in an adversary's communication and transportation infrastructures would cause strategic paralysis and psychological collapse—and do so without the extensive destruction hitherto associated with strategic bombing.[49] The main elements of this theory were implemented in the air phase of Desert Storm, which began on January 17, 1991, and continued until January 23, 1991.[50] It resulted in destroying most Iraqi command-and-control facilities and antiaircraft defenses within hours and featured extensive use of cruise missiles and some sorties by F-117 stealth fighters. With air superiority quickly established, air assets were shifted to knocking out Iraqi armor and artillery pieces. Nearly one-third of Iraqi ground forces were destroyed or rendered combat-ineffective during the air phase, but there was no real evidence that strategic paralysis had been achieved.

In contrast, land-power theory essentially embraced the principles of Air-Land Battle, which held that the key to military success would come from coordinated air-ground maneuver that compelled the enemy to retreat or be destroyed. The chief elements of this theory were essentially validated by the land phase of Desert Storm, which began on February 24, 1991, and lasted "a hundred hours." The decisive air-ground maneuver consisted of a frontal pinning attack by two marine corps divisions and mechanized forces from Egypt, Saudi Arabia, and Kuwait, and horizontal and vertical envelopments by several divisions of US, UK, and French armored and mechanized formations and airborne elements along the Iraqi right flank. Iraqi forces were estimated to have suffered twenty-five thousand to sixty-five thousand casualties; coalition troops incurred fewer than two hundred.[51] The United States and its coalition partners deployed 680,000 troops, three thousand armored vehicles, two thousand aircraft, and one hundred warships against Saddam Hussein's 336,000 troops and nine thousand armored vehicles.[52] The odds were thus approximately 2:1 in the coalition's favor in combat troops, about 1:3 in Saddam's favor in armored vehicles, and overwhelmingly in the coalition's favor with respect to air power. Although Desert Storm validated the principles of AirLand Battle, it was widely acknowledged that Iraqi formations were severely overmatched technologically, as well as with respect to intangibles such as leadership, training, and doctrine.

The 1993 edition of the US Army's *FM 100-5* continued to emphasize the importance of achieving "decisive victory," even though it also acknowledged the Cold War had ended and the nature of the threat had changed. It went on to say that the principal role of the US Army in the post–Cold War era was deterrence and the ability to project power anywhere. However, it also stated that "the objective of the military in war is victory over the opposing military force."[53] Consensus documents, such as *Joint Vision 2010* (1996) and *Joint Vision 2020* (2000), were supposed to outline a way forward for all US military services, and their respective operational approaches, around four interrelated concepts: dominant maneuver, precision engagement, focused logistics, and full-dimensional protection, all of which were to lead to the objective of full-spectrum dominance.[54] However, not only were these documents too aspirational in nature—they also failed to articulate just how the separate services were to function in an integrated manner. In other words, to achieve a genuine paradigm shift, operational science required a forcing function it did not have.

The need for closer integration of the services was made more obvious by the Bosnia (1995) and Kosovo (1999) conflicts. The challenge to operational planners was to stop Serbian aggression and ethnic cleansing but to do so in a manner political leaders could turn on or off quickly and that would neither provoke Serbian reprisals nor increase the political risks for UN or NATO participation. A premium was, therefore, placed on minimizing collateral damage, which at times also meant minimizing harm to Bosnian Serb forces. The American contributions in Operation Deliberate Force (1995) and Operation Allied Force (1999) were initially in the form of air power. However, the US First Armored Division took part as the mainstay of the NATO Implementation Force (IFOR), which consisted of sixty thousand troops from thirty-two nations, more than one dozen of which were non-NATO members.[55] The First Armored Division assured American leadership in the operation and is an example of the use of credible force from the standpoint of land power.

In a move that will likely remain controversial for some time, US political leadership attempted to fight the Kosovo conflict with the proverbial "one hand tied behind its back."[56] Ground combat forces were taken completely off the table from the outset, and "no serious contingency planning for air-land operations was undertaken."[57] That decision was too optimistic about the effects air strikes alone would have and flew in the face of decades of operational science. It reflected a political will divided between wanting to do enough but not too much—and to do it without taking unnecessary casualties and without inflicting unnecessary harm. American pilots flew about two-thirds of the thirty-eight thousand sorties that took place during the seventy-eight-day around-the-clock bombing campaign (March 24 to June 10, 1999) over Kosovo, and the United States contributed over 70 percent of the more than a thousand aircraft used in the operation.[58] It was an effort, in other words, that required most of NATO's operational aircraft, though the reasons Serbian leader Slobodan Milošević conceded were still unclear later.[59] As the air campaign illustrated, the post–Cold War environment did not necessarily suggest that war itself is a last resort for policy, only that the use of land power might be.

The US Air Force had embraced the operational level of war by the time Operation Deliberate Force and Operation Allied Force took place. It had also settled upon something of a methodical approach to the planning and execution of air operations. This method consisted of four basic tasks: envisioning the theater along with the combatant commander and determining when and where to apply what force, creating conditions that maximize the chances of success, assessing the results of each mission and making adjustments accordingly, and exploiting opportunities.[60] These tasks accord with the five interrelated activities that constitute operational science discussed earlier. In both operations, bombing was conducted in accordance with a preapproved target list and strict rules of engagement. These restrictions, in turn, meant greater reliance on precision munitions. In Operation Deliberate Force, nearly 31 percent of NATO's bombs were precision-guided munitions (PGMs).[61] In Operation Allied Force, about 35 percent of NATO's munitions were PGMs. By comparison, less than 9 percent of the munitions used in Desert Storm were PGMs.[62]

As mentioned, UN and NATO political and military leaders were reluctant to use ground forces, though these would have demonstrated political resolve and presented Serbian troops with a second threat. Indigenous forces, such as the Kosovo Liberation Army, were eventually used to provide pressure on the ground as were small numbers of NATO ground troops. However, the success of the Kosovo operation overall gave premature credence to the idea of using local militias and other indigenous forces as a substitute for professional ground forces. Due to the downsizing of the US military that took place in the 1990s, the Kosovo model, which harkened back to the American experiences in the Caribbean and Latin America nearly a century earlier, was too hastily embraced. As Roosevelt, Wilson, Kennedy, and Eisenhower discovered, indigenous partners and allies may well act in ways that promote their own interests over those of the United States. The model thus grew in popularity despite, rather than because of, operational science.

The 1990s also saw the beginning of what has been called the "modern" defense review process, which was to analyze long-term risks and identify required capabilities and how to develop them.[63] This period was also referred to by some analysts—correctly as it turned out—as a "strategic pause" that would allow militaries to transform themselves in ways that would capitalize on new technological opportunities.[64] However, the pause itself lasted less than a decade, and the degree of actual transformation accomplished during it satisfied no one.

The War in Afghanistan

Afghanistan presented an enormous access problem for American operational practice in the autumn of 2001. As a landlocked country, it offered no possibility of transporting troops and materiel directly by sea. Three-quarters of Afghanistan's 650,000 square miles are rugged mountains and highlands, with little in the way of transportation infrastructure (only twenty-five thousand miles of roads, 75 percent of which are unpaved, and fewer than three dozen airports and heliports).[65] These conditions restricted the operational flow of coalition troops and equipment into and within the area when military operations began just two weeks after September 11, 2001. The political aim was regime change: toppling the Taliban and capturing or killing al-Qaeda leadership, Osama bin Laden in particular. The military strategy was thus that of decapitation, at least initially.

Three US carrier battle groups assembled in the Arabian Sea, and several aircraft landed in Uzbekistan with special operations troops.[66] CIA personnel armed with "drones and dollars" were on the ground by September 26, establishing agreements with elements of the Northern Alliance (a multiethnic alliance of Afghans opposed to the Taliban). Coalition military strategy resembled a classic "enemy of my enemy" approach in that it sought alignment with elements of the Northern Alliance and several Pashtun tribes hostile to the Taliban and to strengthen and leverage them in an effort to weaken the Taliban and decimate al-Qaeda. In an example of interdependent maneuver, Operation Enduring Freedom began on October 7, 2001, with special operations forces from the United States and the United Kingdom arriving in country under cover of long-range missile strikes and air-to-ground attacks against Taliban and al-Qaeda targets.[67] Firepower was initially brought to bear in the form of B-52 bombers, B-1 stealth bombers, strike aircraft (F-14s and F/A-18s), and approximately fifty Tomahawk cruise missiles.[68]

On the ground, special operations forces facilitated further long-range air-to-ground attacks while also attempting to solidify relations with the

Northern Alliance. While Defense Secretary Rumsfeld and the press made much of images of modern-day special operations forces on horseback, the technique was as old as that of "hunter and hound"—firepower was used to suppress enemy fire and to facilitate friendly maneuver, which in turn rooted out entrenched fighters through direct assaults. By early December, al-Qaeda and Taliban forces were in full retreat, having been driven from Mazar-i-Sharif, Kabul, Kunduz, and Kandahar into the mountainous areas of eastern and southern Afghanistan. However, the coalition failed to block the escape of key enemy leaders, such as bin Laden, at the Battle of Tora Bora.[69] On December 16, one day before the battle had ended, Secretary of State Colin Powell announced, "We've destroyed al-Qaeda in Afghanistan, and we have ended the role of Afghanistan as a haven for terrorist activity."[70] Powell's announcement was true as far as it went. Taliban and al-Qaeda elements had indeed been "destroyed in" Afghanistan, but they had *not* been destroyed as hostile organizations. Instead they had fled to Pakistan to reconstitute there. In other words, the age-old problem of privileged sanctuary had returned for military planners.

By the end of December, coalition military strategy had changed in character from "divide and conquer" to "search and destroy." A divide-and-conquer approach would have entailed strengthening the anti-Taliban Pashtun base against the likely return of Taliban and al-Qaeda elements. It would undoubtedly have required some long-term commitment in the form of aid and arms programs among other things, none of which need have approximated the scale of social reengineering or nation-building programs of the sort that underpinned most counterinsurgency theories. Instead of a divide-and-conquer strategy, the coalition launched Operation Anaconda in March 2002, followed by a series of smaller but similar undertakings, such as Operation Mountain Sweep. More than two thousand coalition troops—including Americans, Australians, Britons, Canadians, New Zealanders, and Afghans—participated in Anaconda.[71] It was clearly reflective of an annihilation strategy aimed at destroying enemy fighters ensconced in the rugged terrain in eastern and southeastern Afghanistan. Approximately five hundred insurgents were believed to have been killed before it ended, though some one thousand to fifteen hundred fighters were thought to have been in the operations area.[72] Evidence suggested that, as at Tora Bora, some enemy forces fought a determined rear-guard action to enable other elements, including key leaders, to escape into Pakistan.

Between 2002 and 2009, US strategic and operational priorities shifted to Iraq, thus relegating Afghanistan to an "economy of force" mission. That was also the case elsewhere such as the Philippines, where (since 2002) President

Bush's War on Terrorism provided the auspices for reducing the capabilities of such groups as Abu Sayyaf and Jemaah Islamiyah.[73] While the coalition's main effort shifted to Iraq, al-Qaeda and Taliban elements infiltrated back into Afghanistan and reestablished control over provinces in the east and south where coalition presence was weakest. Between 2004 and 2006, insurgent attacks increased more than fivefold, and Taliban control began to strengthen in the regions around Kabul and Kandahar.[74] Coalition conventional forces concentrated on protecting twenty-five provincial reconstruction teams (PRTs), which had been established to promote local governance and stability and to help train Afghan national army and police units.[75] In contrast, special operations forces focused on carrying out decapitation missions against al-Qaeda leadership and other high-value targets, as well as quick-strike operations against Taliban enclaves. This approach culminated in the killing of Osama bin Laden on May 2, 2011, by a joint operation involving SEAL Team 6 and US Army special operations aviators.

Eighteen months prior to that, President Obama had authorized a controversial eighteen-month "surge" of 30,000 US troops to augment the nearly 70,000 already present in Afghanistan, in an effort to reverse the momentum of the Taliban. That increase brought the total of coalition troops to approximately 140,000, who would work alongside some 256,000 members of the Afghan army and police forces. The surge was to accomplish several operational objectives, the two most important of which were to reduce "the Taliban to levels manageable by the Afghan National Security Force (ANSF)" and "to increase the size of the ANSF."[76] Politically, the move was clearly an effort to replicate the counterinsurgency phase of the campaign in Iraq (discussed below) in order to show a good-faith effort to help stabilize Afghanistan on the part of the United States and thus to open the door for an honorable exit in the not-too-distant future. The model was thus "clear-hold-build-transfer," with the transfer to be made as swiftly as possible. A product of that emphasis was Operation Moshtarak ("Together"), a combined effort launched in February 2010 involving 15,000 coalition troops, about half of which were Afghans. Its objective was to liberate the Marja region of Helmand Province from the Taliban by vertically inserting coalition troops in a series of heliborne assaults and expanding their influence much like the so-called ink-spot (or oil-spot) strategy—that is, gradually increasing the areas one controls. The operation was a success: Marja was liberated, and 250 to 300 Taliban fighters were killed, for 48 coalition lives lost. However, the operation may have hurt relations with the Afghan populace.[77]

The Obama administration had essentially shifted to a counterterrorism rather than a counterinsurgency approach, which also occasioned the increased use of drones. As mentioned, drones (unmanned aerial vehicles, or UAVs) had been employed to detect terrorists or insurgents since the autumn of 2001.[78] By 2008, NATO's Joint Air Power Competence Centre reported that there were some 6,700 total UAVs in the inventories of NATO members; by the end of 2010, the US military had some 7,000 UAVs, most of which were smaller reconnaissance drones.[79] Drones appeared to offer one way to address the sanctuary problem: They provided the capability to conduct decapitation attacks against terrorists in areas that were inaccessible for political or logistical reasons. In 2010, about 115 drone attacks were conducted in Pakistan, more than twice the number of attacks the previous year.[80] Yet the shift in strategy was barely noticed as the use of drones drew fire. Criticism came first from those who wished to adhere to a counterinsurgency approach to the war but who failed to acknowledge the strategy had shifted. They argued that drones did little to help build relationships and trust between counterinsurgent forces and the populace. Second, a number of critics raised ethical concerns over the practice of targeted assassinations and the involvement of the CIA.[81] By 2013, criticism of the American use of drones reached fever pitch with questions concerning whether the United States could or would use drone strikes against US citizens on American soil. The US government responded that it would only use unarmed drones for law enforcement purposes and would not, as a matter of policy, use armed drones in strikes against US citizens on American soil.[82] In any case, evidence regarding the effectiveness of drone strikes is mixed.[83] As with any use of force, armed drones can prove effective under conditions in which enemy combatants can be clearly identified and isolated but can be counterproductive in ambiguous situations.[84] Their use did, however, reflect a larger shift in US policy in the direction of maintaining security through a smaller human footprint. Operational practice thus morphed in response to new political direction and new technological means and did so ahead of the ability of operational science to frame the weapon's advantages and disadvantages objectively.

The Iraq War

Military operations began in Iraq in March 2003 after nearly eighteen months' planning time—much more than had been available for the intervention in Afghanistan. By March 19, 2003, the land force component command of Central Command had 122,000 US soldiers and marines, as well as 21,000 British troops, at its disposal.[85] These numbers had been pared down considerably—by a process involving vigorous exchanges between the Office of the

Secretary of Defense and Central Command—from the earliest estimates, which had been as high as 500,000.[86] Military estimates tended to be higher to account for chance and uncertainty and for the likelihood of having to occupy a country of 438,000 square miles with a population of thirty-one million people after combat operations. Defense Secretary Rumsfeld dismissed most of the military's assumptions in favor of his own—namely, that Iraqi resistance would be light, Saddam's demise would be welcomed, if not facilitated, by the Iraqi people, and the ensuing occupation period would be short. The principles of transformation—speed, precision, knowledge, and interoperability (jointness)—would enable a smaller force to accomplish what a larger one would have been needed to do in the twentieth century. A small footprint would also keep costs down and reduce the operation's vulnerability to scrutiny.

The objective of Operation Iraqi Freedom was regime change: removal of Saddam's government from power, destruction or control of the regime's weapons of mass destruction, elimination of its ability to threaten its neighbors, and putting a more acceptable government in its place. Saddam had disposed his forces in series of concentric circles designed to defend against external as well as internal threats. The outer circle consisted of nine regular army divisions, reinforced by two Republican Guard divisions, in a defensive zone in and around Mosul; seven additional regular army divisions were deployed in the south around Basra. The inner circle, which protected Baghdad, comprised four Republican Guard divisions, one special Republican Guard division, one Republican Guard brigade, and one regular army brigade. Saddam's distrust of his own fighting forces was well placed, as coalition intelligence sources indicated that a number of Iraqi units had no intention of fighting and planned to surrender at the first opportunity. The Iraqi army was not as well equipped or motivated as it had been during Desert Storm a decade earlier, but it was still a sizeable force. Estimates varied, but Iraqi ground forces were expected to be in the range of three hundred thousand regular soldiers (sixteen divisions and one brigade), fifty thousand Republican Guard troops (seven divisions and one brigade), and forty-four thousand paramilitary troops, including *Saddam fedayeen* ("Saddam's men of sacrifice").[87]

Special operations forces were on the ground in Iraq by the time the celebrated "shock and awe" strike was executed on March 19 by F-117A stealth fighter-bombers synchronized with volleys of cruise missiles. The strike was an effort to eliminate key Iraqi leaders believed to be at the Dora Farms compound, but those leaders were not among the people killed in the raid. Had they been, coalition ground forces would still have had to invade in order to defeat those units of the Iraqi army that resisted, to disarm those that did not, and to conduct stability operations until a new central leadership was put in place. Extensive psychological operations designed to undermine Iraqi resistance, even buying off Iraqi commanders in some cases, had preceded the attack. Agreements were thus reached in advance with some Iraqi units, though steps were also taken to hedge against deception.

The coalition ground assault began on March 21 and took place along three axes of advance. The US V Corps advanced from Kuwait, west of the Euphrates River, to Baghdad, arriving there on April 7. The US First Marine Division, part of the First Marine Expeditionary Force (First MEF), advanced from Kuwait, east of the Euphrates River, toward Baghdad, arriving there on April 9 and linking up with the US Army's Third Infantry Division. The British First Armored Division, also part of the First MEF, advanced from Kuwait toward Basra on March 22 and arrived there on April 6. A fourth axis of advance from Turkey to Mosul was planned for the US Fourth Infantry Division, but it was canceled when the Turks denied US forces permission to transit. Instead, the 173rd Airborne Brigade assumed that mission.

True to the intelligence forecasts, most of the Iraqi divisions melted away or surrendered. However, some Republican Guard units did fight, though their efforts were not well coordinated and were swiftly crushed by the combined weight of the coalition's air-ground attacks. The *Saddam fedayeen* also occasionally put up fanatical, if fruitless resistance, using pickup trucks to launch frontal assaults against armored formations. Their tactics would change quickly, however, as they discovered that conducting ambushes and raids against supply vehicles was less dangerous and more profitable than taking on tanks and armored personnel carriers. The coalition's rapid advance on Baghdad left attack columns with supply lines as long as four hundred miles in some cases. The lack of "boots on the ground" meant that security was not consistent along the supply routes, nor could Iraqi noncombatants be adequately protected against attempts to ignite a civil war.

To effect regime change, Baghdad, considered by some to be Iraq's center of gravity, had to be captured and the Republican Guard crushed.[88] Those objectives were accomplished by mid-April 2003. At the time, US forces numbered 150,000 personnel (five divisions), and British and other coalition forces added a further 48,000 personnel (two divisions).[89] However, the character of the war changed during the summer and fall of 2003. Long-standing ethnic and sectarian tensions, which Saddam had contained through brutal repression, began to resurface. Ambushes, roadside bombings, and mortar attacks against coalition forces increased: Estimates for the period from September 2003 to October 2004 are that 3,493 attacks took place against coalition military and civilian personnel, resulting in 545 people killed and 1,103 wounded.[90] Mass killings of Iraqi civilians occurred along with uprisings by local warlords and militia leaders, such as Moqtada al-Sadr, in Fallujah and Najaf in 2004. Other violent criminal activities also rose, adding to the aura of disorder.

Coalition forces counterattacked in the fall of 2004 using a systematic approach that combined political preparation of the battlefield, communications campaigns to shape perceptions, and urban assault tactics. One by one over the next four years, urban centers such as Samarra, Fallujah, Ramadi, Najaf, Basra, Sadr City in Baghdad, and others that had become hotbeds for the insurgents were wrested away and restored to coalition control. Controversy still reigns over which tactics proved more effective in restoring control—direct fighting or counterinsurgency. In truth, there was much overlap between the two. US military units not only conducted violent search-and-destroy missions, often with far too liberal doses of firepower—they also searched for and applied other, nonkinetic techniques, and they did so in an iterative "trial and error" fashion until they found procedures that worked.

These techniques included procedures commonly associated with counterinsurgency principles, such as protecting the population, establishing rapport with local leaders, collecting intelligence, and the restrained use of firepower, and they were in evidence as early as 2005, as coalition forces continued their efforts to take back key population centers from the insurgents.[91] The US counterinsurgency manual (*FM 3-24/MCWP 3-33.5*) published in December 2006 codified some of these techniques and placed them within the larger context of classic insurgency and counterinsurgency theory.[92] The manual did not change the US military's mind as its authors seemed to have desired, as much as it validated the main counterinsurgency advice offered to units in the field during the preceding months by numerous defense scholars and consultants. The reorientation of the US military toward counterinsurgency techniques was neither a revolution from above, as many claim, nor a revolution from below, as others argue.[93] It was instead a clear outgrowth of information-age circumstances, which permitted a rapid, lateral exchange of information through e-mails, chat rooms, blogs, and video-teleconferencing. The counterinsurgency manual remained underread for many months after its publication, much to its authors' chagrin. Its publication did, however, coincide with the advice President Bush received from an ad hoc council in December 2006 regarding a potential way ahead for US military strategy in Iraq.

In January 2007, President Bush announced that a "surge" of US combat soldiers would take place that would bring American troop levels from 132,000 to nearly 168,000 by September. The additional soldiers would raise the number of brigade combat teams from fifteen to twenty, providing more operational flexibility. This flexibility was intended to facilitate clearing and holding activities in critical areas and for training Iraqi security forces. Results were mixed, however, as claims touting the measure's success tended to obscure cause and effect; naysayers could rightly point to the lack of political reconciliation but had to admit that violence had decreased.[94] In fact, by the time the surge was announced, considerable momentum was already under way due to the Anbar Awakening, an ethnic and sectarian cleansing that separated warring factions, innovative measures taken by coalition forces at local levels, and modest improvements in the capabilities of Iraqi security forces. The surge did consolidate or enhance some of that momentum. It also demonstrated American resolve at a critical time in the conflict. By mid-February 2008, even cautious defense scholars were able to say that in many places in Iraq—Mosul, Basra, parts of Baghdad, and in much of Diyala Province—"the defeat of al Qaeda was evident."[95] Such analysts were also quick to add, however, that Iraq would still require years of additional support to achieve effective governance. The United States and Iraq signed a security agreement in November 2008, and President Barack Obama established a timetable for withdrawal: US combat troops in Iraq were reduced to zero by January 1, 2012. Months later it was still not clear whether Iraq would prove capable of overcoming its deep sectarian and ethnic divisions to establish durable governance, economic, and security structures.[96] However, by then that problem, while important to many, was officially no longer the concern of the US military.

Conclusion

President Johnson's promise to do "what must be done" and "only what must be done" was rhetorically balanced to serve his administration's interests at the time. Yet it also reflects how successive administrations tended to approach the use of military force during the latter half of the twentieth century into the twenty-first. Even in the Gulf War, where the total weight of US and coalition forces could be considered militarily overwhelming, the destructive potential was unleashed in a controlled manner—and stopped once Iraqi forces abandoned Kuwait. As general practice, however, Johnson's promise was doomed to failure because the line between doing enough and doing too much was rarely the same for the political leaders or the principal institutions involved. The line also moved as American material and moral interests in the conflict increased or decreased. Arguably, the initial successes in Afghanistan and Iraq came too swiftly, and their effects blurred the line between doing too little and doing too much. For some, building viable states in Iraq and Afghanistan were always sufficient and affordable goals; the more those ends grew in cost, the more they became necessary goals. For others, nation-building was always a bridge too far that neither enhanced US security nor came at an affordable price.

By the War on Terrorism, the American way of war was more capable of delivering force in "a measured, limited, controlled, and deliberate way"—the goal expressed by one of McNamara's aides in 1964. This was true of all its weapon systems from firearms to ballistic missiles, as well as how it planned, trained, deployed, fought, resupplied, and refitted. In the process, however, it progressively lost mass, which in turn deprived US policy of flexibility. For all its ability to reach great distances and to extend the hand of US policy, the American way of war found that it had to rely increasingly on the willingness of its allies and coalition partners to help broaden its reach. Fortunately, that realization came in the eleventh hour and not later.

Notes

1. For opposing views on flexible response, see Gaddis, *Strategies of Containment*, 197–217, and Gavin, *Nuclear Statecraft*, 30–56.

2. Gaddis, *Strategies of Containment*, 241.

3. Since 1947, more than thirty US covert operations involving the CIA have taken place. See Daugherty, *Executive Decisions*. However, information regarding the CIA is often sensationalized, and only some actions have been declassified, hence only a sample of US covert operations is presented here.

4. Prados, *Safe for Democracy*, xiv, defines "covert" operations as those that conceal the identity of the sponsor and "clandestine" operations as those that conceal the action itself. See also Berger, "Covert Action," 32–39, which describes the legal authorities for such actions, and Best and Feickert, "Special Operations Forces," which compares the activities of special operations forces and CIA operations.

5. Dujmović, "Drastic Actions," 775–808.

6. Cullather, *Secret History*, 97.

7. Immerman, *CIA in Guatemala*, and ibid., 98–99.

8. The US intervention in Guatemala brought almost immediate criticism from the Western powers, and its political, social, and economic aftereffects have been mixed at best with decades of violence and repression occurring in its wake. Gleijeses, *Shattered Hope*.

9. Gendzier, *Notes*, 304–13.

10. Gambone, *Small Wars*, 25–26, and Geraghty, *Black Ops*, 158–59.

11. Jones, *Bay of Pigs*, 95–111, and Prados, *Safe for Democracy*, 237–38.

12. Prados, *Safe for Democracy*, 203, 312.

13. Grow, *U.S. Presidents*.

14. Ibid., 69. See also Rabe, *U.S. Intervention*.

15. Parker, *Brazil*.

16. Gaddis, *Strategies of Containment*, 235–71.

17. *American Military History*, 632.

18. Herring, *America's Longest War*.

19. MacGarrigle, *United States Army*, 19.

20. Herring, "1st Cavalry."

21. The program's name was changed from "Revolutionary" to "Rural" in 1970. Scoville, *Reorganizing*, v.

22. However, they were not equipped to withstand the final offensive of the NVA in 1975. Cf. Veith, *Black April*; McKenna, *Kontum*; Scoville, *Reorganizing*; Hunt, *Pacification*; and Krepinevich, *Army and Vietnam*.

23. The Phoenix Program also played a role. It was an offshoot of CORDS and was developed to counter Viet Cong infiltration of South Vietnam's political infrastructure. Andradé, *Ashes to Ashes*.

24. Wirtz, *Tet Offensive*, and Stanton, *Rise and Fall*.

25. Clarke, *Advice and Support*.

26. Andradé, *Trial by Fire*.

27. Thompson, "Operations over North Vietnam," and Gentile, "Chimera of Success."

28. Sherwood, *Nixon's Trident*.

29. Gentile, "Chimera of Success," 231–35, offers a negative assessment of pacification.

30. *FM 100-5: Operations*, 1-1.

31. Naveh, *In Pursuit*, 263, describes it as "the longest, most intoxicating and creative professional debate which ever occurred in the history of American military thought."

32. Congressional Budget Office, *Assessing Military Balance*, xvi.

33. *FM 100-5: Operations*, 2–1, 2–2; Swain, "Filling the Void," 159; and English, "Operational Art," 16.

34. English, "Operational Art," 16.

35. Naveh, *In Pursuit*, 292–95.

36. Swain, "Filling the Void," 147–72; Hughes, "Naval Operations," 23–46; and Rubel, "Slicing the Onion," 107–14. By comparison, contemporary British military practitioners talk about four levels: grand-strategic, military-strategic, operational, and tactical. Kiszely, "Thinking about Operational," 38–44.

37. Watts et al., *Uses and Limits*.

38. House, "Operation Urgent Fury."

39. Department of Defense, *Grenada*.

40. Bolger, *Americans at War*, 276–80, describes the process.

41. Aspin, "Operation Just Cause."

42. *Operation Just Cause*, 44. US casualties were 23 killed and 322 wounded. PDF casualties were 314 killed, 124 wounded, and 5,300 taken prisoner. Estimates of civilian casualties range from 200 to several thousand.

43. *United States Forces, Somalia*, and Allard, *Somalia Operations*.

44. Stewart, "Historical Overview," 13.

45. Ibid., and Stevenson, *Losing Mogadishu*.

46. Allard, *Somalia Operations*, 4–7, 79–86, and Hirsch and Oakley, *Somalia*.

47. *JP 3-07: Joint Doctrine for Military Operations Other Than War*.

48. United Nations, Peacekeeping Operations.

49. Olsen, *John Warden*. In brief, Warden maintained that strategic paralysis or psychological collapse would result by attacking critical points in each of five "rings" simultaneously: leadership, organic or system essentials, infrastructure, population, and fielded military forces. Warden, "Enemy as a System."

50. Freedman and Karsh, *Gulf Conflict*, 316–17.

51. Cordesman and Wagner, *Lessons of Modern War*, 588.

52. Brown, "Maturation of Operational Art."

53. *FM 100-5: Operations* (1993), 1-3, 1-4.

54. US Joint Chiefs of Staff, *Joint Vision 2010*, and *Joint Vision 2020*.

55. Wentz, *Lessons from Bosnia*, 477.

56. Nation, *War in the Balkans*, 246.

57. Nardulli et al., *Disjointed War*, 3.

58. Gallis, *Kosovo*, 78–80.

59. Cf. Grant, *Kosovo Campaign*, and Hosmer, *Conflict over Kosovo*. The debate continues.

60. Department of the Air Force, *Air Force Manual 1-1*, 10.

61. Owen, "Operation Deliberate Force," 202.

62. Mason, "Operation Allied Force," 250.

63. Quadrennial Defense Review Independent Panel, *QDR in Perspective*, iii.

64. US Department of the Army, *Knowledge and Speed*.

65. The Afghan population before 2001 was estimated at 23 million people, of whom 78 percent were living in rural areas. Some of the major population centers were Kabul (2.5 million people), Kandahar (512,000), Mazar-i-Sharif (240,000), and Herat (167,000). However, the numbers are notoriously unreliable, due to years of civil war and significant refugee problems.

66. Millett, Maslowski, and Feis, *For the Common Defense*, 640.

67. Described in Echevarria, "Interdependent Maneuver," 95–104, written before 2001.

68. Cordesman, *Lessons of Afghanistan*.

69. Bowman, "Will America Lose," points out that Army rangers could have been inserted to block the escape but were not. See also Bernsten, *Jawbreaker*.

70. Cf. Maley, *Afghanistan Wars*, 222.

71. Summarized in Ballard, Lamm, and Wood, *From Kabul to Baghdad*, 68–72.

72. Naylor, *Not a Good Day*, 20–21.

73. Watts et al., *Uses and Limits*, 69–77. US military operations (Operation Enduring Force–Philippines) remained limited: approximately six hundred sol-

diers and $52 million per year. American efforts have remained tightly focused on counterterrorism and have been successful within that scope.

74. Security incidents increased from 900 in 2004 to 5,000 in 2006, and IED detonations increased from 352 in 2004 to 1,536 in 2006. Ballard, Lamm, and Wood, *From Kabul to Baghdad*, 137.

75. A twenty-sixth PRT was established in 2008. "Provincial Reconstruction Teams."

76. Woodward, *Obama's Wars*, 386.

77. International Council on Security and Development, *Operation Moshtarak*.

78. Harrington, "Briefing," and Singer, *Wired for War*.

79. These ranged from simple remotely controlled vehicles to large UAVs such as Global Hawk and Predator. The CIA flew drones from Langley Air Force Base in Virginia; the Air Force flew UAVs from Creech Air Force Base in Nevada. Singer, "Drones Don't Die."

80. Vanden Brook, "Coalition Attacks."

81. Sloggett, "Attack of the Drones"; Kilcullen and Exum, "Death from Above, Outrage Down Below"; and Peter Bergen and Katherine Tiedemann, *Year of the Drone*.

82. *PBS NewsHour* broadcast, March 7, 2013.

83. For the official military view, see "Kill/Capture" and the June 2011 PBS interview with Gen. David Petraeus.

84. Taj, "Year of the Drone Misinformation."

85. Millett, Maslowski, and Feis, *For the Common Defense*, 656.

86. For further details, see Gordon and Trainor, *Cobra II*, 4–23.

87. "Iraqi Ground Forces Organization."

88. Gordon and Trainor, *Cobra II*, 79.

89. Malkasian, "Counterinsurgency in Iraq," 288.

90. Cordesman with Baetjer, *Iraqi Security Forces*, 32, table 2.1.

91. Russell, *Innovation, Transformation*.

92. The commercially accessible edition is *The U.S. Army–Marine Corps Counterinsurgency Field Manual*.

93. For examples of the former, see Kaplan, *Insurgents*, and Ucko, *New Counterinsurgency Era*. For examples of the latter, see Russell, *Innovation, Transformation*, and Serena, *Revolution*.

94. For a range of opinions, see "Assessing the Synergy Thesis," and Fisher, "3 Years Later."

95. Faughnan, "Cordesman on Iraq."

96. Cordesman and Khazai, *Patterns of Violence in Iraq*.

Conclusions
and Observations

What we believe and what we do today is governed at least as much by the habits of mind we formed in the relatively remote past as by what we did and thought yesterday.

Russell Weigley, 1973

INTEREST IN THE AMERICAN WAY OF WAR may well have begun in earnest in 1973 with Weigley's landmark work. However, it remains strong today largely because of the desire to understand how the United States, the world's sole superpower, might use military force in the future. This is important information not only for Americans, but also for their allies and prospective coalition partners. To return to where this book began, to Weigley's assumption about habits of mind, it is reasonable to believe that the way Americans used war in the past will resemble how they will use it in the future.

However, as this book has shown, some habits of mind regarding the American way of war are based on inaccurate information. They have little in common with the historical record and yet are remarkably difficult to break. What follows are several conclusions concerning the most popular of these habits: the belief that the American approach to war is both apolitical and astrategic and that its chief characteristic is the use of overwhelming force to crush its opponents. The book concludes with observations regarding America's strategic centers of gravity and its way of battle.

American Policy and Politics

Clausewitz was surely right to declare that "war is nothing less than the continuation of policy [*Politik*] by other means."[1] However, as Clausewitz scholars have since reminded readers, the German word *Politik* can mean both policy and politics. Both meanings can, in fact, be applied to the American way of war. The American style of waging war has clearly been the continuation of US policy by other means, where policy is not actually the "collective interests" of a community, as Clausewitz so referred to it, but rather a set of prioritized interests.[2] It is also true that the American way of waging war has been the continuation of American politics, or political interaction, by other means, not only internationally but domestically. Going to war or withdrawing from one tended to crystallize what an administration stood for and prioritized its interests. It is this prioritization, moreover, that invariably draws criticism from the political opposition, which at a minimum can argue that the war is either drawing too much attention or not enough.

That was the case with Federalist opposition to "Mr. Madison's war" in 1812. By the summer of 1814, as much of Washington burned, it was not clear that Madison could administer his war at all, let alone do so without compromising the founding principles of the republic. In contrast, President James K. Polk, elected on an annexationist platform in 1844, was determined to make good on its planks. However, his decision to acquire Mexico's northern territories through military force meant exacerbating the tensions within the American body politic, as well as putting his own and the nation's honor on the line. The great irony of going to war "to extort" respect, as the *New Orleans Bulletin* put it in April 1846, is that respect can be lost even if the war is won.[3] Polk's war had its downturns in 1846 and 1847, and each made the specter of dishonor loom larger. Several times, in fact, the Mexican conflict, self-evidently a war of choice, threatened to become an unmanageable political liability for the Polk administration. Yet he was unable to extract the United States from the war he essentially started without losing the very honor he set out to regain. Some measure of national honor was lost, in any event, due to the atrocities committed by US troops. Ulysses S. Grant, one of America's most acclaimed soldiers and a veteran of that conflict, had good cause indeed to refer to it as a "wicked war."[4]

The relationship between American policy and American politics remained antagonistic and divisive throughout the twentieth century. Divisions ran deep even through the presumed unifying effect of two world wars and the Cold War. Wilson may have believed the United States was chosen to show other nations how to "walk in the paths of liberty."[5] However, many Republican leaders, such as Henry Cabot Lodge, did not share his sentiments and blocked that walk at every opportunity, especially insofar as it required the United States to commit to the League of Nations. Republican opposition to Roosevelt became less vocal when the war broke out but never disappeared; it had less to do with the question of whether to intervene than how and under whose leadership.[6] Until the passage of the Lend-Lease Act in March 1941, Roosevelt was obliged to work around that opposition and the nation's neutrality laws to begin building his "great arsenal of democracy" without which the Allies could not have won the war. Eisenhower's intervention in Guatemala came at the height of Sen. Joseph McCarthy's anticommunist rampage in Congress.[7] A communist regime in Guatemala would not have posed a serious threat to the United States. However, not taking action when action could have been taken would have left Eisenhower looking weak at the time—and American domestic politics in the 1950s called for hard lines and strong stands. Eisenhower later counted the coup in Guatemala among his proudest accomplishments.[8] Kennedy's failed invasion of Cuba in 1961 was in part driven by his desire to stand firm against communist encroachment. However, it was also driven by his need to dispel Republican skepticism, including potential criticism from his predecessor Eisenhower concerning the youth and inexperience of a new generation of American leaders.[9] Johnson probably faced stronger antiwar sentiment and political criticism due to his escalation policies in Vietnam than any other US president in any other war. Domestic opposition to his policies was so strong, in fact, that he believed it was part of an international communist conspiracy, though the CIA found little evidence of any such foreign influence.[10] In 1968, the Vietnam conflict became "Nixon's War" and support for it was again largely divided along party lines; Democrats took the offensive and criticized how the war was being handled while Republicans defended it.[11] Similar results can be found in other American interventions, such as Kosovo, Iraq, and Afghanistan. As a rule, criticism from the opposition party focuses initially on the reasons for the war then shifts to how it is being directed, or rather misdirected, as the war progresses. Casualty numbers are exploited as evidence of an administration's strategic incompetence.

In short, the American way of war has been nothing less than political in every respect and in every period of its history. One may disagree with the policies that issue from the battles and campaigns that make up American politics, yet it is clear that both policy and politics have influenced US military practice. At times that influence has been detrimental to good strategy but not always. As Lincoln demonstrated with Antietam and Roosevelt showed with Midway, military success can be enhanced by the hand of policy.[12] Insofar as war is ever an art, it is less so in the way battles are won than how they are used. If war is truly an instrument of policy, then its success as such depends greatly on the dexterity of the hand wielding it.

American Military Strategy

As these chapters have shown, rather than being astrategic, American military practice drew from a great number of military strategies. From the Revolutionary War through most of the nineteenth century, American military strategy was barely more than a system of expedients, despite the growing influence of Jominian principles on US military doctrine. Overall, its patterns reveal a functional, if uneven, blend of Jominian theorems oriented on controlling positional objectives and Clausewitzian concepts focused on defeating enemy forces. The emphasis shifted between the two approaches according to the situation. In the early stages of the Revolutionary War, Washington's and Greene's operations took place relative to the movements of the British army (enemy-oriented) but were keyed to the locations of towns, mills, and other resupply points (terrain-oriented). American land forces thus maneuvered defensively to protect or deny vital points to the British and generally fought only defensive battles, save for sundry raids as at Trenton and Sullivan's punitive expedition against the Iroquois Confederacy. At sea the Americans practiced an enemy-oriented *guerre de course* that mirrored the guerrilla warfare they carried out on land. By 1781, the situation had changed, and the Americans—with the help of the French and to a lesser extent the Spanish—were able to go on the offensive, maneuvering not just to deny the British control of key positions, but to retake captured ones and to force the enemy into accepting battle under unfavorable conditions.

In the War of 1812, American military practice began with the intention of seizing key positional objectives along the St. Lawrence waterways. It retained that orientation in the North, except for several naval engagements that essentially amounted to battles of annihilation, until British and Canadian counteroffensives forced it onto the defensive. The Americans fought successful defensive battles in the North and the South, but the center—in the vicinity of the Chesapeake Bay and Washington—gave way, allowing government buildings and other city structures to be razed. The Mexican conflict, too, was a blend of Jominian and Clausewitzian approaches. The United States seized key cities and ports, which gave it control of Mexico's northern territories, while Taylor, then Scott, sought to engage the Mexican army in battle and to inflict a defeat severe enough to induce its government to sue for peace. That approach presumed the Mexican government was less committed than it was to retaining its northern territories.

Similarly, Scott's Anaconda Plan during the Civil War hinged on achieving a strategic positional advantage. It aimed at seizing vital lifelines of transportation and commerce and thereby to deprive the South of the wherewithal it needed to resist until Davis's regime capitulated. The strategy obliged the South to spend many of its limited resources defending far-flung points along its perimeter. However, it was not until the Union exerted relentless and devastating pressure against the Confederacy's interior, crushing its main armies and demonstrating that Southern lives and livelihood could no longer be protected, that the Confederacy surrendered. The Civil War was America's asymmetrical conflict of the nineteenth century. Its aims, the amount of physical and psychological effort exerted, and the eventual casualties and destruction were not at all representative of nineteenth-century wars. Regardless, the Civil War continues to be upheld as the benchmark against which other nineteenth-century American wars are compared.

In contrast, in the Spanish–American War, the United States sought a negotiated settlement with Spain. The US Navy won critical battles of annihilation at Manila Bay and Santiago Bay, while the army fought engagements and campaigns to take capitals and major cities, key positional objectives. This division of labor was natural, and it underscored the specific strengths and weaknesses of each service. However, it also highlighted a contemporary capability deficit within the US military. Ground forces could be raised relatively quickly at home, and naval forces could win decisive battles at sea, but without land forces on board or in forward bases, opportunities were lost to exploit the US Navy's initial successes, as McKinley desired. Time and again, it was not lack of tactical training that hampered US military practice, but rather inexperience at coordinating the fire and movement of large combat formations. That was the price of maintaining a small army and marine corps in peacetime.

In addition, Weigley's claim that American military strategy settled into a pattern of attrition or annihilation is not borne out by events. Americans actually employed various types of strategies. These ranged from decapitation as in the pursuit of Pancho Villa, to attrition as in the Great War and the Second World War, to annihilation as in Desert Storm, to terror as in the bombing of Tokyo, Berlin, Hiroshima, Nagasaki, and Hanoi, and to graduated pressure as applied against the Serbs in the 1990s. To these we must add the class of "clear-hold-and-build" counterinsurgency strategies, in the campaigns in Vietnam, Iraq, and Afghanistan, which attempted a blend of reducing enemy influence and controlling terrain. Accordingly, even though planning had routinized the implementation of military strategy, no single type dominated the American way of war for any appreciable length of time. Execution remained at the discretion of local commanders. By the Second World War, the scope and scale of modern armed conflict had grown too great for one type of military strategy to be applied uniformly. Thus military strategy of necessity became much more than the art of the general or admiral in overall command.

Even for America's so-called irregular conflicts—wars fought with and against Native Americans and against the Caribbean *cacos*, as well as the various counterinsurgency and stability operations conducted in the Philippines, Central America, Vietnam, Iraq, and Afghanistan—the functional blend of terrain-oriented and enemy-oriented strategies did not vary profoundly. With respect to the Seminole Wars, the Plains Indian Wars, and the campaigns against different Filipino groups, the prerequisites for a successful strategy were similar: Restrict the movement of hostile elements by securing key positions and expanding one's control, search for and destroy major base areas, and maintain an active presence to provide security for reconciliation and reconstruction. Two classic strategies, one military and one diplomatic, when married with the above techniques, also proved fruitful: "dividing and conquering"—finding tribes or individuals willing to aid the United States with intelligence and other assistance—and the carrot-and-stick approach, which punished undesirable behavior but also helped lure away support from the hostile groups by providing an appealing alternative to suffering or dying for someone else's misdeeds. The distinction between regular and irregular wars is, therefore, a dubious one. Similarly, each American conflict since the eighteenth century has been hybrid in important ways, rendering that descriptor superfluous. It is worth asking whether history can provide examples of any wars that were not hybrid in some way.[13]

Force—Overwhelming and Decisive

As the preceding chapters have also shown, the United States rarely employed overwhelming or decisive military force in its armed conflicts. Except for the final stages of the Civil War, some engagements in the Spanish–American War, and the closing battles of the Second World War, US forces most often fought either outnumbered or at roughly even numbers with its opponents. To be sure, the quantitative inferiority of US regulars was sometimes offset by adding volunteer units, local militias, or indigenous allies, or by using liberal amounts of firepower. Sizeable irregular forces—from Native Americans to volunteers to militiamen to local constabularies—assisted US regulars in virtually every nineteenth-century conflict. However, at times American numerical inferiority stemmed from the very practice of recruiting such irregulars, which joined only for short periods, as in the Mexican War, the Civil

War, and the Spanish–American War. Field generals, such as Winfield Scott, thus had to compensate for such shortfalls by modifying or halting operations to transfer troops from one command to another.

At other times, numerical inferiority resulted from unrealistic expectations concerning what military forces of even a small size ought to be able to accomplish. Perhaps the most egregious example of such expectations is Deputy Defense Secretary Paul Wolfowitz's query to war planners at US Central Command on the eve of the invasion of Iraq in 2003: "We have a brigade on the ground. Why can't we go now?"[14] A popular assumption among Western societies in the eighteenth and nineteenth centuries was that disciplined regulars could prevail over ill-disciplined foes. This assumption remained strong well into the first decade of the twentieth century, as evidenced by the US military's operations in the Caribbean and the Pacific; it was also integral to the tactical debates that occurred prior to the First World War.[15] Again, it was not a uniquely American assumption or practice. The British followed the same pattern in the Zulu Wars, in their campaigns in the Sudan, and in the Boxer Rebellion. The assumption was compromised in the second half of the twentieth century as the proliferation of assault rifles, rocket-propelled grenades, and improvised explosive devices turned even poorly disciplined militias into very destructive foes.

At times, the use of militias or indigenous forces actually increased the risk of failure. Commanders were obliged to rely on troops who, by their nature, were unreliable. This was true of state militias as far back as the eighteenth and nineteenth centuries because their interests did not necessarily align with those of the US government. Operational failures obviously put administrations in uncomfortable positions politically, as evidenced by the War of 1812, the Mexican War, and the Bay of Pigs invasion, among others. Such losses rendered administrations more vulnerable to criticism by the domestic opposition. As Presidents Madison, Polk, Lincoln, McKinley, Kennedy, Clinton, and George W. Bush discovered, the opposing parties were not inclined to show mercy in wartime. On the contrary, the domestic stakes are higher during war, and the game more earnest. Nevertheless, American political leaders frequently accepted the risk of employing limited or even insufficient force, either because they felt doing nothing was worse or because they did not fully understand the potential consequences of failure. In truth, the use of insufficient force sometimes sufficed, making it sufficient after all. The US military's campaigns against the Plains Indians succeeded, as did many (certainly not all) of its interventions in Latin America, Asia, and the Middle East. Many of these required significant escalation over time, as in the Philippine Insurrection and the Vietnam War, until US forces gained a numerical advantage. In others, numerical inferiority was offset by firepower and other technologies. Nonetheless, relying on small forces to accomplish big tasks was standard practice, if not a habit, and was more common than the use of overwhelming force.

Accordingly, American strategic and operational practice was seldom about the application of overwhelming force or even of decisive force. Instead, it was more frequently about employing sufficient means or what we might call "credible" force. In some cases, as in the Gulf War, all US military forces not committed elsewhere were employed, whether or not their sum could be considered overwhelming or decisive. In other cases, US administrations sent only the amount of force they deemed sufficient for enhancing or sustaining American credibility; hence the term *credible force*. More force was sent to remove Noriega from power than proved necessary, in part to enhance US credibility, not only in Latin America but globally. Often this political calculus arrived at an amount of force lower than the military desired, as with the initial levels of force typically approved by Wilson, Eisenhower, Clinton, and George W. Bush. Again, even though the US military often operated with less force than it wanted, it frequently found ways to accomplish its missions. The services' track record of doing more with less is hardly perfect, but it is respectable, and it is enough to undermine the Powell-Weinberger doctrine and its plea for employing only overwhelming force in military situations.

The fact that the amount of force deemed necessary by the military was sometimes overridden by larger political or strategic concerns, such as how an administration wished its actions to be seen on a global stage, makes yet another point. Many criticisms concerning the "astrategic" nature of the American way of war fail to consider US strategy from an appropriate level. American political and strategic decision making was more complex than the literature on strategic theory can capture, particularly once the United States emerged as a superpower after the Second World War. Strategy is typically represented as an art—or, better, a formula—the purpose of which is to balance ends, ways, and means in the service of policy. However, such representations portray strategy too abstractly and nearly sui generis. In practice, strategic decisions were usually taken with the outcomes of previous interventions in mind and with the intention of trying either to undo, set right, or replicate them. America's interventions in Latin America, Asia, and the Middle East thus are more understandable as part of a larger pattern, rather than as isolated events. Although this book is not an analysis of the practice of American grand strategy, which would require an additional volume, it does highlight the linkages between grand strategy and military strategy.

American Operational Practice

American operational practice expanded its repertoire of concepts and methods over more than two centuries, reflecting the influences of its European counterparts as it did so. The missions it had to accomplish ranged from decapitation to punishment to destruction to protection to show of force to evacuation to humanitarian relief, but these did not differ substantially from those in the nineteenth century. However, as mentioned, one critical dissimilarity was the degree to which small arms—assault rifles, rocket-propelled grenades, improvised explosive devices—proliferated within the operational environment and altered it. The successes the United States enjoyed with small numbers of personnel in Latin America and Asia in the early twentieth century were simply not possible one hundred years later due to the increased firepower available to modern paramilitary forces, militias, terrorist groups, and mercenaries. Each operation required more planning and higher levels of training for US personnel. Where once a single marine corps battalion could deal effectively with groups of armed bandits, a balanced task force with dedicated air support was necessary, as in Lebanon in 1983—and even then success was not guaranteed. Another key difference was that American operations in the late twentieth century frequently took place within the context of a coalition effort, whereas US interventions from the late nineteenth century through the Cold War were often done with the aim of preempting or precluding the influence of foreign interests.

As the twentieth century wore on, American operational methods became more sophisticated, with scientific analysis gradually replacing heuristic rules of thumb. Nonetheless, while the process was scientific, it was neither progressive nor linear. Science failed repeatedly throughout this era and for the combination of reasons stated earlier: Individuals and schools of thought were unwilling or unable to see the evidence when it was there or took the evidence further than it could go in order to protect their interests. Moreover, in too many cases, lessons bought dearly in one campaign were painfully relearned in a later one, despite abundant after-action analyses. Knowledge does not exist until it is accessed, which explains why institutional memory is perishable and often fails. As a consequence, operational science was repeated multiple times, making for effective but inefficient recall.

Although sound doctrine already existed for many situations, it was viable only so long as it was accessed and reaffirmed. Archived knowledge was not trusted, particularly in the 1990s, a period perceived to be rife with change. That era, following directly in the wake of the Cold War, was carelessly defined as being unlike any previous one. That definition worked against the

possibility of learning from the past. Noted defense scholars and other lumi-
naries contributed, perhaps unwittingly, to this attitude and helped fashion
a culture of anticipation that drew untenably sharp distinctions between the
past and the present.[16] Traditional ways of thinking or doing business were
hastily dismissed as no longer valid. The new security environment was described as "uncertain, volatile, complex, and ambiguous," and adapting to it
was believed to require a conceptual revolution.[17] Accordingly, operational
science had to be repackaged and sold anew at a rate commensurate with
the perceived pace of change. It is indefensible, in any case, to claim that the
present and the future are, or will be, more uncertain than the past when
the present is still being processed, the future is unknown, and the past is
problematic to access. To be sure, Sovietologists had to redefine themselves
after the Cold War, and the new security environment must have seemed
very unfamiliar to them and to those who had to develop new force-sizing
templates. However, many scholars had spent years studying terrorist groups
and insurgencies, and their collective knowledge was easily accessible.

American operational practice did not benefit from geography as much as
the conventional wisdom claims. Only in the First and Second World Wars
did the oceans prove sufficiently vast to provide the United States additional
time to mobilize, train, and deploy. However, the oceans themselves also became campaign theaters: They had to be fought for, controlled, and defended.
Thus they functioned more like another dimension of conflict than a genuine
barrier. Since 1776, protecting this dimension was a major concern for US
strategists. The conventional wisdom was that, once in theater, American
citizen-soldiers would have sufficient numerical superiority to compensate
for their lack of training and experience. Numerical superiority would thus
enable US troops to learn on the job. However, with some notable exceptions
such as the Allied invasion of North Africa (Operation Torch) in 1942, which
succeeded despite the inexperience of US forces, that luxury was seldom
available. Nor does the conventional wisdom take into account the political
pressures US leadership received from allies and coalition partners, especially during the world wars, to get American combat troops into the conflict quickly and in large numbers. The initial flow of US forces was barely
sufficient to satisfy that demand, even though the expansion of American
combat power actually began several months before the Japanese attack on
Pearl Harbor.

Contrary to popular belief, twentieth-century American operational practice saw few genuine Kuhnian paradigm shifts to revolutionary ways of thinking. Rather, what took place was more akin to paradigm "tiering." Like layers
of sediment, earlier paradigms were partially covered by newer ones but were

never physically displaced. This occurrence was especially true for counter-insurgency doctrine, which in the American context had practical applications going back at least to the eighteenth century. It was also the case for the theories of the celebrated "master strategists," such as Clausewitz, Jomini, or Sun Tzu. Contemporary complexity theory, for instance, did not displace Clausewitz but rather gave his ideas updated terms and new metaphors. Accordingly, despite the rhetoric of the transformation and counterinsurgency (COIN) eras, few genuine military revolutions actually occurred in American military practice. Instead, what took place were renaissances, where ideas and concepts were rediscovered and revised to fit new situations.

Likewise, the RMA that Rumsfeld attempted to carry out was not a revolution but merely a replication of the Cold War model used in Latin America—albeit with the integration of better communications, increased firepower, and stealth technologies. In any case, a revolution is precisely the wrong approach to take in an era believed to be characterized by great uncertainty. Such periods require methods that explore a wide variety of ideas and develop hedging strategies to cope with failed assumptions. Revolutions, on the other hand, create articles of faith around a single way forward. They rely on leaps of faith and dogma, not the logic and rigorous analysis of science. Such revolutions are, in essence, expressions of art in the extreme. The RMA model collapsed in Iraq and Afghanistan for the same reason that the operation in Cuba failed in 1961: It tried too hard to do just enough without doing too much, and the tensions in its bifurcated character were left unresolved. The attempted RMA and COIN revolutions created an uneasy synthesis among the American military's industrial-age and information-age principles of war and its COIN doctrine. Such tension can be healthy, provided the US military follows up with rigorous postaction analyses of its operational successes and failures. However, it is just as likely that individual schools of thought will persist in their claims, with each drawing contrary lessons from the conflict and digging in to protect their interests.

The failed attempt to revive the Cold War model of small-scale, hybrid interventions also suggests a further observation: Operational art and creativity can rarely overcome failures in operational science. One salient example is the concept of center of gravity. The process of determining an opponent's center of gravity grew from a relatively simple task in the early twentieth century, when it was considered to be the enemy's main force, to an exercise in frustration one century later. Some contemporary approaches are more difficult to implement than the original concept and—as a number of practitioners have recently attested—do not necessarily lead to an actual center of gravity. Clausewitz warned against using "elaborate scientific guidelines as if they were a kind of truth apparatus [*Wahrheitsapparat*]" and preferred employing the natural processes of the mind.[18] The concept was never intended to be reduced to a formula. Determining a center of gravity is thus truly a case where operational science failed to contain operational art.

American Centers of Gravity

With that point in mind, it is worth noting that America's commanders in chief have generally been its strategic centers of gravity. Political gains and losses were ultimately evaluated in the minds of the presidents. As noted earlier, a failed or failing operation tends to become a political liability, just as a successful operation has the opposite effect, enhancing the prestige and clout of an administration. This was as true for George Washington's administration in the wars for the Northwest Territory and the Whiskey Rebellion as it was for that of Barak Obama and the conflicts in Iraq and Afghanistan. Presidents decided whether to take military action, whether to appoint or relieve military commanders, and how to set the broad contours of military strategy. In some cases, they even approved specific military actions within those operations. Historically, America's strategic center of gravity has rarely been the will of the public, contrary to conventional wisdom. While American heads of state have taken into account the public's perceived willingness to support military action, presidents from Woodrow Wilson to George W. Bush have acted according to what they believed was in the best interests of the United States, regardless of the public's actual wishes (insofar as they can be known). Even in cases where public opinion seemed particularly strong in one direction or the other, as with the interventions in Vietnam and Somalia, Johnson's and Clinton's decisions revolved around presidential perceptions of public support rather than its actual resolve, which is difficult to measure.

John Adams's handling of the Quasi-War with France and James Madison's direction of the War of 1812 illustrate the point further. Adams avoided yielding to either Federalist or Republican pressures and kept the war limited. In contrast, Madison's inability to develop a sound strategy for the war shows that a weak president can still be a center of gravity.[19] Presidents Polk, Wilson, and Clinton, among others, attempted to apply force in measured ways. Wilson, in particular, did so quite frequently—seven times within a span of four years (1914–18): Mexico (twice), Haiti, Dominican Republic, World War I, northern Russia, and Siberia. In each case, he reserved the right to decide when his political objectives had been met or indeed if they could not be.[20] Lincoln's use of force during the Civil War, described by some as the "supreme emergency of American history," differed but was hardly less controlled.[21]

Whatever image of Lincoln one prefers—political genius or enlightened despot—he was the North's strategic focal point.[22] The fact that the character of a war can change when a president is assassinated or is otherwise succeeded suggests the center of gravity lies more with the individual than with the office. Johnson changed the character of the war in Vietnam after Kennedy's assassination by escalating the conflict, all the while presumably holding out hope for a "favorable settlement."[23] Johnson's policies in 1965 amounted to a significant change, but his desire to avoid being the first US president to lose a war took precedence. Nixon altered the character of the war yet again with his Vietnamization policy and the escalation of the air campaign. To be sure, the War Powers Act (1973) put temporal limitations on the executive branch's use of military force abroad.[24] Nonetheless, as experts acknowledge, it has not been entirely effective at restraining presidential powers.

A Way of Battle

American strategic and operational practice rests, and has long rested, on the assumption that battlefield victories make for successful campaigns, which in turn lead to victorious wars. If the American way of war has shown any consistency over time, it is this belief that tactical victory redounds in favor of strategic success. Negotiations take place *after* and therefore *because of* battlefield victories (or decisive operations, in military parlance). This belief is actually rooted in both Jominian and Clausewitzian doctrine—especially the latter—and is hardly unique to the America way of war. Evidence for it can be found in most contemporary studies of Western operational art. Moreover, the rationale for institutionalizing the operational level of war was ostensibly to strengthen the linkages between tactics and strategy. Obviously, for the American way of war, as well as many others, what happens in the realm of tactics does, in fact, matter. American operational experiences in Vietnam and in Iraq and Afghanistan severely challenged this belief but never truly overturned it. Winning and losing battles has thus remained relevant to the American way of war.

Nevertheless, as an examination of America's wars from the eighteenth century onward shows, a gap often emerged between the final "decisive" battle and the actual signing of the treaty ending the conflict. For the Revolutionary War, for instance, the period from the surrender of Cornwallis's forces at Yorktown on October 19, 1781, and the Treaty of Paris, signed on September 3, 1783, was nearly two years. The principal reason for the delay was that America's allies in the conflict, France and Spain, also had to be satisfied with the terms of the treaty but initially were not. Each held out for the possibility of further concessions from Britain, but the delay also placed greater strain on the American government and US military forces, as they could not be fully disbanded. For the war with Mexico, Scott's forces secured the surrender of Mexico City on September 14, 1847. However, the Treaty of Guadalupe Hidalgo was not signed until February 2, 1848, almost five months later, and not ratified until May 30, 1848, four months after that. Even then, US troops were not fully withdrawn until June 1849, twenty-one months after the surrender of Mexico City. The American Civil War was a somewhat different case, as occupation, though extensive, occurred after the Confederate government was disestablished. For the war with Spain, a period of five months elapsed between the capture of Santiago and the Treaty of Paris, signed on December 10, 1898.

This pattern holds true for many of America's twentieth-century wars as well. The US military routinely had to continue fighting even as negotiations were well under way or had to begin performing extensive occupation duties. Examples of the former are the Korean and Vietnam conflicts. In each of these cases, major military operations continued for some time in the hope of bringing the adversary to the negotiating table. American troops are still present in South Korea, but they are there to prevent North Korea from breaking the terms of the treaty. Even well after a treaty was signed, American troops often had to perform occupation duties, as in the Philippines, China, Panama, Cuba, Nicaragua, Haiti, the Dominican Republic, Germany, Japan, Afghanistan, Iraq, and elsewhere. Some of these duties involved training indigenous security personnel and building or rebuilding critical infrastructure and thus resemble contemporary doctrinal categories of stability operations and support operations. While often tedious and unrewarding, occupation duties nonetheless extend the reach of policy by enforcing a treaty's terms.

Although several studies have examined the problem of "war termination" more closely, the larger point is that a longish interval between victory on the battlefield and a ratified treaty is the rule rather than the exception.[25] Failure to acknowledge the rule has caused the American way of war to become a way of battle more than a way of war. Again, this failure is hardly unique to Americans. It is actually fundamental to Western militaries, most of which see tactical victory as the sine qua non of war. Revising the American way of battle will require redefining the US military's operational framework so it does not suggest that capitulation and peace flow directly from decisive operations. It will also require revisiting the assumption that soldiers should leave the realization of policy objectives to the deft hand of policymakers. In practice, American military personnel have been intimately involved in achieving policy aims. American military theory and doctrine would do well to catch up to American military practice.

This book has endeavored to rediscover the American way of war by examining how it was practiced. It strove to bridge Weigley's history of ideas and the rich and plentiful narratives of America's battles and campaigns. Of necessity, it had to sacrifice some depth for breadth. A truly comprehensive account of the American style of waging war would fill several volumes. One volume would surely have to be a comparison of the American way of war to its British, French, German, and Russian counterparts. However, it would probably reveal that the American version has fared no worse historically than the others. All had their successes and failures, few of which were as clear-cut as the conventional wisdom claims. One point worth bearing in mind is that we can only know a way of war historically—by piecing together what it has done. Such a history offers valuable insights for any scholar or practitioner, particularly regarding the many considerations that have gone into American decisions to use force. However, this knowledge does not permit us to predict what the American way of war will be in the next decade or even in the next half decade. That does not diminish the value of the knowledge—only the uses to which it can be put. Prediction has always been a risky habit of mind in any case.

Notes

1. Clausewitz, Vom Kriege, bk. 1, chap. 1, 210, and On War, 87.

2. Clausewitz, Vom Kriege, bk. 8, chap. 6B, 993, and On War, 607.

3. Cf. Greenberg, Wicked War, 96.

4. Greenberg, Wicked War, viii, citing Grant's Personal Memoirs.

5. Link, Woodrow Wilson, 6–7.

6. Polling data suggest the American public had already begun preparing itself for war psychologically about a year before the attack on Pearl Harbor. Berinsky, In Time of War, 51.

7. For Eisenhower's approach to dealing with McCarthy, see Smith, Eisenhower in War and Peace, 583–95.

8. Immerman, CIA in Guatemala, 5.

9. Freedman, Kennedy's Wars, 127.

10. Andrew, For the President's Eyes, 348.

11. Berinsky, In Time of War, 112–15.

12. Roosevelt, "State of the Union."

13. Other such titles include "compound warfare." See Huber, Compound Warfare. Of note is the exchange between Thomas Huber, Peter Mansoor, and Williamson Murray in the April 2013 Journal of Military History.

14. Cited in Thompson, "How the Iraq War."

15. Echevarria, *After Clausewitz*, 94–120.

16. Key examples are Mearsheimer, "Why We Will Soon"; van Creveld, *Transformation of War*; and Mary Kaldor, *New and Old Wars*.

17. Extracted from course texts for the US Army War College, 1999 to 2009.

18. Clausewitz, *Vom Kriege*, bk. 2, chap. 5, 332; *On War*, 168.

19. Ketchum, *James Madison*. See Taylor, *Civil War of 1812*. For a summary of partisan conflicts between Federalists and Republicans, see Watson, "Trusting." On Britain's other strategic concerns, see Black, "North American Theater."

20. For the opposite view, see Calhoun, *Uses of Force*, especially chapter 9, which maintains that Wilson's goals were realistic and justifiable.

21. Boritt with Pinsker, "Abraham Lincoln," 219.

22. Urwin, "Sowing the Wind," 41–43ff; McPherson, *Tried by War*; and Cohen, *Supreme Command*.

23. Graff, *Tuesday Cabinet*, and Vandiver, *Shadows of Vietnam*.

24. Grimmett, *War Powers Resolution*. The War Powers Resolution provides the following limitations: The constitutional powers of the president as commander in chief to introduce US armed forces into hostilities, or into situations where imminent involvement in hostilities is clearly indicated by the circumstances, are exercised only pursuant to a declaration of war, specific statutory authorization, or a national emergency created by attack upon the United States, its territories or possessions, or its armed forces.

25. For examples, cf. Caraccilo, *Beyond Guns*; Rose, *How Wars End*; Moten, *War Termination*; and Pillar, *Negotiating Peace*.

Bibliography

Adamsky, Dima P. *American Strategic Culture and the US Revolution in Military Affairs*. Oslo: Norwegian Institute for Defence Studies, 2008.

———. "Jihadi Operational Art: The Coming Wave of Jihadi Strategic Studies." *Studies in Conflict and Terrorism* 33, no. 1 (January 2010): 1–18.

Advisor Handbook for Stability Operations. Washington, DC: Department of the Army, 1967.

Allard, Kenneth. *Somalia Operations: Lessons Learned*. Washington, DC: National Defense University Press, 1995.

Ambrose, Steven E. *Halleck: Lincoln's Chief of Staff*. Baton Rouge: Louisiana State University Press, 1962.

American Military History. Washington, DC: US Army Center of Military History, 1989.

Andradé, Dale. *Ashes to Ashes: The Phoenix Program and the Vietnam War*. Lexington: Lexington Books, 1990.

———. *Trial by Fire: The 1972 Easter Offensive, America's Last Vietnam Battle*. New York: Hippocrene, 1995.

Andrew, Christopher. *For the President's Eyes Only: Secret Intelligence and the American Presidency from Washington to Bush*. New York: HarperCollins, 1995.

Appleman, Roy E. *South to the Naktong, North to the Yalu*. Washington, DC: US Army Center of Military History, 1992.

"Armed Forces: Fighting Brush Fires." *Time*, September 29, 1961. http://content.time.com/time/magazine/article/0,9171,895690,00.html (accessed January 21, 2013).

Arms, Anita M. "Strategic Culture: The American Mind." In *Essays on Strategy IX*. Washington, DC: National Defense University Press, 1993.

Aspin, Les. "Operation Just Cause: Lessons and Warnings in the Future Use of Military Force." Report to the House Committee on Armed Services, January 12, 1990.

"Assessing the Synergy Thesis in Iraq: Correspondence from John Hagen, Joshua Kaiser, and Anna Hanson; Jon R. Lindsay and Austin G. Long; Stephen Biddle, Jeffrey Friedman, and Jacob Shapiro," *International Security* 37, no. 4 (Spring 2013): 173–98.

Atkeson, Edward B. "Adapting to the New American Way of War: Postmaneuver Security Operations." *Army* 53, no. 9 (September 2003): 8–11.

Aylwin-Foster, Nigel. "Changing the Army for Counterinsurgency Operations." *Military Review* 85, no. 6 (November–December 2005).

Babits, Lawrence E. *A Devil of a Whipping: The Battle of Cowpens*. Chapel Hill: University of North Carolina Press, 1998.

———. "Greene's Strategy in the Southern Campaign, 1780–1781." In *Adapting to Conditions: War and Society in the Eighteenth Century*, edited by Maarten Ultee, 135–49. Tuscaloosa: University of Alabama Press, 1986.

Ballard, John R., David Lamm, and John K. Wood. *From Kabul to Baghdad and Back: The U.S. at War in Afghanistan and Iraq*. Annapolis, MD: Naval Institute Press, 2012.

Bartley, Robert L. "Thinking Things Over: On the American Way of War," *Wall Street Journal*, July 15, 2002.

Bauer, K. Jack. "The Battles on the Rio Grande: Palo Alto and Resaca de la Palma, 8–9 May 1846." In Heller and Stofft, *America's First Battles*.

———. *The Mexican War 1846–1848*. Lincoln: University of Nebraska Press, 1974.

———. *Surfboats and Horse Marines: U.S. Naval Operations in the Mexican War, 1846–1848*. Annapolis, MD: Naval Institute Press, 1969.

Baylis, John, and Kristan Stoddart. "The British Nuclear Experience: The Role of Ideas and Beliefs (Part One)." *Diplomacy & Statecraft* 23, no. 2 (2012): 331–46.

Bellesiles, Michael A. "Western Violence." In *A Companion to the American West*, edited by William Deverell. Malden, MA: Blackwell, 2007.

Bergen, Peter, and Katherine Tiedemann. *The Year of the Drone: An Analysis of U.S. Strikes in Pakistan, 2004–2010*. Washington, DC: New America Foundation, 2010. www.newamerica.net/sites/newamerica.net/files/policydocs/bergentiedemann2.pdf.

Berger, Joseph B., III. "Covert Action: Title 10, Title 50, and the Chain of Command." *Joint Force Quarterly*, no. 67 (October–December 2012): 32–39.

Berinsky, Adam J. *In Time of War: Understanding American Public Opinion from World War II to Iraq*. Chicago: University of Chicago Press, 2009.

Bernsten, Gary. *Jawbreaker: The Attack on Bin Laden and Al Qaeda*. New York: Crown, 2005.

Best, Richard A., Jr., and Andrew Feickert. "Special Operations Forces (SOF) and CIA Paramilitary Operations: Issues for Congress." RS22017. Washington, DC: Congressional Research Service, 2009.

Biddle, Stephen. "The New Way of War? Debating the Kosovo Model." *Foreign Affairs* 81, no. 3 (May–June 2002): 138–44.

Biddle, Tami Davis. *Rhetoric and Reality in Air Warfare: The Evolution of British and American Ideas about Strategic Bombing, 1914–1945.* Princeton, NJ: Princeton University Press, 2002.

Binnendijk, Hans, and Stuart Johnson, eds. *Transforming for Stabilization and Reconstruction Operations.* Washington, DC: National Defense University Press, 2003.

Birtle, Andrew J. *U.S. Army Counterinsurgency Operations Doctrine, 1860–1941.* Washington, DC: US Army Center of Military History, 1998.

Black, Jeremy. "The North American Theater of the Napoleonic Wars, or, As It Is Sometimes Called, the War of 1812." *Journal of Military History* 76 (October 2012): 1053–66.

———. *Rethinking Military History.* London: Routledge, 2004.

———. *The War of 1812 in the Age of Napoleon.* Norman: University of Oklahoma Press, 2009.

Blumenson, Martin. "Kasserine Pass, 30 January–22 February 1943." In Heller and Stofft, *America's First Battles.*

———. *Patton: The Man behind the Legend.* New York: Morrow, 1985.

Bolger, Daniel P. *Americans at War, 1975–1986: An Era of Violent Peace.* Novato, CA: Presidio, 1988.

Bond, Brian. *Liddell Hart: A Study of His Military Thought.* London: Cassell, 1977.

Bonura, Michael A. *Under the Shadow of Napoleon: French Influence on the American Way of Warfare from the War of 1812 to the Outbreak of WWII.* New York: New York University Press, 2012.

Boot, Max. "Everything You Think You Know about the American Way of War Is Wrong." *Foreign Policy Research Institute.* E-notes, September 12, 2002. www.fpri.org/enotes/americawar.20020912.boot.americanwayofwar.html.

———. "The New American Way of War." *Foreign Affairs* 82, no. 4 (July–August 2003): 41–58.

———. *Savage Wars of Peace: Small Wars and the Rise of American Power.* New York: Basic Books, 2002.

———. "The Struggle to Transform the Military." *Foreign Affairs* 84, no. 2 (March–April 2005): 103–18.

———. *War Made New: Technology, Warfare, and the Course of History: 1500 to Today.* New York: Gotham, 2006.

Booth, Ken. "The Concept of Strategic Culture Affirmed." In Jacobsen, *Strategic Power.*

———. *Strategy and Ethnocentrism.* New York: Holmes & Meier, 1981.

Boritt, Gabor S., with Matthew Pinsker. "Abraham Lincoln." In *The Presidents*, 2nd ed., edited by Henry F. Graff. New York: Macmillan, 1997.

Botjer, George F. *Sideshow War: The Italian Campaign, 1943–45*. College Station: Texas A&M University Press, 1996.

Bowes, John P. "Transformation and Transition: American Indians and the War of 1812 in the Lower Great Lakes." *Journal of Military History* 76 (October 2012): 1129–46.

Bowman, Gary M. "Will America Lose Afghanistan—Again?" *Current History* 110, no. 735 (April 2011): 150–61.

Boyer, Paul S., et al. *The Oxford Companion to United States History*. Oxford: Oxford University Press, 2001.

Brigety, Reuben E., II. *Ethics, Technology and the American Way of War: Cruise Missiles and US Security Policy*. London: Routledge, 2007.

Brighton, Terry. *Patton, Montgomery, Rommel: Masters of War*. New York: Random House, 2008.

Brooks, Victor. *How America Fought Its Wars: Military Strategy from the American Revolution to the Civil War*. Conshohocken, PA: Combined Books, 1999.

Brown, John S. "The Maturation of Operational Art: Operations Desert Shield and Desert Storm." In Krause and Phillips, *Historical Perspectives*, 439–82.

Buley, Benjamin. *The New American Way of War: Military Culture and the Political Utility of Force*. London: Routledge, 2008.

Burk, James. "Public Support for Peacekeeping in Lebanon and Somalia: Assessing the Casualties Hypothesis." *Political Science Quarterly* 144 (1999): 53–78.

Butler, Smedley D. *War Is a Racket*. New York: Roundtable, 1935.

Calhoun, Frederick Sill. *Power and Principle: Armed Intervention in Wilsonian Foreign Policy*. Kent, OH: Kent State University Press, 1986.

———. *Uses of Force and Wilsonian Foreign Policy*. Kent, OH: Kent State University Press, 1993.

———. "The Wilsonian Way of War: American Armed Power from Veracruz to Vladivostok." PhD diss., University of Chicago, 1983.

Callwell, Charles E. *Small Wars: Their Principles and Practice*, 3d ed. East Ardsley, UK: EP Publishing, 1906.

Cann, John P. *Counterinsurgency in Africa: The Portuguese Way of War, 1961–1974*. Westport, CT: Greenwood, 1997.

Caraccilo, Dominic. *Beyond Guns and Steel: A War Termination Strategy*. Santa Barbara, CA: Praeger, 2011.

Cebrowski, Arthur. "The New American Way of War." Speech to the Heritage Foundation, May 13, 2003, reprinted in *Transformation Trends*, May 27, 2003.

Cebrowski, Arthur K., and Thomas P. M. Barnett. "The American Way of War." *Transformation Trends*, January 13, 2003.

Centano, Miguel Angel. *The Western Way of War*. CD presentation. Princeton, NJ: Princeton University, 2002.

"Champion of 'A New American Way of War.'" *Seapower* 46, no. 6 (June 2003): 15–16.

Chandler, David G. *The Campaigns of Napoleon*. New York: Macmillan, 1966.

Cheney, Dick. "A New American Way of War." Speech to the Heritage Foundation, May 1, 2003.

Chief of Staff, US Army. *Field Service Regulations: Special Operations.* Washington, DC: Government Printing Office, 1922.

———. *Field Service Regulations, United States Army: 1923.* Washington, DC: Government Printing Office, 1923.

Citino, Robert M. *Blitzkrieg to Desert Storm: The Evolution of Operational Warfare.* Lawrence: University Press of Kansas, 2004.

———. *The German Way of War from the Thirty Years' War to the Third Reich.* Lawrence: University Press of Kansas, 2005.

Clark, Wesley K. *Waging Modern War: Bosnia, Kosovo and the Future of Combat.* New York: Public Affairs, 2001.

Clarke, Jeffrey. *Advice and Support: The Final Years, 1965–1973.* Washington, DC: US Army Center of Military History, 1988.

Clausewitz, Carl von. *On War.* Edited and translated by Peter Paret and Michael Howard. Princeton, NJ: Princeton University Press, 1976.

———. *Vom Kriege: Hinterlassenes Werk des Generals Carl von Clausewitz,* 19th ed. Edited by Werner Hahlweg. Bonn: Dümmlers, 1991.

Clendinnen, Inga. "'Fierce and Unnatural Cruelty': Cortés and the Conquest of Mexico." *Representations* 33 (1991): 65–100.

Clifford, J. Garry. "World War II: Military and Diplomatic Course." In Boyer et al., *Oxford Companion.*

Coffman, Edward M. "The Meuse–Argonne Offensive: The Final Battle of World War I." In Moten, *War Termination,* 159–69.

———. "A Review of *The American Way of War.*" *Journal of American History* 60 (March 1974): 1090–91.

Cohen, Eliot A. *Conquered into Liberty: Two Centuries of Battles along the Great War Path That Made the American Way of War.* New York: Free Press, 2011.

———. "Kosovo and the New American Way of War." In *War over Kosovo: Politics and Strategy in a Global Age,* edited by Andrew J. Bacevich and Eliot A. Cohen, 38–62. New York: Columbia University Press, 2001.

———. "The Mystique of U.S. Air Power." *Foreign Affairs* 73, no. 1 (January–February 1994): 109–24.

———. *Supreme Command: Soldiers, Statesmen, and Leadership in Wartime.* New York: Anchor, 2003.

Collins, John M. *America's Small Wars: Lessons for the Future.* Washington, DC: Brassey's, 1991.

Congressional Budget Office. *Assessing the NATO–Warsaw Pact Military Balance.* Washington: Government Printing Office, 1977.

Cooper, Robert. "Hubris and False Hopes." *Policy Review* 172 (April 1, 2012): 5–15.

Corbett, J. S. *Some Principles of Maritime Strategy.* London: Longmans, Green.

Cordesman, Anthony H. *The Lessons of Afghanistan: War Fighting, Intelligence, and Force Transformation.* Washington, DC: Center for Strategic and International Studies, 2002.

Cordesman, Anthony, with Patrick Baetjer. *Iraqi Security Forces: A Strategy for Success*. Westport, CT: Praeger Security International, 2006.

Cordesman, Anthony H., and Sam Khazai. *Patterns of Violence in Iraq*. Washington, DC: Center for Strategic and International Studies, 2012. http://csis.org/publication/patterns-violence-iraq.

Cordesman, Anthony H., and Abraham Wagner, *The Lessons of Modern War: Volume IV—The Gulf War*. Washington, DC: Center for Strategic and International Studies, 1994.

Cornish, Paul, and Geoffrey Edwards. "Beyond the EU/NATO Dichotomy: The Beginnings of a European Strategic Culture." *International Affairs* 77, no. 3 (2001): 587–603.

———. "The Strategic Culture of the European Union: A Progress Report." *International Affairs* 81, no. 4 (2005): 801–20.

Cosmas, Graham A. "Daring Raid in the Philippines." *Military History Quarterly* 16, no. 3 (Spring 2004): 18–27.

———. "San Juan Hill and El Chaney." In Heller and Stofft, *America's First Battles*.

Crackel, Theodore. "Battle of Queenston Heights, 13 October 1812." In Heller and Stofft, *America's First Battles*, 35ff.

Craig, Gordon. "Delbrück: The Military Historian." In *Makers of Modern Strategy*, edited by Edward Meade Earle, 272–74. Princeton, NJ: Princeton University Press, 1943.

Crane, Conrad C. *American Airpower Strategy in Korea, 1950–1953*. Lawrence: University Press of Kansas, 2000.

———. "Coercion through Air Pressure: The Final American Campaign in the Korean War." In Moten, *War Termination*, 211–17.

Crowl, Philip A. "Alfred Thayer Mahan: The Naval Historian." In Paret, *Makers of Modern Strategy*.

Cullather, Nick. *Secret History: The CIA's Classified Account of Its Operations in Guatemala, 1952–1954*, 2d ed. Stanford, CA: Stanford University Press, 2006.

Daugherty, William J. *Executive Decisions: Covert Action and the Presidency*. Lexington: University Press of Kentucky, 2004.

Davis, Lance E., and Stanley L. Engerman. *Naval Blockades in Peace and War: An Economic History since 1750*. Cambridge: Cambridge University Press, 2006.

Dawson, Joseph. "Final Campaign of the Mexican–American War: Winfield Scott's Capture of Mexico City and Difficulties with Guerrillas." In Moten, *War Termination*, 95–105.

Department of the Air Force. *Air Force Manual 1-1: Basic Aerospace Doctrine of the United States Air Force*. Washington, DC: Government Printing Office, 1992.

Department of Defense. *Dictionary for Military Terms and Definitions*. Washington, DC: Department of Defense, updated periodically at www.dtic.mil/doctrine/jel/doddict/data/o/index.html (accessed August 7, 2012).

———. *Grenada: October 25 to November 2, 1983*. Washington, DC: Government Printing Office, 1983.

Department of History. *Definitions and Doctrine of the Military Art*. West Point, NY: United States Military Academy, 1979.

———. *History of the Military Art Course Book*. West Point, NY: United States Military Academy, 2001.

Donovan, James. *A Terrible Glory: Custer and the Little Big Horn—The Last Great Battle of the American West*. New York: Little, Brown, 2008.

Doughty, Robert A. *The Evolution of US Army Tactical Doctrine, 1946–1976*. Leavenworth Paper No. 1. Ft. Leavenworth, KS: Command and General Staff College, 1979.

Drezner, Daniel W. "The Power of Economics and Public Opinion." *Policy Review* 172 (April–May 2012), www.hoover.org/publications/policy-review/article/111651.

"Drones and US Strategy: Costs and Benefits." *Parameters* 42/43, no. 4/1 (Winter–Spring 2013): 7–33.

Dugard, Martin. *Training Ground: Grant, Lee, Sherman, and Davis in the Mexican War, 1846–1848*. New York: Little, Brown, 2008.

Dujmović, Nicholas. "Drastic Actions Short of War: The Origins and Application of CIA's Covert Paramilitary Function in the Early Cold War." *Journal of Military History* 76 (July 2012): 775–80.

Dupuy, R. Ernest. *Perish by the Sword: The Czechoslovakian Anabasis and Our Supporting Campaigns in North Russia and Siberia 1918–1920*. Harrisburg, PA: Military Service Publishing, 1939.

Dupuy, R. Ernest, and William Baumer. *The Little Wars of the United States*. New York: Hawthorn, 1968.

Echevarria Antulio J., II. *After Clausewitz: German Military Thinkers before the Great War*. Lawrence: University Press of Kansas, 2000.

———. "The Arms Race: Qualitative and Quantitative Dimensions." In *Cambridge History of War*, vol. 4, edited by Roger Chickering and Dennis Showalter. Cambridge: Cambridge University Press, 2011.

———. *Clausewitz and Contemporary War*. Oxford: Oxford University Press, 2013.

———. *Fourth-Generation War and Other Myths*. Carlisle, PA: Strategic Studies Institute, 2005.

———. *Imagining Future War: The West's Technological Revolution and Visions of Wars to Come, 1880–1914*. Westport, CT: Praeger, 2007.

———. "Interdependent Maneuver for the 21st Century." *Joint Force Quarterly* (Spring 2003): 95–104.

———. "Principles of War or Principles of Battle?" In McIvor, *Rethinking the Principles*, 58–78.

———. *Toward an American Way of War*. Carlisle, PA: US Army War College, Strategic Studies Institute, 2004,

Eisenhower, Dwight D. "Remarks to the National Defense Executive Reserve Conference on November 14, 1957." Dwight D. Eisenhower Library, Abilene, KS.

Eisenhower, John S. D. *Intervention! The United States and the Mexican Revolution 1913–1917*. New York: Norton, 1995.

———. "Polk and His Generals." In *Essays on the Mexican War*, edited by Douglas W. Richmond. College Station: Texas A&M University, 1986.

Engelhardt, Tom. *The American Way of War: How Bush's Wars Became Obama's*. New York: Haymarket, 2010.

English, Allan. "The Operational Art." In *The Operational Art: Canadian Perspectives, Context and Concepts*, edited by Allan English, Daniel Gosselin, Howard Coombs, and Laurence M. Hickey. Kingston, Ontario: Canadian Defence Academy, 2005.

Farrell, Theo. *The Norms of War: Cultural Beliefs and Modern Conflict*. London: Lynne Reinner, 2005.

———. "Strategic Culture and American Empire." *SAIS Review* 25, no. 2 (Summer–Fall 2005): 3–18.

Faughnan, Brian. "Cordesman on Iraq: 'Major Progress in Every Area.'" *Weekly Standard*, February 15, 2008. www.weeklystandard.com/weblogs/TWSFP /2008/02/cordesman_very_real_chance_of.asp.

Fehrenbach, T. R. *This Kind of War*. Washington, DC: Brassey's, 2000.

Feis, William B. "Jefferson Davis and the 'Guerrilla Option': A Reexamination." In *The Collapse of the Confederacy*, edited by Mark Grimsley and Brooks D. Simpson, 104–28. Lincoln: University of Nebraska Press, 2001.

Fischer, Joseph R. *A Well-Executed Failure: The Sullivan Campaign against the Iroquois, July–September 1779*. Columbia: University of South Carolina Press, 1997.

Fisher, Max. "3 Years Later, Did the Iraq Surge Work?" The Atlantic Wire, April 7, 2010. www.theatlanticwire.com/global/2010/04/3-years-later-did-the-iraq -surge-work/24912.

Fitzgerald, David. *Learning to Forget? US Army Counterinsurgency Doctrine and Practice from Vietnam to Iraq*. Stanford, CA: Stanford University Press, 2012.

Fleming, Peter. *The Siege of Peking*. Oxford: Oxford University Press, 1959.

Flint, Roy K. *Confrontation in Asia: The Korean War*. Carlisle Barracks, PA: US Army War College, 2000.

———. "Task Force Smith and the 24th Division: Delay and Withdrawal, 5–19 July 1950." In Heller and Stofft, *America's First Battles*, 265–99.

FM 31-15: Operations against Airborne Attack, Guerilla Action, and Infiltration. Washington, DC: Department of the Army, 1953.

FM 31-15: Operations against Irregular Forces. Washington, DC: Department of the Army, 1961.

FM 31-16: Counterguerrilla Operations. Washington, DC: Department of the Army, 1963, updated 1967.

FM 31-20: Operations against Guerrilla Forces. Washington, DC: Department of the Army, 1951.

FM 31-21: Organization and Conduct of Guerilla Warfare. Washington, DC: Department of the Army, 1951, updated 1955 and 1958.

FM 31-22: U.S. Army Counterinsurgency Forces. Washington, DC: Department of the Army, 1963.

FM 31-73: Advisor Handbook for Counterinsurgencies. Washington, DC: Department of the Army, 1965.

FM 100-5: Field Service Regulations. Washington, DC: Department of the Army, 1954.

FM 100-5: Operations. Washington, DC: Department of the Army, 1976, 1982, 1986, 1993.

Fogelman, Ronald. "Airpower and the American Way of War." US Air Force Association Air Warfare Symposium, Orlando, Florida, February 15, 1996.

Forrest, Morgan. *Compellence and the Strategic Culture of Imperial Japan: Implications for Coercive Diplomacy in the Twenty-First Century.* Westport, CT: Praeger, 2003.

Förster, Stig, and Jörg Nagler, eds. *On the Road to Total War: The American Civil War and the German Wars of Unification, 1861–1871.* Cambridge: Cambridge University Press, 1997.

Freedman, Lawrence. "Alliance and the British Way in Warfare." *Review of International Studies* 21 (1995): 145–58.

———. *Kennedy's Wars: Berlin, Cuba, Laos, and Vietnam.* New York: Oxford University Press, 2000.

Freedman, Lawrence, and Efraim Karsh. *The Gulf Conflict, 1990–1991: Diplomacy and War in the New World Order.* Princeton, NJ: Princeton University Press, 1991.

Freidel, Frank. *The Splendid Little War: The Dramatic Story of the Spanish-American War.* Short Hills, NJ: Burford, 2001.

French, David. *The British Way in Warfare, 1688–2000.* London: Unwin Hyman, 1990.

Friedman, Norman. *Terrorism, Afghanistan and America's New Way of War.* Annapolis, MD: Naval Institute Press, 2003.

Fuller, J. F. C. *The Foundations of the Science of War.* London: Hutchinson, 1926.

Futrell, Robert F. *The United States Air Force in Korea 1950–1953.* Rev. ed. Washington, DC: Office of Air Force History, 1983.

Gaddis, John Lewis. *Strategies of Containment.* Rev. ed. New York: Oxford University Press, 2005.

Gallis, Paul E. *Kosovo: Lessons Learned from Operation Allied Force.* Washington, DC: Congressional Research Service, 1999.

Gambone, Michael D. *Small Wars: Low-Intensity Threats and the American Response since Vietnam.* Knoxville: University of Tennessee Press, 2012.

Gavin, Francis. *Nuclear Statecraft: History and Strategy in America's Atomic Age.* Ithaca, NY: Cornell University Press, 2012.

Geertz, Clifford. *The Interpretation of Cultures: Selected Essays.* New York: Basic Books, 1973.

Gelpi, Christopher, Peter Feaver, and Jason Reifler. *Paying the Human Costs of War: American Public Opinion and Casualties in Military Conflicts.* Princeton, NJ: Princeton University Press, 2009.

Gendzier, Irene L. *Notes from the Minefield: United States Intervention in Lebanon and the Middle East, 1945–1958.* New York: Columbia University Press, 2006.

General Service Schools. *General Tactical Functions of Larger Units.* Ft. Leavenworth, KS: General Service Schools, 1926.

"Generation Kill: A Conversation with Stanley McChrystal." *Foreign Affairs* 92, no. 2 (March–April 2013): 2–8.

Gentile, Gian. "The Chimera of Success: Pacification and the End of the Vietnam War." In Moten, *War Termination*, 225–35.

George, Alexander L. *Forceful Persuasion: Coercive Diplomacy as an Alternative to War.* Washington, DC: United States Institute of Peace, 1997.

Geraghty, Tony. *Black Ops: The Rise of Special Forces in the CIA, the SAS, and Mossad.* New York: Pegasus, 2010.

Glatthaar, Joseph T. "Termination of the Civil War." In Moten, *War Termination*, 107–20.

Gleijeses, Piero. *Shattered Hope: The Guatemalan Revolution and the United States, 1944–1954.* Princeton, NJ: Princeton University Press, 1991.

Gordon, Michael R., and Bernard E. Trainor. *Cobra II: The Inside Story of the Invasion and Occupation of Iraq.* New York: Pantheon, 2006.

Graff, Henry F. *The Tuesday Cabinet: Deliberation and Decision on Peace and War under Lyndon B. Johnson.* Englewood Cliffs, NJ: Prentice Hall, 1970.

Graham, Dominick. *Tug of War: The Battle for Italy, 1943–1945.* New York: St. Martin's, 1986.

Grant, Rebecca. *The Kosovo Campaign: Aerospace Power Made It Work.* Arlington, VA: Air Force Association, 1999.

Grant, Ulysses S. *Personal Memoirs.* 2 vols. Princeton, NJ: Princeton University Press, 1998. First published 1885 by Charles Webster.

Graves, Donald E. "Why the White House Was Burned: An Investigation into the British Destruction of Public Buildings at Washington in August 1814." *Journal of Military History* 76 (October 2012): 1095–1128.

Gray, Colin S. "The American Way of War: Critique and Implications." In McIvor, *Rethinking the Principles*, 13–40.

———. *Irregular Enemies and the Essence of Strategy: Can the American Way of War Adapt?* Carlisle, PA: US Army War College, Strategic Studies Institute, 2006.

———. "National Style in Strategy: The American Example." *International Security* 6, no. 2 (Fall 1981): 35–37.

———. *Nuclear Strategy and National Style.* Lanham, MD: Hamilton, 1986.

———. *Out of the Wilderness: Prime Time for Strategic Culture.* Washington, DC: Defense Threat Reduction Agency, 2006.

———. "Strategic Culture as Context: The First Generation of Theory Strikes Back." *Review of International Studies* 25, no. 1 (1999): 49–69.

———. *The Strategy Bridge: Theory for Practice.* Oxford: Oxford University Press, 2010.

Greenberg, Amy S. *A Wicked War: Polk, Clay, Lincoln, and the 1846 U.S. Invasion of Mexico.* New York: Knopf, 2012.

Grenier, John. *The First Way of War: American War Making on the Frontier, 1607–1814.* New York: Cambridge University Press, 2005.

Griffith, Samuel B. *The War for American Independence: From 1760 to the Surrender at Yorktown in 1781.* Urbana: University of Illinois Press, 2002.

Grimmett, Richard F. *Instances of the Use of United States Armed Forces Abroad, 1798–2009.* CRS Report for Congress RL32170. Washington, DC: Congressional Research Service, 2010.

———. *War Powers Resolution: Presidential Compliance.* Washington, DC: Congressional Research Service, 2012.

Grodzinski, John R. "Opening Shots from the Bicentenary of the War of 1812: A Canadian Perspective on Recent Titles." *Journal of Military History* 76 (October 2012): 1187–1201.

Groom, Winston. *Kearny's March: The Epic Creation of the American West, 1846–1847.* New York: Knopf, 2011.

Grotelueschen, Mark E. *The AEF Way of War: The American Army and Combat in World War I.* Cambridge: Cambridge University Press, 2007.

Grow, Michael. *U.S. Presidents and Latin American Interventions: Pursuing Regime Change in the Cold War.* Lawrence: University Press of Kansas, 2008.

Gruber, Ira D. "America's First Battle: Long Island, 27 August 1776." In Heller and Stofft, *America's First Battles*, 1–32.

———. "From Cowpens to Yorktown: The Final Campaign of the War for American Independence." In Moten, *War Termination*, 31–42.

———. *The Howe Brothers and the American Revolution.* New York: Atheneum, 1972.

Gustavson, Ann T. "Carrizal 1916: A Re-examination." Unpublished manuscript, May 1, 2012.

Hagerman, Edward. "Union Generalship, Political Leadership, and Total War Strategy." In Förster and Nagler, *On the Road*, 141–72.

Hall, John. "Dubious Means and Unworthy Ends: Colonel William Worth's Campaign to End the Second Seminole War." In Moten, *War Termination*, 57–69.

Halleck, H. Wager. *Elements of Military Art and Science*. New York: D. Appleton, 1846; Westport, CT: Greenwood, 1971.

Hämäläinen, Pekka. *The Comanche Empire*. New Haven, CT: Yale University Press, 2008.

Hammond, Grant T. "The U.S. Air Force and the American Way of War." In McIvor, *Rethinking the Principles*, 109–26.

Hammond, Otis G., ed. *The Letters and Papers of Major General John Sullivan, Continental Army*. 3 vols. Concord, NH: New Hampshire Historical Society, 1939.

Hanson, Victor Davis. "The American Way of War." *National Review* 55, 7 (April 21, 2002): 10.

———. *Carnage and Cultures: Landmark Battles in the Rise of Western Power*. New York: Doubleday, 2001.

———. *The Western Way of War: The Infantry Battle in Classical Greece*, 2nd ed. Berkeley: University of California Press, 2000.

Harmon, E. N. "Notes on Combat Experience during the Tunisian and African Campaigns." In *Kasserine Pass Battles*.

Harrington, Caitlin. "Briefing: Unmanned Unbound." *Jane's Defence Weekly*, August 16, 2010.

Harrison, Richard W. *The Russian Way of War: Operational Art, 1904–1940*. Lawrence: University Press of Kansas, 2001.

Hart, Russell A. *How the Allies Won in Normandy*. Norman: University of Oklahoma Press, 2004.

Hassig, Ross. *Mexico and the Spanish Conquest*, 2nd ed. Norman: University of Oklahoma Press, 2006.

Hattaway, Herman, and Archer Jones. *How the North Won: A Military History of the Civil War*. Champaign-Urbana: University of Illinois Press, 1991.

Haw, James. "'Every Thing Here Depends upon Opinion': Nathanael Greene and Public Support in the Southern Campaigns of the American Revolution." *South Carolina Historical Magazine* 109, no. 3 (July 2008): 212–31.

Hayes, Mark L. "War Plans and Preparations and Their Impact on U.S. Naval Operations in the Spanish–American War." Naval Historical Center. www.history.navy.mil/wars/spanam.htm.

Hayward, Joel. *For God and Glory: Lord Nelson and His Way of War*. Annapolis, MD: Naval Institute Press, 2003.

Heilbron, John L., ed. *The Oxford Companion to the History of Modern Science*. New York: Oxford University Press, 2003.

Helfers, John. "Five Generals in Two Years: 1861–1865: The Union Army's Command-Level Failures." In *How to Lose the Civil War: Military Mistakes of the War between the States*, edited by Bill Fawcett, 129–36. New York: Harper, 2011.

Heller, Charles E., and William A. Stofft, eds., *America's First Battles, 1776–1965*. Lawrence: University Press of Kansas, 1986.

Herbert, Edwin. *Small Wars and Skirmishes 1902–18: Early Twentieth Century Colonial Campaigns in Africa, Asia, and the Americas.* Nottingham, UK: Foundry, 2002.

Herring, George C. *America's Longest War: The United States and Vietnam, 1950–1975.* New York: Knopf, 1979.

———. "The 1st Cavalry and the Ia Drang Valley, 18 October–24 November 1965." In Heller and Stofft, *America's First Battles,* 300–326.

Herwig, Holger H. "Innovation Ignored: The Submarine Problem—Germany, Britain, and the United States, 1919–1939." In Murray and Millett, *Military Innovation,* 227–64.

Hewes, James E., Jr. *From Root to McNamara: Army Organization and Administration, 1900–1963.* Washington, DC: Government Printing Office, 1975.

Hickey, Donald R. "1812: Remembering a Forgotten War." *Journal of Military History* 76 (October 2012): 969–72.

Higginbotham, Don. "The Early American Way of War: Reconnaissance and Appraisal." *William and Mary Quarterly* 44 (1987): 230–73.

Hirsch, John L., and Robert B. Oakley. *Somalia and Operation Restore Hope: Reflections on Peacemaking and Peacekeeping.* Washington: United States Institute of Peace, 1995.

Hitchman, James H. "US Control over Cuban Sugar Production 1898–1902." *Journal of American Studies and World Affairs* 12, no. 1 (January 1970): 90–106.

Hittle, James D. *The Military Staff: Its History and Development.* Westport, CT: Praeger, 1975.

Hoffman, F. G. *Decisive Force: The New American Way of War.* Westport, CT: Praeger, 1996.

Hogeland, William. *The Whiskey Rebellion: George Washington, Alexander Hamilton, and the Frontier Rebels Who Challenged America's Newfound Sovereignty.* New York: Simon & Schuster, 2010.

Hopf, Ted. "The Promise of Constructivism in International Relations." *International Security* 23, no. 1 (Summer 1998): 914.

Hosmer, Stephen T. *The Conflict over Kosovo: Why Milosevic Decided to Settle When He Did.* Santa Monica, CA: RAND Corp., 2001.

House, Jonathan M. "Operation Urgent Fury: Grenada, 1983." In *The United States Army in Joint Operations, 1950–1983.* Washington, DC: US Army Center of Military History, 1992.

Howard, Michael. "The British Way in Warfare: A Reappraisal." In Michael Howard, *The Causes of Wars and Other Essays,* 189–207. London: Unwin, 1983.

Howlett, Darryl. "Strategic Culture: Reviewing Recent Literature." *Strategic Insights* 4, no. 10 (October 2005). www.ccc.nps.navy.mil/si/2005/Oct/howlett Oct05.pdf.

Huber, Thomas M., ed. *Compound Warfare: That Fatal Knot.* Ft. Leavenworth, KS: US Army Command and General Staff College, 2002.

Huber, Thomas, Peter Mansoor, and Williamson Murray. "Letters to the Editor." In *Journal of Military History* 77, no. 2 (April 2013): 790–96.

Hughes, Daniel, ed. and trans. *Moltke on the Art of War*. Novato, CA: Presidio, 1993.

Hughes, Wayne P., Jr. "Naval Operations: A Close Look at the Operational Level of War at Sea." *Naval War College Review* 65, no. 3 (Summer 2012): 23–46.

Hunt, Richard A. *Pacification: American Struggle for Vietnam's Hearts and Minds*. Boulder, CO: Westview, 1995.

Huston, James A. *The Sinews of War: Army Logistics, 1775–1953*. Washington, DC: US Army Center of Military History, 1997.

Hutton, Paul Andrew. *Phil Sheridan and His Army*. Lincoln: University of Nebraska Press, 1985.

Ignatieff, Michael. "The New American Way of War." *New York Review of Books*, July 20, 2000.

Immerman, Richard H. *The CIA in Guatemala: The Foreign Policy of Intervention*. Austin: University of Texas Press, 1983.

International Council on Security and Development. *Operation Moshtarak: Lessons Learned*. London: International Council on Security and Development, 2010.

"Iraqi Ground Forces Organization." GlobalSecurity.org. www.globalsecurity.org /military/world/iraq/ground-org.htm.

Jacobsen, Carl G., ed. *Strategic Power: USA/USSR*. New York: St. Martin's, 1990.

James, D. Clayton, with Anne Sharp Wells. *Refighting the Last War: Command and Crisis in Korea 1950–1953*. New York: Free Press, 1993.

Jarecki, Eugene. *The American Way of War: Guided Missiles, Misguided Men, and a Republic in Peril*. New York: Free Press, 2008.

Jefferson, T. H., and George Rippey Stewart. *Map of the Emigrant Road from Independence, Mo., to San Francisco, California*. San Francisco: California Historical Society, 1945. First edition published 1849 by T. H. Jefferson.

Johnson, Robert. *The Afghan Way of War: How and Why They Fight*. New York: Oxford University Press, 2011.

Johnson, Timothy D. *A Gallant Little Army: The Mexico City Campaign*. Lawrence: University Press of Kansas, 2007.

Johnston, Alastair Iain. *Cultural Realism: Strategic Culture and Grand Strategy in Chinese History*. Princeton, NJ: Princeton University Press, 1995.

———. "Thinking about Strategic Culture." *International Security* 19, no. 4 (Spring 1995): 32–64.

Joint Publication 3-0: Joint Operations. Washington, DC: Government Printing Office, 2011.

Jomini, Baron de. *Art of War*. Translated by G. H. Mendell and W. P. Craighill. Philadelphia: Lippincott, 1862.

Jones, Archer. *Elements of Military Strategy: An Historical Approach*. Westport, CT: Greenwood, 1996.

Jones, Archer, and Herman M. Hattaway. *How the North Won: A Military History of the Civil War*. Urbana: University of Illinois, 1983.

Jones, Howard. *The Bay of Pigs*. Oxford: Oxford University Press, 2008.

Jones, Johnny R. *Development of Air Force Basic Doctrine, 1947–1992*. Maxwell AFB, AL: Air University Press, 1997.

JP 3-07: Joint Doctrine for Military Operations Other Than War. Washington, DC: Government Printing Office, 1995.

Kagan, Frederick. *Finding the Target: The Transformation of American Military Policy*. New York: Encounter, 2006.

Kagan, Robert. "A Comment on Context." *Policy Review* no. 172 (March 30, 2012). www.hoover.org/publications/policy-review/article/112376.

———. *Of Paradise and Power: America and Europe in the New World Order*. New York: Knopf, 2003.

———. "Power and Weakness: Why the United States and Europe See the World Differently." *Policy Review* 113 (June–July 2002).

Kaldor, Mary. *New and Old Wars*, 2nd ed. Cambridge, UK: Polity, 2006.

Kaplan, Fred. *The Insurgents: David Petraeus and the Plot to Change the American Way of War*. New York: Simon & Schuster, 2013.

Kasserine Pass Battles: Doctrines and Lessons Learned. Vol. 2, part 3. Washington, DC: US Army Center of Military History, 1993.

Katzenstein, Peter, ed. *The Culture of National Security: Norms and Identity in World Politics*. New York: Columbia University Press, 1996.

Keegan, John. *Six Armies in Normandy: From D-Day to the Liberation of Paris*. New York: Penguin, 1994.

Keithly, David. "Poor, Nasty and Brutish: Guerrilla Operations in America's First Civil War." *Civil Wars* 4, no. 3 (2001): 35–69.

Kelly, Francis J. *US Army Special Forces, 1961–1971*. Washington, DC: Department of the Army, 1973.

Kelly, Justin, and Michael J. Brennan. *Alien: How Operational Art Devoured Strategy*. Carlisle Barracks, PA: Strategic Studies Institute, 2009.

Ketchum, Ralph. *James Madison: A Biography*. New York: Macmillan, 1971.

Kilcullen, David, and Andrew Exum. "Death from Above, Outrage Down Below." *New York Times*, May 16, 2009. www.nytimes.com/2009/05/17/opinion /17exum.html.

"Kill/Capture: Interview; General David Petraeus." *Frontline*, June 14, 2011. www.pbs.org/wgbh/pages/frontline/afghanistan-pakistan/kill-capture /interview-general-david-petraeu/.

Kiszely, John. "Thinking about the Operational Level." *RUSI Journal* 150, no. 6 (December 2005): 38–44.

Kitfield, James. *Prodigal Soldiers: How the Generation of Officers Born of Vietnam Revolutionized the American Style of War*. Washington, DC: Brassey's, 1995.

Klein, Yitzak. "A Theory of Strategic Culture." *Comparative Strategy* 10, no. 1 (1991): 2–12.

Kobbe, William A. *Notes on Strategy and Logistics*. Ft. Monroe, VA: Artillery School, 1896.

Kober, Avi. "What Happened to Israeli Military Thought?" *Journal of Strategic Studies* 34, no. 5 (2011).

Krause, Michael D., and R. Cody Phillips, eds. *Historical Perspectives of the Operational Art*. Washington, DC: US Army Center of Military History, 2005.

Krepenevich, Andrew, Jr. *The Army and Vietnam*. Baltimore: Johns Hopkins University Press, 1986.

Kuhn, Thomas S. *The Structure of Scientific Revolutions*, 2nd ed. Chicago: University of Chicago Press, 1970.

Kupchan, Charles A. "A Still-Strong Alliance." *Policy Review*, no. 172 (April–May 2012): 59–70.

Lambert, Andrew. *The Challenge: Britain against America in the Naval War of 1812*. London: Faber & Faber, 2012.

———. "The Naval War Course, *Some Principles of Maritime Strategy* and the Origins of the 'British Way in Warfare.'" In French, *British Way*, 219–56.

Lambert, Frank. *The Barbary Wars: American Independence in the Atlantic World*. New York: Hill & Wang, 2005.

Langley, Lester. *The Banana Wars: United States Intervention in the Caribbean, 1898–1934*, 2nd ed. Lanham, MD: Rowman & Littlefield, 2001.

Langley, Lester D., and Thomas Schoonover. *The Banana Men: American Mercenaries and Entrepreneurs in Central America, 1880–1930*. Lexington: University Press of Kentucky, 1995.

Lantis, Jeffrey S. "Strategic Culture: From Clausewitz to Constructivism." *Strategic Insights* 4, no. 10 (October 2005). www.ccc.nps.navy.mil/si/2005/Oct/lantis Oct05.pdf.

Laramie, Michael G. *The European Invasion of North America: Colonial Conflict along the Hudson-Champlain Corridor, 1609–1760*. Santa Barbara, CA: Praeger, 2012.

Lee, Wayne E. *Barbarians and Brothers: Anglo-American Warfare, 1500–1865*. Oxford: Oxford University Press, 2011.

———. "The Battles of Plattsburg and Ending the War of 1812." In Moten, *War Termination*, 45–53.

———. "Early American Ways of War: A New Reconnaissance, 1600–1815." *The Historical Journal* 44, no. 1 (2001): 269–89.

———. "The Military Revolution of Native North America: Firearms, Forts, and Polities." In *Empires and Indigenes: Intercultural Alliance, Imperial Expansion, and Warfare in the Early Modern World*, edited by Wayne E. Lee. New York: New York University Press, 2011.

———, ed. *Warfare and Culture in World History*. New York: New York University Press, 2011.

Leland, Anne. *American War and Military Operations Casualties: Lists and Statistics*. Washington, DC: Congressional Research Service, 2012.

Leonhard, Robert R. *The China Relief Expedition: Joint Coalition Warfare in China, Summer 1900*. Laurel, MD: Johns Hopkins Applied Physics Laboratory, 2007.

Levinson, Irving W. *Wars within War: Mexican Guerrillas, Domestic Elites, and the United States of America, 1846–1848*. Ft. Worth: Texas Christian University, 2005.

Lewis, Adrian R. "American Culture of War in the Age of Artificial Limited War." In Lee, *Warfare and Culture*, 187–218.

———. *The American Culture of War: The History of U.S. Military Force from World War II to Operation Iraqi Freedom*. New York: Routledge, 2007.

Liddell Hart, Basil H. *The British Way in Warfare*. London: Faber & Faber, 1932.

———. *The British Way in Warfare: Adaptability and Mobility*. New York: Penguin, 1942.

———. *The Strategy of Indirect Approach*. London: Faber and Faber, 1941.

Lind, Michael. *The American Way of Strategy: US Foreign Policy and the American Way of Life*. Oxford: Oxford University Press, 2006.

Link, Arthur S. *Woodrow Wilson: Revolution, War and Peace*. Arlington, IL: AMH, 1979.

Linn, Brian McAllister. "The American Way of War." *Organization of American Historians Magazine of History* 22, no. 4 (October 2008): 19–23.

———. "*The American Way of War* Revisited." *Journal of Military History* 66, no. 2 (April 2002): 501–30.

———. *The Echo of Battle: The Army's Way of War*. Cambridge: Harvard University Press, 2007.

———. *The Philippine War, 1899–1902*. Lawrence: University Press of Kansas, 1989.

Lock-Pullen, Richard. "The U.S. Way of War and the 'War on Terror.'" *Politics & Policy* 34, no. 2 (2006): 374–99.

Long, John W. "American Intervention in Russia: The North Russia Expedition, 1918–19." *Diplomatic History* 6, no. 4 (Sept 1982): 45–68.

Lord, Carnes. "American Strategic Culture." *Comparative Strategy* 5, no. 3 (1985): 289–90.

Luttwak, Edward N. "A Post-Heroic Military Policy: The New Season of Bellicosity." *Foreign Affairs* 75, no. 4 (July–August 1996): 33–44.

———. "Toward Post-Heroic Warfare." *Foreign Affairs* 74, no. 3 (May–June 1995): 109–22.

Luvaas, Jay. *The Military Legacy of the Civil War: The European Inheritance*. Lawrence: University Press of Kansas, 1988.

Lynn, John A. *Battle: A History of Combat and Culture*. Boulder, CO: Westview, 2003.

MacGarrigle, George L. *The United States Army in Vietnam: Combat Operations, Taking the Offensive, October 1966 to October 1967*. Washington, DC: US Army Center of Military History, 1998.

Mahnken, Thomas G. *Technology and the American Way of War since 1945*. New York: Columbia University Press, 2008.

——. *United States Strategic Culture*. Defense Threat Reduction Agency: SAIC, 2006.

Maley, William. *The Afghanistan Wars*, 2d ed. New York: Palgrave Macmillan, 2009.

Malkasian, Carter. "Counterinsurgency in Iraq: May 2003–January 2010," in Marston and Malkasian, *Counterinsurgency*.

Malone, Patrick M. *The Skulking Way of War: Technology and Tactics among the New England Indians*. Lanham, MD: Madison Books, 1991.

Mann, Charles C. *1491: New Revelations of the Americas before Columbus*. New York: Knopf, 2005.

——. *1493: Uncovering the New World Columbus Created*. New York: Knopf, 2011.

Marston, Daniel, and Carter Malkasian, eds. *Counterinsurgency in Modern Warfare*. Oxford: Osprey, 2010.

Maslowski, P. "To the Edge of Greatness: The United States, 1783-1865." In Murray et al., *Making of Modern Strategy*, 205–41.

Mason, Tony. "Operation Allied Force, 1999." In Olsen, *History of Air Warfare*.

Matheny, Michael R. *Carrying the War to the Enemy: American Operational Art to 1945*. Norman: Oklahoma University Press, 2011.

Matthew, Laura, and Michael R. Oudijk, eds. *Indian Conquistadors: Indigenous Allies in the Conquest of Mesoamerica*. Norman: University of Oklahoma Press, 2008.

McCranie, Kevin D. "The War of 1812 in the Ongoing Napoleonic Wars: The Response of Britain's Royal Navy." *Journal of Military History* 76 (October 2012): 1067–95.

McGinnis, Anthony R. *Counting Coup and Cutting Horses: Intertribal Warfare on the Northern Plains, 1738–1889*. Lincoln: University of Nebraska Press, 2010.

——. "When Courage Was Not Enough: Plains Indians at War with the United States Army." *Journal of Military History* 76 (April 2012): 455–73.

McInness, Colin. *Hot War, Cold War: The British Army's Way in Warfare, 1945–95*. London: Brassey's, 1995.

McIvor, Anthony D., ed. *Rethinking the Principles of War*. Annapolis, MD: Naval Institute Press, 2005.

McKenna, Thomas P. *Kontum: The Battle to Save South Vietnam*. Lexington: University Press of Kentucky, 2011.

McPherson, James M. *Battle Cry of Freedom: The Civil War Era*. Oxford: Oxford University Press, 1988.

——. "From Limited War to Total War in America." In Förster and Nagler, *On the Road*, 295–310.

——. *Tried by War: Abraham Lincoln as Commander in Chief*. New York: Penguin, 2008.

———. *War on the Waters: Union and Confederate Navies, 1861–1865*. Chapel Hill: University of North Carolina Press, 2012.

Mearsheimer, John J. "Why We Will Soon Miss the Cold War." *The Atlantic Monthly* 266, no. 2 (August 1990): 35–50.

Meilinger, Phillip S. *Paths of Heaven: The Evolution of Airpower Theory*. Maxwell AFB, AL: Air University Press, 1997.

Melton, Carol W. *Between War and Peace: Woodrow Wilson and the American Expeditionary Force in Siberia, 1981–1921*. Macon, GA: Mercer University Press, 2001.

Melville, Sarah. "The Last Campaign: The Assyrian Way of War and the Collapse of the Empire." In Lee, *Warfare and Culture*, 13–33.

Meyers, Richard B. "The New American Way of War." *Military Technology* 27, no. 6 (June 2003): 64–74.

———. "The New American Way of War: Keeping the Legacy Alive." Speech delivered at the Navy League Air Space Exposition, Washington, DC, April 16, 2003.

Milkowski, Stanlis D. "After Inch'on: MacArthur's 1950 Campaign in North Korea." In Krause and Phillips, *Historical Perspectives*, 415–38.

Millett, Alan R. "Assault from the Sea: The Development of Amphibious Warfare between the Wars." In Murray and Millett, *Military Innovation*, 50–95.

———. "Cantigny, 28–31 May 1918." In Heller and Stofft, *America's First Battles*, 149–85.

———. *The Politics of Intervention: The Military Occupation of Cuba, 1906–1909*. Columbus: Ohio State University Press, 1968.

Millett, Allan R., Peter Maslowski, and William B. Feis. *For the Common Defense: A Military History of the United States from 1607 to 2012*. New York: Free Press, 2012.

Mitchell, William. *Skyways: A Book on Modern Aeronautics*. Philadelphia: Lippincott, 1930.

Moltke, Helmuth von. "Über Strategie." In *Moltkes Militärisches Werke*, 14 vols., edited by Großer Generalstab, vol. 4, part 2, 287–93. Berlin: E. S. Mittler, 1892–1912.

Moran, Daniel. "Operational Level of War." In *Oxford Companion to Military History*, edited by Richard Holmes. Oxford: Oxford University Press, 2001.

Morrison, Samuel Eliot. *Oxford History of the American People, Vol. 2: 1789 through Reconstruction*. Oxford: Oxford University Press, 1995.

Moten, Matthew, ed. *War Termination: The Proceedings of the War Termination Conference*. Ft. Leavenworth, KS: Combat Studies Institute, 2010.

Mullen, Michael G. *Officer Professional Military Education Policy*. Washington, DC: J-7, Joint Chiefs of Staff, 2009.

Muller, Richard R. "Close Air Support: The German, British, and American Experiences, 1918–1941." In Murray and Millett, *Military Innovation*, 144–90.

Murfin, James V. *The Gleam of Bayonets: The Battle of Antietam and Robert E. Lee's Maryland Campaign, September 1862*. Baton Rouge: Louisiana State University Press, 1965.

Murray, Williamson. "The American Civil War." In Olsen and Gray, *Practice of Strategy*, 199–218.

———. *Military Adaptation in War: With Fear of Change*. Cambridge: Cambridge University Press, 2011.

———. "Strategic Bombing: The British, American, and German Experiences." In Murray and Millett, *Military Innovation*, 96–143.

Murray, Williamson, and Allan R. Millett. *A War to Be Won: Fighting the Second World War*. Cambridge: Harvard University Press, 2000.

———, eds. *Military Innovation in the Interwar Period*. Cambridge: Cambridge University Press, 1996.

Murray, Williamson, Macgregor Knox, and Alvin Bernstein, eds. *The Making of Strategy: Rulers, States, and War*. Cambridge, UK: Cambridge University Press, 1994.

Musicant, Ivan. *The Banana Wars: A History of United States Military Intervention in Latin American from the Spanish–American War to the Invasion of Panama*. New York: Macmillan, 1990.

Nardulli, Bruce R., Walter L. Perry, Bruce Pirnie, John Gordon IV, and John G. McGinn. *Disjointed War: Military Operations in Kosovo, 1999*. Santa Monica, CA: RAND Corp., 2002.

Nation, R. Craig. *War in the Balkans, 1991–2002*. Carlisle, PA: Strategic Studies Institute, 2003.

Naveh, Shimon. *In Pursuit of Military Excellence: The Evolution of Operational Theory*. London: Frank Cass, 1997.

Naylor, Sean. *Not a Good Day to Die: The Untold Story of Operation Anaconda*. New York: Berkley, 2006.

Naylor, William K. *The Principles of Strategy*. Ft. Leavenworth, KS: General Service Schools, 1920.

Neely, Mark E., Jr. "Was the Civil War a Total War?" In Förster and Nagler, *On the Road*, 29–52.

Neilson, Keith, and Greg Kennedy, eds. *The British Way in Warfare: Power and the International System, 1856–1956*. Burlington, VT: Ashgate, 2010.

Nelson, Harold. "The Origins of Operational Art." In Krause and Phillips, *Historical Perspectives*.

Nenninger, Timothy K. "American Military Effectiveness in the First World War." In *Military Effectiveness: Volume I, The First World War*, edited by Allan R. Millett and Williamson Murray. Boston: Unwin Hyman, 1987.

Newell, Clayton R., and Charles R. Shrader. "The US Army's Transition to Peace, 1865–66." *Journal of Military History* 77, no. 3 (July 2013): 867–94.

Nofi, Albert A. *The Spanish-American War 1898*. Conshohocken, PA: Combined Books, 1996.

O'Hanlon, Michael E. *The Science of War: Defense Budgeting, Military Technology, Logistics, and Combat Outcomes*. Princeton, NJ: Princeton University Press, 2009.

O'Shaughnessy, Andrew J. *An Empire Divided: The American Revolution and the British Caribbean*. Philadelphia: University of Pennsylvania Press, 2000.

———. *The Men Who Lost America: British Leadership, the American Revolution, and the Fate of Empire*. New Haven, CT: Yale University Press, 2013.

O'Toole, G. J. A. *The Spanish War: An American Epic 1898*. New York: Norton, 1984.

Odom, William O. *After the Trenches: The Transformation of the U.S. Army, 1918–1939*. College Station: Texas A&M University, 1999.

Offner, John L. *An Unwanted War: The Diplomacy of the United States and Spain over Cuba, 1895–1898*. Chapel Hill: University of North Carolina Press, 1992.

Olsen, John Andreas, ed. *A History of Air Warfare*. Washington, DC: Potomac Books, 2010.

———. *John Warden and the Renaissance of American Air Power*. Washington, DC: Potomac Books, 2007.

Olsen, John Andreas, and Colin S. Gray, eds. *The Practice of Strategy: From Alexander the Great to the Present*. Oxford: Oxford University Press, 2011.

Operation Just Cause: The Incursion into Panama. Washington, DC: US Army Center of Military History, 2004.

Osanka, Franklin Mark, ed. *Modern Guerrilla Warfare: Fighting Communist Guerrilla Movements, 1941–1961*. New York: Free Press, 1962.

Overy, Richard J. *The Air War, 1939–1945*. Washington, DC: Potomac Books, 2005.

———. *Why the Allies Won*. New York: Norton, 1997.

Owen, Robert C. "Operation Deliberate Force, 1995." In Olsen, *History of Air Warfare*.

Owens, Christopher S. "Unlikely Partners: Preemption and the American Way of War." In *Essays 2003*, 1–16. Washington, DC: National Defense University Press, 2003.

Owens, Mackubin T. "The American Way of War." Editorial, *Jerusalem Post*, December 2003.

Palmer, Dave R. *George Washington's Military Genius*. Washington, DC: Regnery, 2012.

Palmer, Michael A. *Stoddert's War: Naval Operations during the Quasi-War with France, 1798–1801*. Columbia: University of South Carolina Press, 1987.

Paludan, Philip S. "'The Better Angels of Our Nature': Lincoln, Propaganda, and Public Opinion in the North during the Civil War." In Förster and Nagler, *On the Road*.

Paret, Peter, ed. *Makers of Modern Strategy: From Machiavelli to the Nuclear Age*. Princeton, NJ: Princeton University Press, 1986.

Parker, Phyllis R. *Brazil and the Quiet Intervention, 1964*. Austin: University of Texas Press, 1979.

Patton, George S. Jr. "Success in War." *Cavalry Journal* 40 (January 1931): 26–30.

Pedraja, René de la. *Wars of Latin America, 1899–1941*. Jefferson, NC: McFarland, 2006.

Pershing, John J. *Punitive Expedition. Report of Operations of the Punitive Expedition to June 30, 1916*. Colonia Dublan, Mexico: Headquarters, Punitive Expedition, US Army, October 20, 1916.

Peters, Ralph. "Speed the Kill: Updating the American Way of War." In McIvor, *Rethinking the Principles*, 95–108.

Phillips, Kevin. *1775: A Good Year for Revolution*. New York: Viking, 2012.

Piecuch, Jim, ed. *Cavalry of the American Revolution*. Yardley, PA: Westholme, 2012.

Pillar, Paul R. *Negotiating Peace: War Termination as a Bargaining Process*. Princeton, NJ: Princeton University Press, 1984.

Poore, Stuart. "What Is the Context? A Reply to the Gray-Johnston Debate on Strategic Culture." *Review of International Studies* 29, no. 2 (2003): 279–84.

Porter, Patrick. *Military Orientalism: Eastern War through Western Eyes*. London: Hurst, 2011.

Prados, John. *Safe for Democracy: The Secret Wars of the CIA*. Chicago: Ivan Dee, 2006.

The Principles of Strategy for an Independent Corps or Army in a Theater of Operations. Ft. Leavenworth, KS: Command and General Staff College, 1936.

"Provincial Reconstruction Teams." GlobalSecurity.org. www.globalsecurity.org/military/ops/oef-prt.htm.

Pusey, Merlo J. *The Way We Go to War*. Boston: Houghton Mifflin, 1969.

Quadrennial Defense Review Independent Panel. *The QDR in Perspective: Meeting America's National Security Needs in the 21st Century*. Washington, DC: United States Institute of Peace, 2010.

Quirk, Robert E. *A Matter of Honor: Woodrow Wilson and the Occupation of Veracruz*. New York: Norton, 1967.

Rabe, Stephen G. *U.S. Intervention in British Guiana: A Cold War Story*. Chapel Hill: University of North Carolina Press, 2005.

Record, Jeffrey. *The American Way of War: Cultural Barriers to Successful Counterinsurgency*. Policy Analysis No. 577. Washington, DC: Cato Institute, 2006.

———. "Collapsed Countries, Casualty Dread, and the New American Way of War." *Parameters* 32, no. 2 (Summer 2002): 4–23.

Richard, Carl. "'The Shadow of a Plan': The Rationale behind Wilson's 1918 Siberian Intervention." *Historian* 49 (1986): 83.

Robertson, W. Glenn. "First Bull Run, 19 July 1861." In Heller and Stofft, *America's First Battles*.

Rockoff, Hugh. *America's Economic Way of War: War and the US Economy from the Spanish-American War to the Persian Gulf War.* Cambridge: Cambridge University Press, 2012.

Rodgers, Thomas E. "Saving the Republic: Turnout, Ideology, and Republicanism in the Election of 1860." In *The Election of 1860 Reconsidered*, edited by A. James Fuller, 165–92. Kent, OH: Kent State University Press, 2013.

Roeder, George H. *The Censored War: American Visual Experience during World War II.* New Haven, CT: Yale University Press, 1993.

Roosevelt, Franklin D. "State of the Union Address," January 7, 1943. The American Presidency Project, edited by Gerhard Peters and John T. Woolley. www.presidency.ucsb.edu/ws/?pid=16386.

Roosevelt, Theodore. *The Rough Riders.* New York: Modern Library, 1999.

Rose, Gideon. *How Wars End: Why We Always Fight the Last Battle.* New York: Simon & Schuster, 2010.

Ross, Steven T. *American War Plans, 1890–1939.* London: Frank Cass, 2002.

———. *American War Plans, 1941–1945.* London: Routledge 1997.

———. *American War Plans, 1945–1950.* London: Frank Cass, 1996.

Rostow, Walter W. *Concept and Controversy: Sixty Years of Taking Ideas to Market.* Austin: University of Texas Press, 2003.

Roth, David. *Sacred Honor: A Biography of Colin Powell.* San Francisco: Harper, 1993.

Rubel, Robert C. "Slicing the Onion Differently: Seapower and the Levels of War." *Joint Force Quarterly*, no. 64 (January 2012): 107–14.

Rumsfeld, Donald H. "Transforming the Military." *Foreign Affairs* 81, no. 3 (May–June 2002): 20–32.

Rumsfeld, Donald H., and Tommy R. Franks, "Summary of Lessons Learned in OIF," Prepared Testimony for the Senate Armed Services Committee, July 9, 2003.

Russell, James A. *Innovation, Transformation, and War: Counterinsurgency Operations in Anbar and Ninewa Provinces, Iraq, 2005–2007.* Stanford, CA: Stanford University Press, 2011.

Sale, Richard. *Clinton's Secret Wars: The Evolution of a Commander in Chief.* New York: St. Martin's, 2009.

Sarotte, Mary Elise. "Deciding to Be Mars." In *Policy Review*, no. 172 (April–May 2012).

Scheina, Robert L. *Latin America's Wars.* Vol. 2. Washington, DC: Brassey's, 2003.

Schelling, Thomas C. *Arms and Influence.* New Haven, CT: Yale University Press, 1966.

Schmidt, Hans. *United States Occupation of Haiti 1915–1934.* New Brunswick, NJ: Rutgers University Press, 1995.

Schnabel, James F. *Policy and Direction: The First Year.* Washington, DC: US Army Center of Military History, 1992.

Schwartz, Benjamin. "The Post-Powell Doctrine: Two Conservative Analysts Argue the American Military Has Become too Cautious about Waging War." *New York Times Book Review*, July 21, 2002, 11–12.

Scott, Henry L. *Military Dictionary*. New York: Van Nostrand, 1864.

Scott, William B. "New Way of War: Strategies Based on 'Annihilation and Attrition' Are Relegated to History." *Aviation Week & Space Technology* 158, no. 19 (May 12, 2003): 38–39.

Scoville, Thomas W. *Reorganizing for Pacification Support*. Washington, DC: US Army Center of Military History, 1999.

Serena, Chad. *A Revolution in Military Adaptation: The US Army in the Iraq War*. Washington, DC: Georgetown University Press, 2011.

Shannon, Timothy. "The Native American Way of War in the Age of Revolutions, 1754–1814." In *War in an Age of Revolution*, edited by Roger Chickering and Stig Förster, 139–43. Cambridge: Cambridge University Press, 2010.

Shaw, Martin. *The New Western Way of War: Risk-Transfer War and Its Crisis in Iraq*. Cambridge, UK: Polity, 2005.

Sherwood, John D. *Nixon's Trident: Naval Power in Southeast Asia, 1968–1972*. Washington, DC: Government Printing Office, 2009.

Showalter, Dennis. *Patton and Rommel: Men of War in the Twentieth Century*. New York: Berkley, 2005.

———. *The Wars of Frederick the Great*. London: Longman, 1996.

Singer, Peter W. "Drones Don't Die." *Military History* 28, no. 2 (July 2011): 66–69.

———. *Wired for War: The Robotics Revolution and Conflict in the 21st Century*. New York: Penguin, 2009.

Singletary, Otis A. *The Mexican War*. Chicago: University of Chicago Press, 1962.

Skaggs, David Curtis. *Oliver Hazard Perry: Honor, Courage, and Patriotism in the Early U.S. Navy*. Annapolis, MD: Naval Institute Press, 2006.

———. *Thomas Macdonough: Master of Command in the Early Navy*. Annapolis, MD: Naval Institute Press, 2006.

Skaggs, David C., and Larry L. Nelson, eds. *The Sixty Years' War for the Great Lakes, 1754–1814*. East Lansing: Michigan State University, 2001.

Sloggett, Dave. "Attack of the Drones: The Utility of UAVs in Fighting Terrorism." *Jane's Intelligence Review*, July 16, 2010.

Smith, Jean Edward. *Eisenhower in War and Peace*. New York: Random House, 2013.

Snell, J. C. "A Review of *The American Way of War*." *Annals of the American Academy*, no. 410 (November 1973): 224.

Snyder, Jack. "The Concept of Strategic Culture: Caveat Emptor." In Jacobsen, *Strategic Power*.

———. *The Soviet Strategic Culture: Implications for Nuclear Options*. Santa Monica, CA: RAND Corp., 1977.

Solana, Javier. "A Secure Europe in a Better World: European Security Strategy." Brussels: European Council, December 12, 2003. www.envirosecurity.org/ges /ESS12Dec2003.pdf.

Sondhaus, Lawrence. *Naval Warfare, 1815–1914*. London: Routledge, 2001.

———. *Strategic Culture and Ways of War*. London: Routledge, 2006.

Spector, Ronald. "The Military Effectiveness of the U.S. Armed Forces, 1919– 1939." In *Military Effectiveness: Vol. II: The Interwar Period*, edited by Allan R. Millett and Williamson Murray. Boston: Unwin Hyman, 1990.

Stagg, J. C. A. *The War of 1812: Conflict for a Continent*. West Nyack, NY: Cambridge University Press, 2012.

Stanton, Shelby L. *The Rise and Fall of an American Army: US Ground Forces in Vietnam*. Novato, CA: Praeger, 1985.

Starkey, Armstrong. *European and Native American Warfare, 1675–1815*. Norman: University of Oklahoma Press, 1998.

Stevenson, Jonathan. *Losing Mogadishu: Testing US Policy in Somalia*. Annapolis, MD: Naval Institute Press, 1995.

Stewart, Richard W. "Historical Overview: The United States Army in Somalia, 1992–1994." In *United States Forces, Somalia*.

Stoker, Donald. *The Grand Design: Strategy and the U.S. Civil War*. New York: Oxford University Press, 2010.

Strachan, Hew. "British National Strategy: Who Makes It?" *Parameters* 43, no. 2 (Summer 2013): 33–41.

———. "The British Way in Warfare Revisited." *The Historical Journal* 26, no. 2 (June 1983): 447–61.

———. "The Meaning of Strategy: Historical Perspectives." in *The Direction of War: Contemporary Strategy in Historical Perspective*, edited by Hew Strachan. Cambridge: Cambridge University Press, 2014.

———. "Operational Art and Britain, 1909–2009." In *The Evolution of Operational Art from Napoleon to the Present*, edited by John Andreas Olsen and Martin van Creveld. Oxford: Oxford University Press, 2011.

———. "Strategy or Alibi? Obama, McChrystal and the Operational Level of War." *Survival* 52, no. 5 (2010): 157–82.

Sutherland, Daniel E. "The Union's Counterguerrilla War, 1861–1865." In *Hybrid Warfare: Fighting Complex Opponents from the Ancient World to the Present*, edited by Williamson Murray and Peter R. Mansoor. Cambridge: Cambridge University Press, 2012.

Swain, Richard M. "Filling the Void: The Operational Art and the U.S. Army." In *The Operational Art: Developments in the Theories of War*, edited by B. J. C. McKercher and Michael A. Hennessy. Westport, CT: Praeger, 1996.

———, ed. *Selected Papers of General William E. DePuy*. Ft. Leavenworth, KS: Combat Studies Institute, 1994.

Sword, Wiley. *President Washington's Indian War: The Struggle for the Old Northwest 1790–1795*. Norman: University of Oklahoma Press, 1993.

Symonds, Craig L. *The Civil War at Sea*. New York: Oxford University Press, 2012.

Taj, Farhat. "The Year of the Drone Misinformation." *Small Wars & Insurgencies* 21, no. 3 (September 2010): 529–35.

Taylor, Alan. *The Civil War of 1812: American Citizens, British Subjects, Irish Rebels, and Indian Allies*. New York: Random House, 2010.

Telp, Claus. *The Evolution of Operational Art, 1740–1813: From Frederick the Great to Napoleon*. London: Routledge, 2013.

Thompson, Mark. "How the Iraq War Got Off on the Wrong Foot." *Time*, June 19, 2013. http://nation.time.com/2013/06/19/how-the-iraq-war-got-off-on-the -wrong-foot.

Thompson, Wayne. "Operations over North Vietnam, 1965–1973." In Olsen, *History of Air Warfare*, 107–26.

Tierney, Dominic. *How We Fight: Crusades, Quagmires, and The American Way of War*. New York: Little, Brown, 2010.

Till, Geoffrey. "Adopting the Aircraft Carrier: The British, American, and Japanese Case Studies." In Murray and Millett, *Military Innovation*, 191–226.

Tomes, Robert R. *US Defense Strategy from Vietnam to Operation Iraqi Freedom: Military Innovation and the New American Way of War, 1973– 2003*. London: Routledge, 2007.

Toner, James H. "Candide as Constable: The American Way of War and Peace in Korea, 1950–1953." PhD diss., Notre Dame University, 1976.

Tooze, Adam J. *The Wages of Destruction: The Making and Breaking of the Nazi Economy*. New York: Penguin, 2007.

Trask, David. "The Entry of the USA into the War and Its Effects." In *World War I: A History*, edited by Hew Strachan, 239–52. Oxford: Oxford University Press, 1998.

———. *The War with Spain in 1898*. New York: Bison Books, 1996.

Trautsch, Jasper. "The Causes of the War of 1812: 200 Years of Debate." *Journal of Military History* 77, no. 1 (January 2013): 273–93.

Trudeau, Noah Andre. "Battle for the West: 'Hard War' on the Southern Plains." *Military History Quarterly* 23, no. 4 (Summer 2011): 26–37.

Tucker, Spencer, ed. *The Encyclopedia of the Spanish-American and Philippine-American Wars: A Political, Social, and Military History*. Vol. 1. Santa Barbara, CA: ABC-CLIO, 2009.

Turner, Robert F. "President Thomas Jefferson and the Barbary Pirates." In *Piracy and Maritime Crime: Historical and Modern Case Studies*, edited by Bruce A. Ellerman, Andrew Forbes, and David Rosenberg, 157–72. Newport, RI: Naval War College Press, 2010.

Ucko, David H. *The New Counterinsurgency Era: Transforming the U.S. Military for Modern Wars*. Washington, DC: Georgetown University Press, 2009.

United Nations. Peacekeeping Operations. www.un.org/en/peacekeeping /documents/operationslist.pdf (accessed August 6, 2012).

United States Forces, Somalia after Action Report. Washington, DC: Government Printing Office, 1995.

United States Strategic Bombing Survey: Summary Report (European War). Washington, DC: Department of Defense, September 30, 1945.

United States Strategic Bombing Survey (Pacific War). Washington, DC: Department of Defense, July 1, 1946.

Urwin, Gregory J. W. "Sowing the Wind and Reaping the Whirlwind: Abraham Lincoln as a War President." In *Lincoln and Leadership: Military, Political, and Religious Decision Making,* edited by Randall M. Miller, 39–59. New York: Fordham University Press, 2012.

US Army. *General Tactical Functions of Larger Units.* Fort Leavenworth, KS: General Service Schools Press, 1926.

US Army Center of Military History. "Medal of Honor Recipients: Statistics." www.history.army./html/moh/mohstats.html.

The U.S. Army–Marine Corps Counterinsurgency Field Manual. Chicago: University of Chicago Press, 2007.

US Department of the Army. *Knowledge and Speed: The Annual Report on the Army After Next Report Project to the Chief of Staff of the Army.* Ft. Monroe, VA: Army Training and Doctrine Command, 1996.

US Joint Chiefs of Staff, *Joint Vision 2010.* Washington, DC: Government Printing Office, 1996.

———. *Joint Vision 2020.* Washington, DC: Government Printing Office, 2000.

US Marine Corps. *Small Wars Manual.* Washington, DC: Government Printing Office, 1935, 1940.

———. *Tentative Manual for Landing Operations.* Quantico, VA: Marine Corps Schools, 1934–35.

US War Department. *Manual for Commanders of Large Units.* Washington, DC: Government Printing Office, 1930.

Utley, Robert M. "Total War on the American Frontier." In *Anticipating Total War: The German and American Experiences, 1871–1914,* edited by Manfred F. Boemeke, Roger Chickering, and Stig Förster, 399–414. Cambridge: Cambridge University Press, 1999.

van Creveld, Martin. *The Transformation of War.* New York: Free Press, 1991.

Vanden Brook, Tom. "Coalition Attacks Sap Key Insurgents in Afghanistan." *USA Today,* December 28, 2010. www.usatoday.com/news/world/afghanistan/2010-12-29-dronestrikes29_ST_N.htm.

Vandiver, Frank. *Shadows of Vietnam: Lyndon Johnson's Wars.* College Station: Texas A&M Press, 1997.

Van Riper, Paul. "The Foundation of Strategic Thinking." *Infinity Journal* 2, no. 3 (Summer 2012): 4–10.

Vásquez, Josefina Zoraida. "War and Peace with the United States." In *Oxford History of Mexico,* edited by Michael C. Meyer and William H. Beezley. New York: Oxford University Press, 2000.

Vego, Milan. "Science vs. the Art of War." *Joint Force Quarterly* 66 (2012): 62–70.

Veith, George J. *Black April: The Fall of South Vietnam, 1973–75.* New York: Encounter, 2012.

Votaw, John F., and Steven Weingartner, eds., *In the Wake of the Storm: Gulf War Commanders Discuss Desert Storm.* Cantigny, IL: First Division Foundation, 2000.

Wang, Yuan-Kang. *Harmony and War: Confucian Culture and Chinese Power Politics.* New York: Columbia University Press, 2011.

Warden, John A., III. "The Enemy as a System." *Airpower Journal* 9, no. 1 (Spring 1995): 40–45.

War Department. "Training Lessons from the Tunisian Campaign." Reprint of "Training Memorandum 44, 4 August 1943." In *Kasserine Pass Battles.*

Wass de Czege, Huba. "Systemic Operational Design: Learning and Adapting in Complex Missions." *Military Review* 89, no. 1 (January–February 2009): 2–12.

"Was There a Russian Enlightenment?" Conference. Ertegun House, Oxford University, November 10, 2012. http://podcasts.ox.ac.uk/series/was-there-russian-enlightenment.

Watson, Samuel. "Trusting to 'the Chapter of Accidents': Contingency, Necessity, and Self-Constraint in Jeffersonian National Security Policy." *Journal of Military History* 76 (October 2012): 973–1000.

Watts, Barry, and Williamson Murray. "Military Innovation in Peacetime." In Murray and Millett, *Military Innovation,* 369–400.

Watts, Stephen, Caroline Baxter, Molly Dunigan, and Christopher Rizzi. *The Uses and Limits of Small-Scale Military Interventions.* Santa Monica, CA: RAND Corp., 2012.

Weddle, Kevin J. "'A Change of Both Men and Measures': British Reassessment of Military Strategy after Saratoga, 1777–1778." *Journal of Military History* 77, no. 3 (July 2013): 837–66.

Weigley, Russell F. "American Strategy from Its Beginnings through the First World War." In Paret, *Makers of Modern Strategy.*

———. *The American Way of War: A History of U.S. Military Strategy and Policy.* Bloomington: Indiana University Press, 1973.

———. *A Great Civil War: A Military and Political History, 1861–1865.* Bloomington: Indiana University Press, 2000.

———. *History of the United States Army.* New York: Macmillan, 1967.

———. "A New Way of War? Review of F. G. Hoffman, *Decisive Force: The New American Way of War.*" *Naval War College Review* 52, no. 1 (Winter 1999): 130.

———. "Normandy to Falaise: A Critique of Allied Operational Planning in 1944." In Krause and Phillips, *Historical Perspectives,* 393–414.

———. "The Political and Strategic Dimensions of Military Effectiveness." In *Military Effectiveness: Volume 3, The Second World War,* edited by Williamson Murray and Allan R. Millett. Boston: Allen & Unwin, 1988.

———. "Response to Brian McAllister Linn." *Journal of Military History* 66, no. 2 (April 2002): 531–33.

Wentz, Larry, ed. *Lessons from Bosnia: The IFOR Experience.* Washington, DC: National Defense University Press, 1997.

Wheelan, Joseph. *Invading Mexico: America's Continental Dream and the Mexican War, 1846–1848.* New York: Avalon, 2007.

Williams, Glenn F. *Year of the Hangman: George Washington's Campaign against the Iroquois.* Yardley, PA: Westholme, 2005.

Wilson, David K. *The Southern Strategy: Britain's Conquest of South Carolina and Georgia, 1775–1780.* Columbia: University of South Carolina Press, 2005.

Wilson, Isaiah. *Thinking beyond War: Civil-Military Relations and Why America Fails to Win the Peace.* New York: Palgrave Macmillan, 2007.

Wirtz, James J. *The Tet Offensive: Intelligence Failure in War.* Ithaca, NY: Cornell University Press, 1991.

Wood, Gordon S. "The War We Lost—and Won." *New York Review of Books,* October 28, 2010.

Woodward, Bob. *Obama's Wars.* New York: Simon & Schuster, 2010.

Yenne, Bill. *Indian Wars: The Campaign for the American West.* Yardley, PA: Westholme, 2008.

Index